Towards the Conservation
and Restoration
of Historic Organs

Michael Gillingham (1933–99)

The social highlight of the Liverpool conference was the conference dinner, enlivened by a speech given by Michael Gillingham, the first chairman of the British Institute of Organ Studies. After a difficult personal period, it was obvious that he had recovered his old form, but this was to be his last public-speaking engagement. It came as a great blow to hear of his untimely death on 29 October 1999. His knowledge, understanding and generosity cannot be replaced. This volume is a modest acknowledgement of the inspiration he offered. At his memorial service, we pondered John Betjeman's words:

> The Church's Restoration
> In eighteen-eighty-three
> Has left for contemplation
> Not what there used to be . . .[1]

Perhaps when we meet again more of what there used to be may survive. That would please him.

Towards the Conservation and Restoration of Historic Organs

A record of the Liverpool Conference,
23–26 August 1999

Edited by Jim Berrow

CHURCH HOUSE PUBLISHING

Church House Publishing
Church House
Great Smith Street
London
SW1P 3NZ

ISBN 0 7151 7586 6

Published 2000 for the Council for the Care of Churches by Church House Publishing.

Front cover illustration: St Peter's Chapel, Tower of London. Detail from a photogrammetric record.

Cover design: Sarah Hopper

Typeset in 10 on 13 point Stone Serif.

Printed and bound in England by J. W. Arrowsmith Ltd

Contents

List of illustrations

Biographies of contributors and chairs

Jonathan Ambrosino specializes in the historical review of the twentieth-century American organ. Originally trained in journalism, Jonathan has worked both in organ restoration and building, from restorers Nelson Barden (Boston) and Douglass Hunt (New York City) to builders Austin (Hartford) and Rosales (Los Angeles). He has now withdrawn from full-time association with any particular company, and combines historical studies with periodic involvement in organ building, consultation and tonal finishing projects. Among his many writing projects, he co-authored the script for the film *Pulling Out all the Stops* and recently completed a series on present-day American organ building for *Choir and Organ*.

Andrew Argyrakis was appointed Conservation Officer of the Council for the Care of Churches in 1990. Prior to this he worked at the Passmore Edwards Museum where he was Principal Assistant Curator – Conservation. Andrew was involved in the Area Museums Service for South Eastern England and was a member of its Archaeology Panel and Chairman of its Care of Collections Panel.

Ian Bell started organ building in 1960 as an apprentice in the voicing shops of the John Compton Organ Company. From 1963 to 1993 he worked with N. P. Mander Ltd in London, being at various times Head Voicer, Workshop Manager, in charge of the design office, and a director of the company. During that period he supervised most of the firm's larger restoration or rebuilding projects, in addition to sharing in the design of new organs. In 1993 he left to become an independent organ adviser; his present caseload includes seven new organs, in addition to numerous restoration projects including the 1831 Bishop organ at St James, Bermondsey, Gloucester Cathedral, and the Royal Albert Hall.

Jim Berrow was apprenticed as an organ builder. As an executive producer with Central Television, he made many programmes about the arts, including twentieth-century music, and is attracted by the impact of the contemporary arts on traditional forms of aesthetic experience. He now sits on the City of Birmingham Symphony Orchestra Board, was Founder-Chair of Birmingham Contemporary Music Group and is a trustee or board member of several other cultural organizations. He was Secretary of the British Institute of Organ Studies at the time of the conference, is an Honorary Research Fellow at the University of Birmingham (his doctoral dissertation investigated an organ-building dynasty), is a member of the Council for the Care of Churches Organs Committee and advises several other organizations.

John Clare is an independent consultant, with experience of practical conservation and the preparation of conservation plans. He is a member of both the Institute of Historic Building Conservation and the British Institute of Organ Studies.

Barrie Clark was an English Heritage Historic Buildings architect. He began to advise English Heritage on matters relating to organs from about 1970. Later, from 1988, he represented them on the Organs Committee Council for the Care of Churches. He was officially made English Heritage Organs Adviser in 1992 and this continued after his retirement, as a consultant, advising in particular the Government Historic Buildings Advisory Unit. He is now one of the organ advisers to the Diocese of Southwark.

William Drake culminated his apprenticeship and work as a journeyman with the building of a small two-manual and pedal organ, for which the Chamber of Commerce in Stuttgart awarded him the German Certificate of Master Organ Builder in 1974. He established his workshop in Buckfastleigh in 1974. The work of the firm has developed towards creating organs with a strong stylistic identity, greatly influenced by the restoration of several English organs. Current new work takes its inspiration from English organs of the eighteenth and early-nineteenth centuries. All instruments built by the firm have mechanical key and stop action.

Michael Gillingham, CBE, FSA, HonRCO. Founder-chairman of the British Institute of Organ Studies, 1976–83; Advisory Board for Redundant Churches, 1989–99 (member since 1979); London Diocesan Advisory Committee (member since 1965). Member, Organs Advisory Committee of the Council for the Care of Churches, 1967–91; Westminster Abbey Fabric Commission, 1990–; Trustee of the Fitzwilliam Museum Trust, 1990–; Trustee of the Fitzwilliam Museum Trust, 1990–; Friend of Christ Church Spitalfields and of Care for St Ann's Limehouse. He was Consultant for the restoration of organs at St Michael, Framlingham, 1968; St Mary-at-Hill, City of London, 1971; St James, Clerkenwell, 1978; Peterborough Cathedral, 1980; Chichester Cathedral, 1986; for new organs at Corpus Christi College, Cambridge (with Sir John Dykes Bower), 1968; St Michael, Paternoster Royal, 1968; St Giles, Cripplegate, 1969; St Andrew, Holborn, 1989; St Matthew, Westminster, 1989; for the restoration of the organ-cases at Gloucester Cathedral, 1971 and Stanford-on-Avon, 1969. Special interests included English organ cases and the aesthetic approach to organ restoration. Michael Gillingham attended the conference on behalf of the Royal College of Organists.

Martin Goetze trained at the firm of Grant Degens and Bradbeer from 1970. Further experience was obtained with Karl Lötzerich in Germany and Gabriel Kney in Canada, before returning to Northampton to set up a workshop with Dominic Gwynn in 1980, and moving to larger premises at Welbeck in 1985. Interest in the restoration and conservation of organs was spurred in 1976 with a visit to Poland, where the documentation and restoration of their historic instruments were well established. Martin's attitudes towards old organs were fundamentally changed, and although it is the earlier period that inspires him most, there is still interest in all organ types, particularly through their conservation. Membership includes the United Kingdom Institute for Conservation, Metals Section.

Göran Grahn is Curator of Stiftelsen Musikkulturens Främjande (Nydahl Collection) in Stockholm. This collection holds about 550 instruments, 2,000 music autographs and 6,000 autograph letters from various composers. He is also active as a consultant on organ restoration and since 1990 has worked voluntarily in Estonia, Latvia and Lithuania, where many historic organs are well preserved. This work has been aimed at preventing their organ builders from repeating the mistakes of Western Europe. Apart from extensive travel in these countries, he has invited their organ builders and cultural heritage protection officials to study recent restorations in Sweden. He is also Organist at the Anglican Church of St Peter and St Sigfrid, Stockholm.

Dominic Gwynn is an organ builder, one of the partners of Goetze and Gwynn at Welbeck in North Nottinghamshire. They have specialized in making new organs based on the English classical tradition, and restoring organs to museum standards. Dominic has also organized conferences, given lectures and published a number of articles on British organ history.

John Harper became Director General of the Royal School of Church Music in the summer of 1998, and is developing new initiatives in music and music education for the Church. His career is that of administrator, composer, choral director, university teacher and scholar. He directed the choir of Magdalen College, Oxford, in the 1980s, and St Chad's Cathedral, Birmingham, in the 1970s. He taught at the universities of Birmingham and Oxford, and was Professor of Music at the University of Wales, Bangor, where he remains a Research Professor. His *Forms and Orders of Western Liturgy from the Tenth to the Eighteenth Century* is used widely throughout the world. His interest in early British organs and liturgical organ music is longstanding, and a book on the subject is in progress.

Peter Horton was born in 1953 and read music at Magdalen College, Oxford. After graduating he embarked on research into the music of Samuel Sebastian Wesley (D.Phil. 1983) and has since continued his work on Wesley with an edition of his complete anthems for *Musica Britannica* and various articles (including one on the organ in St George's Hall, Liverpool, for the 1998 *Journal of the British Institute of Organ Studies*), and is currently working on a study of Wesley's life and music. He is Reference Librarian and Research coordinator at the Royal College of Music, London.

Christopher Kent is Senior Lecturer in Music at the University of Reading and Co-ordinator of the Lady Susi Jeans Centre for Organ Historiography. He was Honorary Secretary of the British Institute of Organ Studies between 1987 and 1996 and spent nine years as an organ adviser for the Diocese of Oxford before recently joining the Salisbury Diocesan Advisory Committee in a similar capacity. Dr Kent is a committee member of the International Association for Organ Documentation and a member of the Association of Independent Organ Advisers. He has published widely in the fields of Elgar and organ studies and is Honorary Organist at the Chapelry of St Nicholas, Tytherton Lucas, Wiltshire.

John Kitchen is a Senior Lecturer and University Organist in the University of Edinburgh. He also directs the University Singers, and is Organist of Old St Paul's Episcopal Church. For many years he played regularly with the Scottish Early Music Consort as a harpsichordist, organist and fortepianist, and now plays with several other ensembles. He gives many solo recitals, and is much in demand as a continuo player, accompanist, lecturer and reviewer. His CD recordings include seventeenth- and eighteenth-century German music, played on the Ahrend organ in the Reid Concert Hall, Edinburgh, in the *Great European Organs* series, published by Priory Records. Further recording ventures are planned.

David Knight is currently completing his dissertation on the history of the organs and their music at Westminster Abbey for a Ph.D. at King's College London and has published on various aspects of this research, Renatus Harris, the eighteenth-century swell organ and approaches to organ restoration. He has spoken at conferences in the UK and at the Göteborg Organ Academy, for whom he works part-time as a research assistant for the performance-practice project. He has been with the Council for the Care of Churches since 1996 as a member of the Conservation Department.

John Mander became Managing Director of N. P. Mander Ltd. on the retirement of his father in 1983. He served his apprenticeship with Rudolf von Beckerath of Hamburg. Following his three-and-a-half-year apprenticeship, which included the organ builders' course at the technical college dedicated to musical instrument making at Ludwigsburg, he remained with Beckerath to further his knowledge in voicing and organ design, culminating in the design of a Choir organ for the Petrikirche in Hamburg. Following his return to London after five years in Hamburg, he worked in the drawing office and was responsible for the conception and design of a number of small mechanical-action organs. In 1979 he directed the historic reconstruction of the early-eighteenth-century organ at Pembroke College, Cambridge. In 1980 he returned to Germany to prepare for the Master Organ Builders' examination which he completed successfully in that year, making him one of a handful of builders with that qualification outside Germany. He takes an active part in the conception and realization of the firm's work, frequently directing the tonal finishing of organs on site all over the world. For six years he served on the board of the International Society of Organ Builders and is a founder member of the Institute of British Organ Building which has been formed to further the education of organ builders in Britain. He lectures on a wide variety of topics, and is often called upon to advise on unequal temperaments, of which he has made a special study.

John Norman is a member of the Cathedrals Fabric Commission for England, the Organs Committee of the Council for the Care of Churches and of the London Diocesan Advisory Committee. He is Editor of *The Organbuilder* and a regular columnist for *Organists' Review*. John studied acoustics under Dr R. W. B. Stephens at Imperial College, London, and organ under H. A. Roberts. At Hill, Norman & Beard he learned voicing from Robert Lamb and tonal finishing from Mark Fairhead, working on seven cathedral organs before leaving in 1974. John is an accredited professional organ consultant and a founder member of the Association of Independent Organ Advisers. His most recent assignment was the new organ in the crypt chapel of the Houses of Parliament.

Gordon Stewart was born in Scotland and studied at the Royal Manchester College of Music and the Geneva Conservatoire, gaining a performer's diploma with distinction at the former and a *Premier Prix de Virtuosie* from the latter. For eleven years he was Organist of Manchester Cathedral and has been Borough Organist of Kirklees for the past eight years, where he is Organist of Huddersfield Town Hall. Organ playing has taken him to countries across Europe, to the USA, Canada, South Africa and New Zealand. Gordon is in demand as a teacher and has given masterclasses for the Royal College of Organists, the Royal College of Music, the Göteborg Organ Academy and various other colleges and organizations. He is a regular musical director for the BBC *Daily Service* and has recently conducted three programmes for the television series *Songs of Praise*. He serves on the Royal College of Organists' Education Working Party. In June 1999 he was a judge at the International Bach Competition in Alkmaar where he played in the opening concert and gave a lecture and masterclass on the organ music of Henry Purcell. Gordon Stewart attended the conference on behalf of the Incorporated Association of Organists.

Nicholas Thistlethwaite is author of *The Making of the Victorian Organ* and joint editor of *The Cambridge Companion to the Organ*, and has written monographs, articles and reviews concerned with the organ, its history and conservation. He was the founding Secretary of the British Institute of Organ Studies, later serving as Chairman. As an organ consultant he has been responsible for projects at Birmingham Town Hall, Eton College Chapel, Chelmsford Cathedral, St John's College, Cambridge, and Buckingham Palace, among others. He is an Anglican priest and Canon Precentor at Guildford Cathedral.

Alan Thurlow read music at Sheffield University before going on to Emmanuel College, Cambridge, from 1968 to 1971 to research pre-Reformation English church music. In 1973 he was appointed Sub-organist at Durham Cathedral, where he combined his duties with those of Director of Music at the Chorister School and a part-time lecturer in music at the University. In 1980 he was appointed Organist and Master of the Choristers at Chichester Cathedral. Alan is a member of the executive of the Friends of Pallant House, an organ adviser in the Chichester diocese, Chairman of the Friends of Cathedral Music and a trustee of the ON Organ Fund. He has been President of the Cathedral Organists Association. During his time at Chichester the cathedral's historic pipe organ has been restored to use after a silence of 14 years.

Axel Unnerbäck, Fil.Dr is Senior Executive Officer at the Swedish Central Board of National Antiquities and, since the middle of the 1960s, has been responsible for questions concerning the preservation and care of historic organs in Sweden. As a researcher he is attached to the Göteborg Organ Art Center at the Göteborg University.

John R. Watson was formally trained in music, and his dual career began in church music and instrument making. Using historic instruments as 'primary documents' he has made 30 reproductions including spinets, regals, fortepianos, clavichords, and harpsichords. His 14 publications are in organology and conservation ethics. His book on the collaborative conservation of organs is forthcoming. He is also editing proceedings of an organ restoration colloquium which took place in 1999 in Smithfield, Virginia. John Watson set up the musical instrument conservation laboratory at the Colonial Williamsburg Foundation in Williamsburg, Virginia, where he is Conservator of Instruments.

David C. Wickens is a founder member of the British Institute of Organ Studies. He has contributed several articles to the *Journal of the British Institute of Organ Studies* and his study of Samuel Green's methods of organ building was published by Macmillan. He is currently editing the *Freeman-Edmonds Directory of British Organ Builders*, manages the British Organ Archive index and is Director of Music at the parish church of St Helen, Abingdon. He served in Hong Kong in the Intelligence Corps, and has taught English in the South Pacific and in Central Africa.

Acknowledgements

The conference was organized by Jim Berrow, Dominic Gwynn and David Knight. Valued support came from the Chairman and Council of the British Institute of Organ Studies; the Secretary of the Council for the Care of Churches and, especially, the Conservation Officer (Andrew Argyrakis) and the Chairman and members of the Organs Committee (Alan Thurlow, Jim Berrow, Ian Bell, Peter Cavanagh, Barrie Clark, Peter Collins, Dominic Gwynn, Richard Hird, John Norman, Nicholas Thistlethwaite); and the President and the Council of the Institute of British Organ Building and their past and present administrators.

These essays represent the views of the individual contributors and not necessarily those of the conference organizers or publisher.

The editor is grateful to Sarah Roberts and Tracey Messenger of Church House Publishing for their assistance in compiling this volume.

Thanks to:

- Peter Burman and the Secretary of the Council for the Care of Churches, Thomas Cocke for their initial advice;
- the staff of the Conservation Centre, Liverpool, especially David Abbott, Janet Berry, Tracey Seddon and Graham Usher;
- John Kitchen, Gordon Stewart and Ian Wells for their recitals;
- David Wells, organ builder, for advice, assistance and local support above and beyond the call of duty;
- all the other helpers, delegates, contributors and speakers;
- the Radcliffe Trust for a grant towards this publication.

Organizing such an event costs money and although we had the backing of three leading organizations, the conference had to be self-supporting. Congratulations are due to those firms who sent employees, and those self-employed organ builders, advisers and performers who paid their own way.

This event would not have happened without the commitment of David Knight (Conservation Adviser, Council for the Care of Churches), who worked so hard behind the scenes to bring us all together and helped facilitate the production of this book.

Jim Berrow

Copyright acknowledgements

The editor and publisher would like to thank the following organizations for permission to reproduce copyright material in this book. Every effort has been made to trace and contact copyright holders. If there are any inadvertent omissions we apologize to those concerned and undertake to include suitable acknowledgements in all future editions. Page numbers are indicated in parentheses.

Australia ICOMOS: for the Burra Charter (129)

The British Institute of Organ Studies (BIOS): extracts from *Sound Advice: The Care of Your Pipe Organ* (162) and the BIOS guidelines for conservation and restoration, 1991 (156).

Historic Royal Palaces: Figure 8.5 (65), which is Crown copyright and reproduced by permission under licence from the Controller of Her Majesty's Stationery Office.

John Murray (Publishers) Ltd: Extract from John Betjeman, 'Hymn', from *John Betjeman's Collected Poems*, 2nd edn, London, 1962, pp. 3–4 (half-title verso).

The NSW Heritage Office and the Organ Historical Trust of Australia: extracts from the *NSW Heritage: Pipe Organ Conservation and Maintenance Guide*, 1998 (143).

The Organ Historical Society: for the OHS guidelines for conservation and restoration, 1986 (153).

Conventions used

Notation and compass

The system adopted for notation refers to the keyboard or pedalboard note and not the pitch or pipe length of the stop:

$$GG\text{-}C\text{-}c^0\text{-}c^1\text{-}c^2\text{-}c^3\text{-}c^4$$

where GG is the bottom G of a long compass keyboard, i.e. the G below the bottom C of a modern, German-principle, organ key or pedalboard, and c^4 is the top note of a modern five-octave keyboard.

Acronyms

See Appendix 1: Relevant organizations.

Locations

All locations are in the United Kingdom, unless otherwise stated.

Terminology

In general, technical spelling follows the conventions set out in Wilfried Praet *et al.*, *Orgelwoordenboek* (*Organ Dictionary*). Zwijndrecht, Belgium, 1989, pp. 255–62.

Introduction

Jim Berrow

These pages attempt to convey the substance of a conference held in Liverpool from 23 to 26 August 1999, when over 80 players, builders, advisers, curators and owners of organs met under the auspices of the British Institute of Organ Studies (BIOS), the Council for the Care of Churches (CCC) and the Institute of British Organ Building (IBO). This lively event replaced the usual BIOS and the CCC Organ Advisers' annual residential conferences, and was billed under the rather dry and almost-accurate title of *Ethics and the Conservation of the Organ*.

If asked to produce a model compendium of use to all concerned, a *vade mecum* of historic organ conservation and restoration, rest assured few would start from here. But here we were. The editorial task has sought not to judge, distort or impose personal views on what the speakers brought to the table, but rather to provide a useful record and other documents for reference, consideration and review. For many reasons, not least the frailty of the organizers, these are not formal proceedings, if only because some participants did not present their contributions in a formal way. Not all the sessions were recorded and this is not a reflection on their value, but rather that some were presented in workshop fashion and, along with the panels, round-table sessions and informal discussions, are impossible to translate to the printed page in the time available. As always, the chance to meet and talk informally was the most valuable ingredient, again, something this volume cannot reflect. Several speakers, notably Drs John Harper, Peter Horton and Nicholas Thistlethwaite, complemented parallel recitals and events not strictly relevant to this volume, to enrich our understanding of those activities, and their papers will appear elsewhere. As well as opening doors into the world of professional museum conservation, we attempted to show what was happening 'over there', in Europe and the USA, and some of the most powerful and illuminating contributions came from sources who claimed to know little about the British organ, but were prepared to recount their own experiences for our benefit.

Why were we there? The catalyst (apart from the celebration of the coming of age of BIOS) was the continuous stream of requests to the organizing bodies for more technical education, along with the production of allied publications. The successful launch of the IBO, with its accreditation process, the availability of some public funds for conservation work, and a growing awareness of the importance of these matters in the wider museum and heritage field, made it obvious that there is a hunger for information and debate of quality. As a result three of us attempted to produce an agenda, draw together some experts from this country and abroad, find a suitable location and share what we had found. There was a realization, through the research work of BIOS members, the growing

enlightenment of various grant-giving bodies and the concern of many professional organ builders, that all was not well. We were aware that established
international standards existed in the conservation field, and that we must
become more familiar with these and adopt them. While such criteria have been
applied to other musical instruments, the organ has tended to remain uninflu-
enced by them, and the first step was to search for, and establish, general
philosophies that could guide our day-to-day work. Liverpool was, as Dominic
Gwynn aptly remarked, 'an event whose time had come', and your feedback and
participation are now essential to the process of furthering this endeavour.

We met in Liverpool because it is a friendly and interesting place and easy to
reach from most parts of the country and abroad;[1] it has some interesting organs
which, in the hands of our player-delegates, could provide illumination and
entertainment to the agenda, and stimulate thought-provoking discussion on the
why and how of conserving the three monsters we visited (at St George's Hall and
the two cathedrals); but, primarily, the recent establishment of the Conservation
Centre in the heart of the city had brought together a group of skilled conservators, working with advanced facilities, who care for objects as diverse as
mummified Egyptian crocodiles, public sculptures and space satellites.[2]

The contribution of the Liverpool conservators to our debate demonstrated that
we do not face unique problems. We must never be misled into thinking that the
organ and its repertoire are outside mainstream music-making. Like few other
historic musical instruments, organs are at the mercy of passing fashion. There are
those who feel so confident about their skills and knowledge that they incremen-
tally encourage the destruction of the instruments in their care, using organ
builders willing to take on inappropriate work, regardless of the consequences.
Special circumstances do exist, because most *historic* organs have a dual role, both
as heritage objects and as musical instruments in regular use, often expected to
service a repertoire for which they were not designed, but we ignore the accumulated knowledge of those who care for other large, complicated, heritage objects at
our peril. We have much to learn from those who manage the continued use,
repair and survival of objects as diverse as railway locomotives, boats of all shapes
and sizes, working looms, and so on. If they survive as historic objects to study,
copy or use, we can investigate the underlying philosophies which their curators
have adopted in order to resolve the difficult decisions which govern their
integrity and survival. Certainly, the parallels between the organ and other objects
which interest us through use, rather than as static exhibits, are convincing. It was
this sort of thinking that we wanted to encourage at Liverpool, in order to step
outside an intellectually confining world, and attempt to learn from the best practice readily available around us. Who organs know, who only organs know?

When it comes to considering the restoration of a good Edwardian organ, I sometimes feel that it is as if a modern-day aviator, having experienced the advanced
cockpit of a modern wide-bodied aircraft, comes across a vintage *Vickers Vimy*

biplane and attempts to modify it, in order to fulfil some of the benefits of the former. The result would be of little or no use to crew, passengers, historians or, especially, the owner.[3] Both vehicles are of their time and fulfil parallel (and admirable) functions. I cannot resist quoting from Jonathan Ambrosino:

> it would have been far kinder to history and church finances alike to secure organists who actually like a given instrument rather than to fund the desires of an organist who does not, and for a congregation that in all likelihood neither knows the difference nor much cares.

Perhaps it would be helpful to offer a thumb-nail sketch here of some twentieth-century western developments in the conservation world. International concerns led to the Athens Charter of 1931, the foundation for much later progress. A conference held in Venice brought about a charter of that name in 1964, 'for the conservation and restoration of monuments and sites'. This successful model led to others – Florence, on historic gardens (1981), Washington, on towns and urban areas (1987), and Lausanne, on the protection and management of archive heritage, especially with reference to legislation and economic prototypes (1989). The Australians brought a fresh approach to heritage matters (we know the value of their unique collection of nineteenth-century British organs), and adapted these grand texts to their own needs in the down-to-earth Burra Charter on the conservation of places of cultural significance (1979, with later refinements, see Appendix 2). Like many Australian wines, this document has travelled well and is a perfect starting point for us. Its precise and intelligent definitions should be hung on the wall of any one who professes to care for historic organs or, indeed, organs which might *become* historic. You must interpret its terms carefully and substitute 'organ' for 'place' but the subtleties (especially of the word 'significance') will become apparent. A popular journal for players has recently become exercised about some of these issues, but in so doing appears to have missed an important point (perhaps the single most important point): we cannot continue to make so-called conservation choices from a menu of flexible principles, picking and choosing at will – restored key-actions good, altered pedalboards, pitch, compass and swell-pedal mechanisms even better! British organ literature has a tendency to describe but not explain, especially in publicity material and organ builders' standard schedules – where rebuild, reconstruct, recast, refurbish, renovate, restore and renew are (wrongly) interchangeable words.

In the wider conservation world, excellent exchanges of ideas and information take place through organizations such as the International Council on Monuments and Sites (ICOMOS), the International Committee of Musical Instrument Museums and Collections (CIMCIM, founded in 1960) and their parent body, the International Council of Museums (ICOM). The Museums and Galleries Commission published standards for the care of musical instruments in 1995,[4] but this is mainly devoted to environmental issues within a museum context and leaves most of our problems unresolved.

It might be thought that the work and publications of professional museum conservators would shame similar attempts in our narrow sphere of interest. We came away from the Conservation Centre realizing that *best* practice in our field was good by any standard. Knowledge, skill and expensively gained experience are alive and well in British organ building (for builders, advisers and players) for those who conscientiously seek it but, it appears, we lack time, resources and sometimes the confidence to set out our views. This may be the result of the unusual fusion of craft, design, aesthetics and performance skills which make up the organ world, where we are nourished by enthusiasm rather than adequate funds.

The activity surrounding the Burra Charter may have played some part in inspiring the admirable Organ Historical Trust of Australia (OHTA) to produce their contemporary *Preservation Standards* for the treatment of historic pipe organs (1979, with revisions, see Appendix 3).[5] With the benefit of this example, BIOS published similar guidelines in 1991, which have never been revised, but stand up remarkably well today (Appendix 5).[6] The first major paper on the topic in the *BIOS Journal* was contributed by Grant O'Brien in 1982. It remains essential reading (although its author now feels less comfortable about various points, especially the issue of reversibility). He cautioned that, 'As we advance into the future, the number of early instruments will become less and less, and the rate at which new historical instruments will be discovered will decrease . . .'[7] and, 'Because no two historical instruments are ever exactly the same, they must be treated by the restorer as a unique document of the practice of some historical period . . . There is no such thing as a definitive restoration.'[8] Six years later, BIOS re-examined the topic, but still in a climate where such ideas were thought more appropriate to antiquarians.

But here, a warning. We can only explore past methods and the use of historic materials through the evidence of instruments which survive, as near as possible, in their original condition (the best reason for minimal intervention). That may mean, indeed it probably does mean, that some organs will never be played again, as at Stanford-on-Avon, where too little is left for such an exercise. Otherwise, incremental alterations by the well-meaning, nibble away at the soul of good instruments and eventually turn them into an assembly of meaningless bits and pieces, usually fuelled by just enough funds to do something, but not enough to employ those who know what should, or should not, be done. 'Poverty', as Michael Gillingham used to say, 'is a great preserver.'

The essays which follow do not claim to encompass all the needs of those questing for information on this thorny topic but, it is hoped, they will encourage debate and provide the foundation for another conference (and a more complete summary) in, say, five years or so. We would respond to those who might counsel the commission of further papers to fill some of the gaps in this volume, that the delay this would entail would be unwise. Everyone, including those who did not attend, must have the opportunity to play their part through feedback, so this volume does not represent an end, so much as the end of the beginning.

However, we made one exception. John Clare spoke from the floor on the issue of conservation plans, a subject neglected in our agenda, and so we commissioned a short paper from him on that topic given its importance, especially to those who seek grants. There remain some interesting dilemmas we did not fully explore – what should we do about an old organ that has somehow survived, but is 'not and probably never has been good'?

> An organ, whose foundation is not good, is generally rendered worse by attempts at mending it. Snetzler, a celebrated organ builder at Frankfort, [*sic*] told some churchwardens, who asked him, what he thought an old organ, which they wanted to have repaired, was worth, and what would be the expense of mending it: he appraised it at one hundred pounds, and said, if they would lay out another hundred upon it, it would then, perhaps, be worth fifty.[9]

Do organ builders, or their successor firms, have the right to modify their own work? The latter is an issue now concerning relatively recent, and once influential, instruments of the organ-reform movement. There is a reluctance in Britain to recognize the heritage value of organs and, as Barrie Clark points out in his contribution, there are no effective statutory controls which can be exercised over their survival. Should we pursue the notion of asking the appropriate authorities to recognize immobile organs as 'large objects' under the terms of existing legislation? One of the disadvantages of a reasonably successful campaign by BIOS against the destruction of good organs, is that diocesan Chancellors have taken to agreeing the removal of historic instruments (where their location, especially in a spacious chamber, is ear-marked for crèche or coffee-bar) on condition that a good home is found. At a stroke, these well-meaning decisions disconnect organs from the buildings for which they were commissioned. I understand that when a listed building is moved (not an impossible occurrence with today's technical skills), it automatically loses its status – unless, like a signal-box, it is a structure designed to be de-mountable.[10] Has BIOS yet refined its HOCS policy to withdraw a certificate attached to such peripatetic organs? Our discussions in this area attempted to draw together these points and some might criticize the conference organizers for not presenting model guidelines that could be held up (at least for the time being) as an ideal for care of organs in the new millennium, prescribing an approach to greater protection (and with it greater funding). But pain and gain often go together, and it is necessary for all the stakeholders to have the opportunity to participate in this debate, and contribute to a more complete conclusion. As previously mentioned, it would be premature and unproductive to rush into print with yesterday's manifesto, so these thoughts from three continents are offered for your consideration. The chapters are intended to be sampled individually; if they add up to more than the sum of their individual parts, they may have served some purpose.

What did we carry away from the conference? These are some personal thoughts:

- There is a danger that we undervalue *British* organ heritage, while recognizing its importance abroad.

- The issue of 'listing' is critical. We must refine our definition of what constitutes a historic organ (in whole or part) and ensure a uniform approach to their inclusion in a published record. BIOS is ideally suited to continue this process and should refine the excellent work of the NPOR and HOCS. We cannot expect to attract statutory recognition for the protection of historic organs, nor serious grant support, unless we do, and a thorough field trial is essential.

- Without compromising standards, all of those working on the research and *heritage* side must do their best to be 'user-friendly' and win their arguments through explanation and understanding other points of view.

- There appeared to be a feeling from the organ builders present that organ scholars could take on specialized (especially archival) research and reporting tasks on behalf of organ builders. This could be to their mutual benefit.

- Much better documentation *prior* to the commencement of restoration work is necessary. While new work is often well-documented, accurate descriptions of instruments or historic components as they stand are not.

- Tomorrow's researchers and restorers will be grateful to today's organ builders if their *new* instruments are fully documented.

- As so few organ journals are indexed, reading lists should be produced, especially covering conservation materials and techniques.

- The training of organ builders, particularly in an unsympathetic financial climate (see John Mander's thoughtful essay) must be reviewed.

- The Church must take more responsibility for the future provision of organists.

- We must encourage clergy, ecclesiastical officials and their committees to be aware of their responsibilities to keep historic instruments intact, and in their original locations, despite the pressures of passing liturgical and musical fashions.

- The IBO representatives mentioned plans to refine their accreditation process and this was welcomed.

- Might there be a consolidation of some of the organizations who now represent the craft, performers and scholars, along with a more sensible delegation of responsibilities? Certainly, the creation of a central forum which could speak with one voice when the occasion warranted must be worth considering. Such an umbrella organization might play a key role in preparing the next conference.

- 'Any statements we make about the past are at the same time statements about ourselves . . .'[11] With the benefit of hindsight, how some of us must be concerned with earlier, unwitting self-exposure in these changing times!

There was one other item of business before we went home, perhaps a first for a British organ conference (maybe the first in Europe since Freiberg in 1927!). We unanimously endorsed the proposal that:

> This conference expresses its grave concern about the continuing depletion of the nation's stock of historic organs owing to the inadequate protection of these instruments and lack of funding from public bodies for their repair and conservation. It calls upon Government to take steps, as a matter of urgency, to ensure that these instruments are listed, recorded and adequately protected, and also to make regular funding available to assist the custodians of these instruments with their repair and conservation.

Who will listen? In a world where the management style of the motorway service station is a model for guiding the Arts Council, and celebrity status is the preferred qualification for cultural recognition by the Department of Culture, Media and Sport, these words will only be converted into action if widely publicized, endorsed and then communicated to the politicians and civil servants who control the purse strings. But that's up to you!

1

What is a historic organ?

David Knight

An attempt to create greater understanding of the term 'historic' in organ building, and a view of how this might inform our approach to organ restoration

We are used to hearing the word 'historic' to describe a variety of things: historic houses, palaces, battles and cities. Doubtless some image is conjured up in our minds when we hear, for example, the phrase 'a historic castle'. How helpful are these ideas when we try to define what makes a historic organ? Although defining a historic organ is challenging, understanding its value is relatively easy. For example, Edward Rimbault said in his College of Organists lecture in 1864:

> The Organist cannot be too minutely acquainted with the history of his instrument in order that he may reason upon the various points that may arise in the course of his studies, and draw his inferences from correct data.[1]

In common with other nineteenth-century writers, Rimbault did not use the term historic, preferring to talk about *old* organs. Similarly, in Charles Pearce's late nineteenth-century book about organs in the City of London churches, the word historic does not even appear (with regard to organs) in the introductory preface. The *historic* organ appears to be a twentieth-century concept.

Outside the world of organ literature, the term 'early' is used far more than 'historic'. Recently, Peter Holman wrote that the early music movement began with instruments, but in recent years the focus has shifted to the fascinating relationship between instruments and the music written for them.[2] Note here the use of the term 'early music' not 'historic music' and the emphasis on the relationship between the instruments and their music. They are seen as part of a musical tradition that is still alive, even if parts of it had to be resurrected.

Most articles in journals like *Early Music* include details about instruments alongside examples in music manuscript relating them to their repertoire. Such associations are nearly always absent in writing about the organ as an instrument, but the benefits are obvious. An early or historic organ with some apparently anachronistic device can become a living musical instrument in the right context. William McVicker gives a good example of such a union of music and instrument in another recent article on the swell pedal. A hitch-down swell pedal in Franck's organ music makes perfect sense of his crescendo and diminuendo indications and puts a device which is found uncomfortable by some players into an appropriate musical context.[3]

What is a historic organ? The then Organ Advisory Committee of the Council for the Care of Churches (CCC) suggested a definition in 1956. In their list of historic organs, instruments were primarily included because of their cases, 'but where the pipes only are important, this is specifically stated'. The introduction to a list of 116 organs states, 'Where not otherwise stated, the case only is of importance.'[4] An organ case is often a significant furnishing in a church, and may well have a historical value of its own, independent of the organ it contains. This view is now seen as a weakness, not a strength, and may have given rise to the organ case being considered of more merit than its contents by organizations such as English Heritage. Another list of 'historically significant' instruments (including examples which qualified only for their cases or pipes) was included in Clutton and Niland's seminal book, *The British Organ* (1963). The introduction to the gazetteer section extended the definition of historic by saying that 'it is arguable that all surviving work prior to 1900 has a prima facie claim to historical significance'.[5] This will almost certainly include organs where the case is arguably of less importance.

In 1994, the British Institute of Organ Studies attempted a response to the question in their pamphlet, *Sound Advice*:

> This is a difficult question to answer concisely, but an arbitrary answer might be that an historic organ is one that . . .
>
> – is a good and intact example of its style or period;
>
> – incorporates material (e.g. pipework) from an earlier instrument of good quality; or
>
> – retains an interesting or architecturally distinguished case.[6]

This definition included the case of an instrument, along with its contents, and allows old materials in new locations to be regarded as historic.

The way we understand what makes an organ historic has changed in the last 20 or so years. The 'Guide to surviving English organs' which concludes Stephen Bicknell's *History of the English Organ*, sets out his philosophy of the value of old (rather than historic) organs:

> there are relatively few examples of old English organs that have been left as they were originally built . . . thus although it is in theory possible to draw up a long list of historic material surviving in the British Isles . . . much of this would be of academic interest, consisting only of casework or of instruments that are no longer representative of the style of the original builder.[7]

This introduces two ideas that were not present in the earlier lists. First, organ cases have a much lower priority than previously and the concept of an organ representing the style of the original builder is elevated to a new importance. An organ should be regarded as a complete entity, and a collection of historic material may not be the same as a historic organ. You will have noticed an absence of music references in these four examples.

Now consider the difference between a historic and a historical organ. A historic organ is one that has a famous or important place in history. A historical instrument is one that tells us about history, or one that can be established by evidence of earlier organ-building practice. Therefore the Alexandra Palace organ is *historic* because of its place in history, whereas the Gray & Davison organ at St Anne's, Limehouse, London, is historic because of its place in history and is historical because it survives in basically original condition as an example of Gray & Davison's organ building. All organs tell us about their building history, and can loosely be called historical. For the purposes of a working definition, a historical organ will be considered to be one that maintains the character and style of a definite period of organ building. This may not always be the organ's original condition, and could be the result of later rebuilding, giving it a new and cohesive identity.

The *historic* nature of an organ is not something we can influence. The *historical* nature of an instrument can be preserved or lost by what we do to it today, and will concern us in what follows.

Changes of fashion affect our understanding of an instrument, and our approach when it is being considered for restoration. This may result in organ parts being placed in a context never conceived by their original builder – for example eighteenth-century pipework played through a twentieth-century electric-action. Is the historic value of the pipework intrinsic to it and unaffected by its new location or not? According to the BIOS definition it is. In any musical use related to repertoire this is more difficult to defend.

What is historical? Is everything historical until proven otherwise?

The Organs Committee is the only one of the CCC's conservation committees to include age in the definition of a historical object. To help achieve the preservation of our organ-building heritage should the basic premise be that everything is historical until proven otherwise? Is scarcity a criterion for historicity? Is an organ less historic if there are several similar examples extant? Organs grant-aided by the Organs Committee in 1998 included some by lesser-known builders with few surviving instruments to their name such as Gardner, Abbott, Banfield and Thomas Smith, alongside those by Harrison & Harrison, T. C. Lewis and J.W. Walker whose work is better represented.

Some nineteenth-century organ builders were prolific, to say the least. In the mid-1860s Hill & Sons were producing 500 new stops per annum.[8] There is only one Hill organ from the years 1860–69 with a historic Organ Certificate, so what has happened to all the others? Although this is only a rough and ready figure, it is a suitable reminder that organs from major builders need to be respected and, arguably, conserved before we unwittingly lose the last one. What is common now will be scarce tomorrow if we treat it in a cavalier fashion to meet present-day expediency.

The emergence of the Victorian period as worthy of study and conservation has caused considerable change to the way Victorian organs are approached. Nicholas Thistlethwaite comments that:

> It is gradually coming to be realised that the years between 1840 and 1914 represented a veritable 'golden age' in the history of English organ building . . . Sadly this realisation has begun to dawn on us long after most of the grandest efforts of the Victorian and Edwardian organ-builders have been destroyed or pitifully modified by insensitive – if well-meaning – hands.[9]

The changes deprecated include modern pedalboards, electrification of actions, balanced swell pedals and tonal *improvements*.[10] Stephen Bicknell comments:

> Changes in musical fashion repeatedly intervene to render yesterday's instruments 'out of date', as some might say. The players and organbuilders who together arrange the care of many church organs on behalf of their owners frequently conspire to remove anything conspicuously old or unusual – just the very features most in need of preservation.[11]

Our attitude to what is historical will affect our philosophical approach to an organ for restoration or other work, and this attitude will change with time.

Practical music-making and conservation

The organ is a musical instrument, so how far do repertoire and performance – practice issues affect our definition of a historic or historical organ? This question remains unanswered in much of the debate about conservation, although I am pleased to see that some of the contributors to this conference compensate for this.

Should an organ with a body of repertoire be more strongly defended as historic? The long-compass English organ – that which we enjoyed in this country before succumbing to the desire to play the works of Bach on an organ with Continental compass – was all but lost over the late nineteenth and early twentieth centuries. This has left a body of English organ music, from the eighteenth-century and earlier, whose merits it is harder to appreciate as there are very few places where it can be played to advantage.

An organ can be considered historic for a range of reasons. Simon Webb, writing about the Albert Hall organ, stated that:

> The finest players of each generation have been attracted to the Royal Albert Hall. In August 1871 Anton Bruckner, then Court Organist of

Vienna, gave six recitals for £50. Saint-Saens was another of the early recitalists; while nearly a century later the French virtuoso Marcel Dupré gave his last recital on the instrument . . . The Royal Albert Hall organ is a national treasure and, in keeping with the character of the hall, a living monument to Victorian grandeur. It holds a secure place in the hearts of Promenaders.[12]

The reasons for the organ being historic are its location and musical associations, not just what is inside the case. On the same lines, the organ of the Temple Church, London, can be considered historic on account of its association with the long tenure of Sir George Thalben-Ball as organist.

Are organs with no body of repertoire, or identifiable performance practice, of less historic value? How much can an organ exist in a vacuum with no repertoire and still be historic? Is the Grant, Degens and Rippin organ in St John's, Boscombe, Bournemouth, historic? It was built in 1965 and is in many ways a picture of organ building in that era. It has electric-action, a romantically voiced Swell and Great, and classically voiced Choir and Solo. The pedal is arranged with some stops in each style. A full range of couplers, super- and sub-octave couplers, thumb and toe pistons is provided, along with a Fanfare Trumpet of ear-splitting volume. Although it is difficult to identify to what repertoire it is especially suited, the instrument as a whole is a bold statement for the eclectic organ, with an honesty few builders now have the courage to emulate.

In a world where fashions and ideas change rapidly this organ seems vaguely anachronistic. Is this a reason to preserve it or to lose it? Would you defend it as historic or not?

The question posed at the start of the paper – what is a historic organ? – still remains unanswered. We have seen that it includes elements related to the organ's age, case, pipework and repertoire along with people and events associated with it. We may still think we could recognize a historic organ when we see one, although the range of instruments considered historic by the delegates to this conference would probably be wide enough to surprise some of us and too narrow to satisfy the rest. This in itself shows the need for caution when we consider what approach to adopt when work is needed. It throws into relief the need for an ethical code to release us from a cycle of 'change and decay' and ensure a safe future for our pipe-organ heritage.

2

Protection of historic organs: European legislation and British isolation

Barrie Clark

In almost every mainland European country where organs represent a significant part of the musical history, they are protected by law and preserved with the help of the state, regardless of the government's political colour. Former eastern European countries, as far as they have been able, have taken the same attitude as western states. The United Kingdom is one of very few countries having no such statutory protection or recognition that organs in their own right are important to our cultural heritage. However, Historic Scotland has begun to include organs in list descriptions, and is prepared to consider listing a building because of the importance of an organ. Until recently the only central funds available in England were minor grants from English Heritage for casework repairs (recognition, at most, that they are pieces of furniture), but solely in Grade I and Grade II* listed buildings, and the National Heritage Memorial Fund have on a few occasions given grants to organs. The launch of the *Joint Grant Scheme for Churches and Other Places of Worship*, funded by English Heritage and the Heritage Lottery Fund (HLF),[1] led to a brief period of financial help for organs, not necessarily of national importance, but still only if in Grade I or Grade II* buildings, except in what is termed 'targeted areas' of the country. This anticipation was to be deflated shortly after by a sudden restriction of funds, and organ grants are now only given in exceptional circumstances.

When it comes to the preservation of an important organ in this country, there is no consistency of protection and sometimes, it must be said, of expert advice. It is complicated by the ecclesiastical exemption for churches in use, which sets them outside listed building controls, although growing consultation with local authorities, at least for buildings, is to be welcomed. The Church of England has its own protection system, together with Diocesan Organ Advisers, but there is no consensus in their appointment or required expertise, and some are not even conservation orientated. The Roman Catholic Church has set up an advisory body and the Methodists also have appointed advisers, but the Baptists and United Reformed Church are still struggling to set up similar systems.

In theory organs in secular buildings are protected by listed building legislation, but only as part of a building. Confusion in law about what constitutes a fixture and therefore part of a building, and what is a moveable object has exercised the courts from time to time and, as yet, there is no clear definition. Organs not physically built into a structure or within a chamber specifically built for an organ are sometimes regarded as moveable. This certainly applies to chamber organs which are to some extent more portable. John Norbury was perceptive in stating in his *Box of Whistles* (1877)[2]: 'Remember that an organ is built, other musical instruments are made.' In the United Kingdom since the war there has been a growing unease about this unsatisfactory situation. The Anglican Church recognized the problem and set up an Organs Advisory Committee in 1954, under the Council for the Care of Churches. On the other hand, one of English Heritage's conditions for grants to churches gives them freedom to comment on alterations, and this could be taken to include organs, but they choose not to exercise that right, not seeing it as an appropriate role.

In 1976 the destruction or drastic alteration of so many fine historic organs (usually regretted with hindsight) led to the setting up of the British Institute of Organ Studies (BIOS) to press for the preservation of historic organs in the United Kingdom. It has had growing success in drawing attention to particular problems and has highlighted the plight of organs threatened by destruction or alteration, but such changes of fate should not depend on the work and influence of a private pressure group. The radical changes to the organ in Sherborne Abbey, when it was rebuilt and enlarged in 1954, were undertaken on the advice of two important musicians. It should never have happened and in other countries, with statutory protection, would no doubt have been prevented. Ecclesiastical exemption was insufficient to prevent the Sherborne alterations but, on the other hand, legislation ought to be effective in protecting organs in secular buildings, but is it?

The problem of adequate legal protection is particularly acute with town hall organs, where the future of an instrument may be decided by the vote of councillors who often consider economy before aesthetics and may have little interest in artistic or historic matters. The fate of the organ in Preston Public Hall is well known and although now in store its future gets bleaker as time passes.

The Cavaillé-Coll organ in Parr Hall, Warrington, is the only instrument of any size in the United Kingdom by this French master-craftsman that has not been tonally altered to any great extent. In 1969 the Warrington Corporation decided that an estimate of £9,000 for repairs was not worth the expenditure and proposed its disposal. It was saved only by the efforts of the specially formed Cavaillé-Coll Organ Retention Committee which began to raise money for its repair. The Corporation eventually gave an undertaking that if sufficient funds could be raised, the organ would be retained. The future of an artistic treasure such as this should not be decided in such a manner.

The organ in Reading Town Hall raises the same issues. Until recently it would appear that the local authority did not have a high regard for this very important instrument, and proposed to reduce the dimensions of the concert hall in which it stands by inserting an extra floor. This would have seriously altered the acoustics, to the detriment of the substantially unaltered and, therefore, extremely important early Willis concert organ. (Most of his other examples have been drastically altered, for instance those in the Albert Hall, London, and Huddersfield Town Hall.) After worries about its future for several years, the restoration and re-erection of the Reading organ has taken place and the alterations reversed, but there is no statutory power which would have guaranteed its reinstatement.

To illustrate how isolated the United Kingdom is regarding organ preservation, I have looked at how a number of European countries deal with such matters. The information has largely come from an exchange of letters with various government departments and also some organ advisers, charged with the preservation of organs, who gave details of their legislation.

Italy

Italian historic organs are protected by law as historic monuments. The work is divided between the state and the regional governments, and a superintendent covers groups of provinces. In Tuscany, for example, there are three – for Florence and Pistoia; Pisa, Lucca and Livorno; and Massa, Siena, Arezzo and Grosseto. Each has a director of restoration and Florence has a special director for historic organs. Grants for restoration are available and applicants must work with an organ builder chosen from an approved list. Work can either be controlled by the superintendent working through his director of restoration, or more usually by national experts appointed by the Ministry of Culture and the Environment; these make a report to the regional director who makes the final decision. A problem is that some superintendents have different ideas about restoration and, so far, attempts to establish a relevant charter have not been successful.

Alternatively, organs can be restored directly by the state, or in the form of a one-third grant to the owner. Regional, provincial or city administrations can also give grants, but in this case the state does not contribute. Private funds are encouraged through tax concessions and, as an example, one of the Veronese banks has largely paid for the major restoration of the two organs in the *Duomo* of that city. In those circumstances, public money is not given and the church pays any shortfall in cost.

The Netherlands

The Dutch system of control has operated for just over 40 years. This small country has designated over 800 organs as historic monuments, the majority belonging to the Dutch Reformed Church. These come under the control of the National Trust (a government department) which decides if an organ is historic or not – usually instruments prior to about 1900 although, no doubt, this will change. There is a National Trust central adviser who is a civil servant.

The Dutch Reformed Church has an Organ Commission, drawn from the general board of the Church. A parish first goes to them for advice; they are given a list of ten advisers and the church is free to choose one. In practice some are specialists in organs by particular builders, two have a technical bias, and in some instances the parish is advised to select the one with the greatest appropriate expertise. These advisers must spend half of their time on advisory work, studying organ builders' works and visiting similar examples in other countries. They are paid 5 per cent of the restoration costs and the Commission also charges up to an additional 2 per cent for administration costs. The advisers' study time is not paid for. There is no formal system for appointing or training organ advisers, but the National Trust oversees their work and all restoration reports are deposited with them. There is a twice-yearly meeting of the advisers to maintain consistency and discuss any problems. The Roman Catholic Church has a similar Commission with an adviser specially appointed for restoration work. The smaller denominations can go direct to the National Trust and then use any of the Dutch Reformed Church advisers or the Roman Catholic adviser. (Maybe, for the present, the Church of England could help the Baptist and United Reformed Church in a similar way.)

The advisers are independent of all organ builders. If a church disagrees with the adviser's report the National Trust makes the final decision. The adviser's fee is paid directly by the church concerned. Advisers can also be involved in the design of new organs, but there is no state aid for these, or for recreating missing parts of historic instruments. There is a presumption that the builder who maintains the organ will carry out the work, but a specialist in a particular builder's historic work may be suggested.

State funds for grants in general are divided between the regions, depending on the number of historic monuments, and regional administrations must then decide on priorities. This is a fairly new system to strengthen regional decision-making, but informal opinion prefers the old system whereby the National Trust had its own central budget and could take a balanced national overview. Perhaps an example of 'if it works don't fix it'.

Until 1977 grants for all historic monuments were 80 per cent, but this is now reduced to 70 per cent which the provincial government can top up by 10 per cent. In special cases of hardship (for instance a small rural population) and where an organ is of great importance, churches can obtain grants approaching 100 per cent, often a compelling reason for organists to live with a restricted compass, mean-tone temperament and no playing aids. There are also special funds from cultural foundations such as the Prince Bernhardt Fund. Where an organ has a complicated history, there has been a growing assumption of conservation, rather than restoration to a perceived original, so preserving a musical entity.

France

In France organs are protected under the law of 31 December 1913, with its various amendments, which applies equally to all historic monuments.[3] Organs are not referred to specifically but are included in the general category of moveable furniture. In *Notes et Etudes Documentaires* (24 September 1974) there are sections which set out the procedures for the classification of historic organs, the measures for their protection and the general principles to be applied to their conservation.

The majority of organs in France are in public ownership. The cathedral organs are owned and wholly funded by the state and most parish church organs belong to the local commune. There is therefore a high level of tax-payers' money spent on their repair and restoration. Within the Ministry of Culture, the Directorate of Heritage is responsible for historic organs, and the Directorate of Music and Dance is empowered to aid the restoration of unprotected organs, or the building of new ones. The latter department is also responsible for the modern parts of a historic organ. An example is Notre Dame, Paris, where, because the action from console to soundboards is not original, both directorates are involved.

A breakdown of funding for a typical parish church organ might be: 50 per cent from the state, the region 10 per cent, the department 25 per cent and the commune 15 per cent, but this varies from region to region. An inventory was begun in 1980 and so far 8,500 organs are now recorded. Of these 900 are protected in their own right, in the same way as buildings, and of these 100 are in a special category. In addition, 400 organ cases are classified under the same law as items of furniture.

The listing of, and conservation work to, historic organs is controlled by a section of the Superior Commission of Historic Monuments formed of organ specialists, usually historians and renowned organists. Only certain organ builders in France are registered to carry out historic organ restorations, and these have passed special examinations in conservation techniques.

When work is to be carried out, a detailed report is written by an organ adviser for the Commission who then nominates one of their members to oversee the project. The system is regarded by some as complicated and confusing.

Germany

Germany, until after the Second World War, like the United Kingdom, only gave money to restore organ cases and not instruments themselves. The federal government has devolved all responsibility for the preservation of cultural objects and buildings to the regional (*Länder*) governments, but organs are not separately protected except as part of a building.

Nearly all organs belong to the church, and they take the primary responsibility for funding necessary work. If important enough, the repair of a historic organ may be assisted financially by the *Denkmalschutzbehorde* or Office of Monuments.

In ordinary situations some funds are raised locally by the parishes themselves but most will come from the church tax. District councils can also help financially if they have part ownership of an organ. Before work can be carried out, each project must be examined by an organ adviser (who can be over-ruled by the priest) who is on the church authorities' approved list. The parish can choose which one to appoint. There is a problem of hierarchy here because organ advisers, who are usually organists, rank lower than priests in authority.

Austria

In Austria there are laws for the protection of monuments which include organs.[4] *Das Bundesdenkmalamt* or Federal Monuments Office has two departments responsible for organs – the musical department, which deals with the instruments, and the architecture department, responsible for the cases.

Secular organs are dealt with by one of the nine regional offices of the Monuments Office. The Roman Catholic Church looks after its own organs and each diocese appoints experts. In most cases methods of restoration are agreed between the diocese and the Monuments Office, and this includes alterations or the move of an organ to a new site.

The parishes pay for most restorations but the state will contribute to the restoration of particularly valuable instruments. This, however, only amounts to an average of 5 per cent, but the diocese frequently offers parishes interest-free loans. The Protestant churches administer a similar system.

The Czech Republic

In the Czech Republic, formerly Bohemia and Moravia, almost all historic organs come under state protection (there are still some remote areas which to date have escaped the state listing of moveable monuments). The state Monuments Office has no organ experts and, since 1984, Dr Jiri Sehnal has been co-ordinating a survey on their behalf, carried out by volunteers, to document all organs according to a set of agreed criteria. The Monuments Office makes use of unpaid experts, not on their staff, but not all areas have such a person. There are normally no state funds available for restoration.

Some Roman Catholic dioceses, such as Prague, Brno and Königgräz have their own unpaid experts, but others have none. The parishes almost always pay for restorations, but in exceptional circumstances state funds have been provided. There is great reluctance on the part of a large number of organists to accept historical restoration, without modern improvements, but lack of money often leads to inferior alterations. The Monuments Office is only an advisory body without power to take legal action. Prior to the Communist regime this was not the situation, and no doubt in time the legislation will be strengthened.

Spain

In Spain the federal government has devolved most of its powers for monument protection to the autonomous regions, and they have all set up their own systems and legislation. Funds for restoration are available for organs registered as historical monuments in the form of grants or loans. Some regions have attempted to, or intend to, draw up inventories of their stock of organs.

As an example, the region of Navarra is willing to grant aid up to 75 per cent of the cost of restoration, depending on the importance and quality of the instrument. Parishes or local authorities forward applications to the region, and technical supervision is delegated to the *Association Navarra de Amigos de los Organos* (Navarra Association of Friends of the Organ), the Navarra region's equivalent of BIOS. They produce a report before payment is made.[5]

In some regions the Roman Catholic Church plays a greater role in a self-regulatory way, with the regional government helping with funds.

The Ministry of Culture in Madrid has a department charged with preserving items deemed to form part of the national heritage, which can include just about any important historic work of art. A catalogue of cathedral organs is planned but, as far as I know, has not yet been compiled. The Ministry can in theory fund organ restoration but, in reality, can only afford to spend on prestigious examples such as cathedral organs.

I have no detailed information about other European countries, but although the systems for protection differ in effectiveness, there is at least a common intent to protect historic organs. For instance in Poland, the first order for the protection of a historic organ was made in 1918.[6] To date about 2,000 historic organs have been surveyed and there is a restoration workshop in Krakow. Croatia with all its political problems has a full survey of pipe organs, carried out in the mid 1970s. Last, but most important in setting an example to the *old country* is:

Australia

Our former colonies relied on England to provide the majority of their major instruments, and in Australia many examples of English organ-builders' work remain virtually unaltered. The state of New South Wales has recently set a good example by establishing a register of historic organs and has protected them by legislation. The Organs Historical Trust of Australia (OHTA) was founded in 1977 as a national organization for the conservation of their organ heritage. The New South Wales Heritage Act (1977) acts as model legislation for state involvement in conservation. The Heritage Council of New South Wales gives funds to the OHTA for the latter to administer on its behalf, and this can include the relocation of historic organs where this is essential. Work on organs can be tax deductible if classified by the National Trust of Australia. Although they did not actually provide funding for the recent restoration of the 1891 Lewis organ in St Paul's Cathedral, Melbourne, the National Trust agreed to sponsor the appeal for $500,000, thereby acknowledging the importance of the project.

One other example is Victoria, where pipe organs are covered by legislation for the protection of historic buildings. Organs may be listed on the Register of Buildings, and any proposed work or alteration must be approved by the Historic Buildings Preservation Council.[7]

United Kingdom

As for the United Kingdom, the time has surely come when we should face the problem of organ preservation and enact legislation for their proper protection and, in particular, recognize that mechanism is also most important. In this country organs are regarded only as musical instruments and not as part of our national heritage or history of technology for, during the nineteenth century, we led in the development and patenting of ingenious devices for more efficient control of the instrument. We acknowledge the archaeological importance of machinery from our industrial revolution – why should organs be excluded from this?

The Newman Report has given special mention to organs, a small acknowledgement that our lobby has at least a foot in the door, and the government has now given its official response. On matters relating to organs, it *notes* John Newman's suggestions rather than proposing action. One important Newman proposal for the Church of England faculty system was that 'certain controversial cases which turned exclusively on conservation issues should be adjudicated by someone with conservation expertise'.[8] The Department for Culture, Media and Sport (DCMS) noted this, but advised caution and a wait and see policy. No hasty decisions there! The key statement on organs in the Newman report said:

> All the relevant committees of exempt denominations should appoint organs advisers, one of whose principal tasks should be to compile the relevant list of historic organs in liaison with BIOS or other such body. Where an organ has been identified as being of historic significance permission to move it should not be given until serious efforts have been made to find it a suitable new home.[9]

The DCMS response merely notes that the denominations are working towards this state of *nirvana*.

In February 1999, a meeting was hosted by the Anglican Council for the Care of Churches with the exempt churches and bodies closely connected with historic churches and organs, such as English Heritage, BIOS, the National Heritage Memorial Fund and the Churches Conservation Trust, to discuss this official response to Newman. Perhaps significance could be attached to the fact that the DCMS sent its apologies! The outcome was a proposal to seek a meeting with DCMS to discuss the following issues:

- a method of funding the completion of an accurate national list of pipe organs;
- protection of organs in unlisted buildings;

- the listing of whole instruments, not just cases;
- the inclusion of organs in the listing description of a building;
- the listing of historic parts of an organ in their own right.

The DCMS has now responded negatively to a meeting and seems unwilling, for the present, to consider the statutory listing of organs.

It appears that the government does not see itself taking a lead in organ matters, and is relying on BIOS to do the job. This would be fine if it would fund the work and raise BIOS to the status of a statutory consultation body, such as the Georgian Group and Victorian Society, but as BIOS has set up the National Pipe Organ Register (NPOR) it is probably in the best position to complete the job. There are now about 25,000 entries in the NPOR, which may be about half the total number of organs in the country. The cost of completing this work is difficult to estimate, but could be as high as £80,000, depending on the contribution from volunteer workers.

In April 1999, representatives of the British Institute of Organ Building (IBO) and BIOS met with the Heritage Lottery Fund, to put the case for increased lottery funding for organs, but the situation will not improve in the immediate future.

The listing and statutory protection of organs need to be given in their own right, and not as part of a building. This would then give a clear indication of an instrument's independent importance, overcome the problem of organs in unlisted buildings and protect them against displacement, sale abroad, alteration or other inappropriate work. In other words a full continental-European system of protection. As long as ecclesiastical exemption exists, new legislation will not directly help church organs, but could at least establish guidelines which are difficult to ignore.

The BIOS Historic Organ Certificate has now been given to about 200 owners of qualifying organs and it is a good start, but offers no actual protection to the instruments. It should not be a substitute for statutory listing. If the DCMS eventually agrees to statutory protection it will need specific proposals for listing before taking matters further, and therefore the guidelines laid down must be clear so that the result is consistent and logical.

In December 1989, during House of Commons question time, Tony Banks, then a back-bench MP, made a special plea for the protection of organs in redundant churches. He was quoted as saying that:

> the fine musical instruments found in many old churches were not given adequate protection as they are in other European countries. An inventory of the organs within any area should be drawn up so that adequate protection could be extended to them.

Until recently he was a parliamentary under-secretary within the DCMS. Hopefully he still has some influence and, perhaps, should be reminded of his enthusiasm of ten years ago.[10]

We are not alone in this venture and other bodies are pursuing similar aims. In 1992 the National Historic Ships Committee (NHSC), whose chairman is Admiral of the Fleet Sir Julian Oswald, set up a National Register of Historic Vessels and the National Maritime Museum and the Heritage Lottery Fund support this. An important point to note is that the NHSC advises central government and heritage-funding agencies on historic vessel preservation in the United Kingdom. Where did we go wrong?

The distinguished architectural historian and academic, Peter Burman, once said, 'The organ remains the Cinderella of church furnishings and works of art.' Certainly both Cinderella and organs involve Buttons, but is it not time for this particular situation to end? In true pantomime fashion, when the government responds negatively to statutory listing of organs, 'Oh no we won't', you will know what to reply.

I recently bought a second-hand book called *Amsterdam, City of the 70s*, published in the Netherlands, in English – a very general book covering all aspects of the city's life. What I find significant is that one page is a full-colour picture of the Westerkerk organ showing that such instruments are regarded as a natural part of Dutch culture. This is only part of my point as the caption reads, 'Largest part built in 1686 by Johannes Duyschot.' Where, other than the Netherlands, would a publisher assume that such obscure information would be of interest to the general reader? I think he has certainly misjudged his English readers. That says it all and I rest my case.

3

A USA perspective: 1

Jonathan Ambrosino

The title given to my paper has, to me, an old-time journalistic ring to it; one can faintly hear the teletype machine in the background. To clue you in a bit further, I was specifically asked to discuss America's treatment and care of twentieth-century organs, perhaps as something vaguely preparatory to our visit to Liverpool's Metropolitan Cathedral, with its landmark instrument from a period we may not yet consider historic. Or do we? I've never heard the organ, so cannot comment. But on the topic of whether we have actually restored any organ of the twentieth century in the twentieth century in my own country I have much to say.

In America, as in England, presenting a historic entity to a modern public often brings with it radical alteration of the entity in question. Independence Hall in Philadelphia is no longer a seat of government; it has become the embodiment of its historical icon, the cradle of liberty, for all to walk through and see. Walking through implies ramps for the handicapped, elevators for the weary, air-conditioning for our sweat and radiators for our chill, not to mention wiring, plumbing, lighting, telephones and security systems. The cradle of liberty is now cradled in laser-beam motion detectors. As a culture we are conditioned to having our history pre-digested, sized up in convenient individual portions, so that we are not so much visitors to a shrine but more consumers of history as a marketed tourist item. If we have 'done it, bought the T-shirt (or *tea*-towel, as Jim Berrow has helpfully suggested)', chances are that we have gone into a structure that, even with much sensitivity and thought, has been shamelessly altered to keep pace with modern expectations, even of an experience that is supposed to be 'historic'.

Our old organs are increasingly becoming the equal of these types of 'historic' experiences. Not only is this bad in and of itself, but it tends to make genuine conservation-oriented restoration some kind of fluke exception to the more normal sort of intrusive rebuild, or even that kind of rebuilding which masquerades as restoration.

I came here not from Philadelphia, which is my home, but from Montreal, where the Organ Historical Society's annual convention is still in progress. It is our Society's first convention outside the United States, and is a fascinating but chilling preview of what I fear future conventions may be like. Simply put, Montreal has almost no organs in original condition. Although we regularly hear new

23

organs at our OHS conventions, this is the first time new organs comprise the majority of those seen. Those not from the nineteenth century, or not modern organ-reform-movement instruments, have all, every one of them, been changed.

Most were Casavant organs to begin with, rebuilt either by Casavant themselves or one of the more recently prominent firms such as Guilbault-Thérien or Létourneau. The most famous of these old Casavants, the 1915 organ at the Eglise de Très Saint Nom de Jesus in the Maisonneuve section of Montreal, would have suggested itself a prime candidate for pristine restoration; instead it was completely rebuilt by Casavant. Even more interesting, Casavant's philosophy is available for all to savour. I quote from a pamphlet issued by them, in conjunction with the church:

> From a tonal standpoint the organ is representative of the large instruments produced by Casavant in those days. While it shows the influence of the nineteenth-century French-symphonic aesthetics favoured by the Casavant brothers, it also reflects the Anglo-American style then in fashion.

> The organ . . . earned praise from many quarters. The famous organist Lynnwood Farnam, who played it a few months after it was installed, emphasized that 'balance and finish were everywhere apparent'. In 1924, the renowned English organ builder Henry Willis III visited the Casavant brothers while on a trip to the United States and Canada. He wrote, 'The organ which gave me the most pleasure, and which I consider the Casavant chef d'oeuvre, is that in the Church of the Sacred Name of Jesus, Maisonneuve, Montreal.'

> A restoration committee was formed in the early 1980s. Four renowned organists drew up specifications, while organologist Massimo Rossi made an exhaustive review of the pipework. While everyone involved agreed on the historical and tonal value of the instrument, it was felt that the work should be done in keeping with the French symphonic tradition, since the organ had obvious roots in that style.

You can guess the rest, which goes on to say that the console was entirely rebuilt, the Great chorus entirely recast, and the Great reeds revoiced with new shallots. A hiatus occurred due to lack of funding, but a decade later it was possible to resume work. 'The key elements of the original restoration plan were respected, although it was simplified somewhat, in particular through greater re-use of the pipework.' Two choice quotes end my citation, this first from Christopher Jackson of Concordia University:

> It is not surprising that I enthusiastically agreed to act as a consultant for the proposed restoration in 1984, later to be joined by several of my colleague organists. After extensive debate and discussion we agreed that the organ should not only be restored but brought to a

closer approximation of the French symphonic instruments it was intended to emulate.

And from Casavant's associate tonal director Jacqueline Rochette:

> In keeping with our tradition, we took particular care with the voicing, tone regulation and balance between the different tonal syntheses. The 'balance and finish' praised in 1915 by Farnam can still be heard in this wonderful instrument, part of Quebec's musical heritage.

On a recent Internet discussion forum devoted to organ matters, John Panning, the tonal director of Dobson Pipe Organ Builders, summed up my reaction more politely than I would have. I quote:

> Apparently, the instrument is a great success. Why, then, is there this bowing and scraping to the idea that the organ has been 'restored', when it's clearly been rebuilt and revoiced? Is there something dishonourable about this, especially if the result is excellent? Will the organ be more highly regarded because of this fiction that it's been 'restored'?

If we are not clear in our definition of 'restore', it will soon mean nothing.

I don't wish to point at Casavant as an example of what every builder in America has done at sometime or other. What I find so glaring is the double-speak. For one thing, the early Casavant aesthetic, with its closed-shallot chorus reeds, roller-bearded strings, leathered diapasons and prolific wooden flutes, relates to nineteenth-century French traditions in nomenclature only: it was never, as Mr Jackson would have us believe, intended to emulate anything but a personal style of Claver Casavant, one of the original brothers. More to the point, it demonstrates how in North America the word restoration is applied indiscriminately across a wide range of treatments, very few of which have anything to do with true restorative preservation work.

This troubling development almost seems a retrogression from the heady ideals in force at the beginning of the conservation movement. In the 1970s when a real restoration ethic started to emerge simultaneously in both tracker and electric-action realms, restoration meant just that: making the organ go again by cleaning it up and changing only those perishable materials the builder expected would be renewed over the long-term life of the instrument.

These days the word restoration is more often invoked as a marketing ploy rather than as an indication of serious intent to preserve the past. Perhaps this is to be expected of America. History is a very great and sentimental thing to many Americans, much in the manner of the Bible. Like the Bible, however, history is something few Americans have read or actually understand, much less wish to grasp. They like the notion of history, as we all do. It is comforting to have come from something and from somewhere, but otherwise the awe of the ancient makes us glaze over, pining instead for storybook myth over real historical wonder and example.

As soon as organs began to be restored there was both celebration and opposition. People who were tired of seeing organs either spoilt or discarded rejoiced at new-found sensitivity and respect for organ heritage. Those who had been all too happy to change, enlarge and 'update' their instruments looked upon the restorers as trouble-makers who had come to spoil the party. Moreover, these same people grew increasingly uncomfortable with any unwelcome attention upon the machinations of their hoped-for rebuilds.

Why are organists and builders so afraid to keep old organs old? In some cases, they have been the ones to change an organ, and they have no desire to go back to a sound and musical effect they consider inferior. One famous instance involved a 1930s Aeolian-Skinner, designed and finished by G. Donald Harrison. The organ was mostly on pressures of between three and four inches and was undoubtedly mild; texture, clarity of tone and seamless blend were the objectives here, not raw decibels: an anti-heroic rather than anti-romantic organ. Over a period of many years, the organist had systematically loudened the organ, first by having the shallots of the chorus reeds filled with wax and let out to the limit, then by having the toes cut full open on the two Great mixtures, scraping nicks and widening windways on the remainder of the chorus to balance. The result was a hideous, shrieking mess without blend, balance or clarity. The final touch came in the addition of not one but two half-length 32' reeds, shoved into the organ at either end like overgrown news kiosks.

Not surprisingly, the church suspected that something was wrong. Not only did the organ sound somewhat tortured, it was a disorganized mess inside. This state of affairs was confirmed by the fact that every independent evaluator recommended putting the organ back exactly as it had been, and commented in no uncertain terms upon the quality of the rebuilding work. The organist, who hired a consultant perhaps with the goal of protection from the 'historical mob', did not realize how committed to restoration his consultant actually was. The poor organist was now not only upset at the prospect of losing his new-found tonal excitement; he was humiliated to lose the support of his church. Rather than suffer the fate of his own decision-making, he resigned. The restoration work continued under the guidance of the same consultant and a new, supportive organist; all pipework was restored, including chipping the wax out of the slender Bertouneche-style shallots, at great expense but with convincing results.

This is one of the few instances where the organist left. It was an uncomfortable and unhappy situation for all parties – except, of course, for the organ. Since egos mend faster than organs, it was perhaps for the best. In most other instances the organist will be annoyed by restoration because he had hoped to use the rehabilitation process as a means of getting the organ reconfigured according to his own liking. After all, he plays it Sunday by Sunday, who better should know its flaws? And why should flaws not be corrected? If the argument is set up on these false premises, no reasonable hand will win. The fact of the matter is that if we don't leave organs alone, we will never understand a thing about them, let alone be open to the lessons that they alone can teach.

In a nineteenth-century instrument of earlier vintage, the desire to reconfigure is sometimes more about logistics than personal tonal whim. The major obstacles always seem to be compass, pitch and action: no pedalboard, a GG and a c° Swell, and a heavy-handed nineteenth-century balanced action are conventionally seen to limit the range of repertoire an instrument will accommodate. In a twentieth-century instrument, the impatience is greater, the reasoning thinner, the means of change much easier, and to my mind the consequences just as grave. Another example: again, an organ by Aeolian-Skinner, this time from the early 1950s in a prosperous church. The organ was formerly distinguished not only by its completeness but also by the presence of Great reeds, something of a rarity in a Harrison instrument of about 50 stops.

A consortium of firms recently rebuilt the organ. On the plus side, it was discovered that the floor supporting the organ was giving way; this was rectified. On the other hand, a new console was introduced, several stops switched around, certain existing stops made playable at more than one pitch, the former barbaric Pedal reed choked down and made into a Great double reed, several new ranks of pipes added, and numbers of new electronic stops to go with them, including a monstrous 32′ plus 16′ pedal-reed 'effect'.

However, since this is the era of historical awareness, the church authorities knew they would have to answer to someone. To demonstrate historical sensitivity, they placed the original console in a gallery some 140 feet away from the chancel and main organ, and wired it to the original specification. The awfully nice organist related that he had accomplished much of the funding for the project by using the R word, which was impossible to deduce until he said 'Restoration'. Is adding electronic voices, at least easier to reverse in the future, less invasive than changes and additions to the pipes?

Whatever the answer, these kinds of events cause one to review positive attitude about recent trends. For example, as recently as three years ago, I was able to write rather smugly in the *Journal* of the then-new IBO:

> The Organ Historical Society happily celebrates its fortieth anniversary this year. Since its inception in 1956, the OHS has fought vigorously and effectively for the cause of the historic American organ. Their efforts have paid off: more and more organs, large and small, are restored according to their Guidelines for Conservation and Restoration. This simple page, authored more than twenty years ago by restorer and tracker organ builder George Bozeman and modified only slightly since then, sets forth a simple code of good restoration conduct: if something has worked reliably, then refurbish it according to the original manufacture and techniques used to build it; if it has proven unreliable, or secondary conditions prevent reliable operation, then – and only then – alter it with the greatest sensitivity and make your work easy to undo at a later time.[1]

While there is no untruth in the above statement, it must be conceded that we have still a very great distance to come in the recognition and genuine conservation of our heritage. There is no question that things have improved. Historical awareness has developed, research has been considerable, and appreciation and understanding have grown tremendously. People used to guard their opinions for fear of reprisal when their organs were out of fashion. Now, tolerance is at a much greater level, and almost every kind of instrument enjoys some degree of appreciation. People confess to liking Schlickers, others have stopped holding monthly village swell-box burnings.

However, a considerable gap continues to exist between acknowledging historical significance and a consistent, honest and serious restoration ethic. In organs that have been even slightly changed, people seem too eager to jump on the change-and-addition bandwagon, since the door has been opened. In organs that were once very significant but are now considerably altered, most people have less interest in recapturing what was once potentially magnificent, preferring instead to take an easier, less challenging route towards what is invariably a more modern stop-list and musical result. Thus the outcome is neither new nor old, and it requires a builder of considerable genius to produce distinguished results.

Players and builders alike share a role in the outcome, and the results, like the culture, touch all extremes. Don't misunderstand, numerous instruments have been the objects of thoughtful preservation, but as I surveyed the examples for this talk, it dawned on me anew that such examples remain the exception to normal practice. Real restoration – that is, keeping organs entirely original with no changes whatsoever – continues to be seen as an extremist and impractical treatment set against modern expectations of what any organ should be called upon to perform. Old tracker organs continue to be rebuilt with new actions (to better approximate the action in new organs) and routinely receive tonal alterations (to better approximate modern desires in performing a broader range of music). While such changes occur less frequently than was the case in the 1960s and 1970s, one wonders why it is still going on at all: wasn't this supposed to be the domain of new organs? Has the preservation movement in fact failed? It is easy to be cynical in concluding that most organists really aren't interested in the past, and most organ builders are all too happy for the work. Few other conclusions present themselves, however.

Twentieth-century electric-action organs see the greatest casualties. Almost without exception their electrical systems are replaced, and consoles are either rebuilt or replaced outright. This disregards the all-important original builder's tactile and environmental intentions: after all, did not the twentieth century lavish incredible attention on console feel, look, touch? Worst of all, such organs never seem to escape some kind of tonal alteration or augmentation. It used to be bad enough that every second electric-action organ could not be re-leathered without growing a trompette-en-chamade in the process. These stops were installed everywhere: east walls, west walls, transept walls, tower walls, high above pointing at nothing and, most frighteningly, in vertical arrangements sticking out like machine artillery from chancel columns. The 1990s has another solution for us, in that instruments can be 'completed' without regard for spatial consideration by the introduction of electronic (pardon me! *digital*) voices. (This splitting of hairs is something akin to calling leatherette Naugahyde, but apparently it means a great deal to those who know the difference.)

Not that there are many more unaltered organs to compromise. Consider the 750 organs that Ernest Skinner's company built from 1901 to 1931; about 11 per cent of those instruments, just about 80, survive without alteration of any kind, save standard re-leathering or renewal work. By alteration of any kind, I am applying what some might consider a strict standard but which constitutes the only definition that can apply: those that survive with no tonal or interior mechanical alterations whatever, and with their original consoles and electrical systems intact. If one were to be more lax, and accept the number of organs that have been added to, or electrically changed, but at whose core one can still experience the original musical results, the figure would grow to perhaps 25 per cent. By any count this is alarming, but few seem to care much.

Aeolian-Skinner organs have fared only slightly better, and certainly most of the landmark organs have been already altered a good deal. Famous instruments such as Boston's Church of the Advent are celebrated as a testament to the legend of G. Donald Harrison, yet only 8 of its 57 stops speak either on their original wind pressure or in their original voice. The Groton School organ of 1935, a seminal instrument in the history of American organ reform and the first instance of an unenclosed-Positiv division in any Aeolian-Skinner, has not *one single stop* speaking in its original voice or wind pressure. Naturally these instruments are still destinations of pilgrimage, and while they continue to have musical merits, they are hardly historic documents any longer.

Even modern organs do not escape the revisionist's hand. The C. B. Fisk company has in fact revised a number of Charlie Fisk's early organs. Take the 1963 instrument for King's Chapel and the 1967 organ for Harvard University: poor-quality supply-house reeds replaced with new, actions re-engineered, mixtures re-composed, stop-action solenoids replaced (the last hard to protest). Murray Somerville, organist of the landmark Harvard Fisk, finds himself in a major quandary: the organ cannot be called a consummate accompanimental organ and lacks any truly romantic voices. Can and should he change it? Are we prepared to preserve the bad with the good? Are we really capable of judging any organ built only 32 years ago? History suggests that we are probably not. (Perhaps Professor Somerville has decided to grit his teeth and programme a lot of unaccompanied music: I haven't checked his service leaflets lately.)

Of course, it would be handy to blame all the organists for the destruction of these instruments, but the first prize often belongs to the original builders themselves. G. Donald Harrison set a precedent by repeatedly revising some of the earliest and most important Aeolian-Skinners: he revised the Groton School organ in many details before his death, his successors doing still more and probably feeling that they were simply carrying on the tradition of experimentation and refinement. Harrison altered several other of his landmark organs during his lifetime, among them St Mary the Virgin in New York City, All Saints' in Worcester, and Grace Cathedral in San Francisco, not to mention countless examples of Ernest Skinner's work. And although we rarely consider Skinner in the rebuilder's light, he did it too, although the fact that he was replacing tracker organs with electric often meant that he was called to rebuild organs far less frequently. In dealing with his own work, Skinner usually added new features and rarely revamped an organ's basic philosophy.

In each case, Skinner and Harrison were trying to superimpose a later aesthetic on more youthful efforts, but in so doing they paved the way, and not without at least rhetorical justification, for modern builders to say, 'Well, since these builders recognized the flaws in their own work and changed them accordingly, why can't we?' It takes an unusually level head to deal with this very thorny issue.

Theoretically, the restoration of an electro-pneumatic organ should be no different from any other. The very nature of such instruments, however, invites a perspective that sees a chain of separate elements rather than an integrated whole. Even a bad tracker organ is an unmistakable entity: console connected to action, connected to chests; chests connected to bellows, connected to wind system. Usually, the building frame is all one piece, and the organ is as integrated in its construction as in its design. It is easier to apply a restoration ethic to such an instrument, because changing one part of it, as in any tracker organ, will inevitably affect the whole. Even if you don't care about restoration, you may be less likely to introduce that kind of domino-effect trouble into your work.

Now consider a 1930 Skinner organ. It may be housed in one location, with the console in another; the divisions may be together or located separately. Even if they are together, each division can be regarded as a self-contained unit, with individual wind supplies, tremulants, etc. Unlike even a tubular-pneumatic organ, or so many English organs with mechanically operated shutter mechanisms over great distances, there exist no hard-and-fast mechanical ties between any section of the instrument. The separation of elements, the isolated identity of the console, the stand-apart nature of the electrical system, and the freedom to alter individual pressures and pipe placement without regard for impact on key action, certainly paves an easier road for changes both trifling and drastic.

Add to this a certain derisive modern perspective which regards this style of organ building as the result of a haphazard design philosophy, and the temptation to alter such an instrument grows larger still. Will not the righteous rebuilder know in his heart that there is no harm in compromising an already inherently flawed work? And, as if all of this weren't already a potent recipe for change, consider one final dynamic: in its every phase the twentieth-century organ has received absolutely rotten press right on the eve of decline in each of its phases. Call this phenomenon the 'enormous condescension of posterity' at a speeded-up, twentieth-century pace.

In the years after the First World War, most nineteenth-century organs were dismissed because they were difficult to play, had too many mixtures, overly bright and unrefined reeds, and few console aids to permit the convincing performance of transcribed music. In the 1930s, most organs of the 1920s were dismissed because they lacked clarity, they had no mixtures and the reeds were too dark. In the years following the Second World War, most pre-war organs were dismissed because they contained chorus reeds in unthinkable places (the Great organ, for example) and the mixtures, though present, were too tame, and there was still too much fundamental, so how was Bach to be played? Around the mid-1960s, most of the post-war organs were dismissed because they didn't play Bach authentically (whatever that meant, means or will mean).

In the 1990s, most post-1960s organs were dismissed as exercises in false scholarship at worst, or indicative of a pure and unapologetic modernist bent at best (I think of Beckerath here, almost all of whose American organs survive without any alteration because of their inherent quality). Not only are the neo-classical organs rather unlike their supposed inspiration, but authenticity itself may now be unravelling as any kind of decisive parameter. Rather the better builders confess that they are building new organs in an old style, hoping to create their own art, even if the stylistic debt is enormous. In time we will tire of this also, and a more straightforward kind of ego will return to high-echelon organ building.

From a preservation standpoint, this revolving cycle of our regard for new organs has a potentially disastrous correlative effect on our regard for old ones, particularly those from the immediate past. I don't think we are completely unable to trust our own judgement where old organs of the recent past are concerned but, if history is any guide, no organ culture gets a high score in this area. The only barometer to worthiness of preservation must rest with the instrument itself, and unless we are prepared to deny an instrument reaching its future admirers, we must give it every benefit of the doubt.

If we look in again at our hypothetical unaltered 1930 Skinner, it has now been out of fashion for three different generations at three increasing levels of bad taste. The latest phase, that of the late 1980s and 1990s, adds its own twist by viewing the Skinner as a significant and unaltered relic, something like an heirloom and just as perplexing. The instrument isn't really out of the fire just yet. In this last round of scorn its apparent lack of literature will condemn it to the curiosity category – under the strange and utterly modern premise that organ building becomes great only when it inspires great literature (as if the instrument itself is supposed to be in the delivery room with the baby Franck and Widor, counterpoint text at the ready). So the comments one hears about the unaltered Skinner will run something like – 'This Swell five-rank mixture is terrific, but how do you use the Dolce Cornet?' Or another favourite, and admittedly with good reason, 'Why is there a Nazard but no 2' Piccolo in my Choir organ?'

Uncannily, with all these changes in taste, our hypothetically unaltered 1930 Skinner has undergone no changes, only ageing. It is our perspective that is the wild variable, the moving target, and the thing to fear most because it makes the organ the victim of whim. Once realizing this phenomenon, we will arrive at the two most important elements of organ restoration. First, if perspective is at the bottom of so much organ changing, then it turns out that we have been changing things for the wrong reasons. If we wanted something different would we have been better to have started afresh? It would have been far kinder to history and church finances alike to secure organists who actually like a given instrument rather than to fund the desires of an organist who doesn't, and for a congregation that in all likelihood neither knows the difference nor much cares.

I realize these are not the kindest words, but when a Hook won't play Karg-Elert or a Skinner won't play Scheidt, the simplest thing to do is put a different score on the music rack and put away our proposals. In America at least, organists and organ builders are equally guilty of doing the wrong thing more often than the right; but it is the organist who gets the ball rolling by uninformed and insensitive demands of history, and the organ builder who, out of desperation or an equal degree of misunderstanding, too often goes right along with the script, lest he empty his order book and bank account.

One might legitimately conclude that there is no hope for the cause of organ preservation and restoration in the United States. In fact, there is great hope. However, advances and progress in preservation must be realistically viewed in the context of an environment both benignly uninformed and occasionally hostile towards preservation's aims. In Chapter 10 we will survey the good news: developments and milestones in restoration and preservation over the last quarter of a century.

4

The preservation and restoration of old organs in Sweden

Axel Unnerbäck

There are about 450 to 500 historic organs preserved in Sweden, about 250 of them from the classical and early-romantic period and about the same number from late-romantic times. Most are small instruments with eight to fifteen stops, with one manual and pedals, permanently coupled to the manual without independent stops, but there are also some larger organs. Instruments before 1860 are well known, thanks to the thorough, published inventories and researches of the 1940s and 1950s, produced by the organ historian Dr Einar Erici. A corresponding survey of the organs from the late romantic period (about 1860 to the 1920s) is planned.

All churches and their furnishings belonging to the Church of Sweden are protected under the Heritage Act. Any alteration to them requires the approval of the heritage management authorities (which, from 1995, means the county administrative boards, with the Central Board of National Antiquities as their expert advisory body). This rule has consistently been applied to organs since the early 1960s and provides good opportunities for the preservation of not only old instruments, but also organs of our own time. Additionally, it is possible to safeguard some old material, such as single stops, in organs which cannot be termed completely historic.

No distinct code existed before the 1960s and visible changes, such as alterations to an organ case, could be prevented, but the instrument itself was not protected. When the Central Board sought to preserve an old organ, it was mostly through recommendations rather than prohibitions or injunctions. Very often alterations were made without consultation with the Board, thus organists assumed a high degree of responsibility for the preservation or loss of historic instruments.

Old organs have, as we know, been constantly threatened with destruction, alteration or change, for technical and musical reasons. In Sweden, as in other countries with cold winter climates, church heating and low humidity have caused serious technical problems and damage, and the organs require continuous maintenance.

Musical demands have caused many organs to be rebuilt or destroyed and, when the late-romantic organ arrived, the existing Swedish organs appeared musically outdated. In almost all the large town churches, and in a good many country churches as well, instruments from the baroque and early-romantic period made way for new organs. Another wave of rebuilding in the 1920s and 1930s affected both classical instruments and the first generation of late-romantic organs, with pneumatic actions replacing slider chests and tracker action. When the organ-reform movement arrived, the romantic organ was the prime target of its reaction and, paradoxically, classical organ cases of the eighteenth and early nineteenth century were also under threat, because they did not satisfy the demands of the *Orgelbewegung* for a distinct *werk* structure and speaking front-pipes.

A pressing problem concerning classical and late-romantic organs is their limited size. The typical Swedish single-manual organ has, since the 1920s, been looked upon as inadequate for service and recital use, and there has been intense pressure to provide two-manual instruments, even in small country churches.

Albert Schweitzer visited Sweden during the 1910s and 1920s and drew attention to our organ heritage. Dr Bertil Wester prepared programmes for restorations in the 1930s but, in the 1940s and 1950s, Einar Erici, a physician colleague and friend of Schweitzer, became the leading expert. His listing of preserved historic organs, along with research and other activities, saved the most valuable instruments from rebuilding and his work was of the utmost importance and laid the ground for further care.

Also in the 1930s, Dr Wester and the cathedral organist, Henry Weman, published an article about the problems of preserving old Swedish instruments.[1] They considered historic organs inadequate and old-fashioned, but proposed different ways to solve the problem. Wester maintained that valuable instruments should be conserved and left intact and, if inadequate, an additional instrument should be installed in the building. Weman, on the other hand, argued for modernization and the addition of supposedly missing facilities, such as a second manual, independent pedals and modern action. Sometimes Wester's principles carried the day, as in Fröslunda with its gothic case and 1730s wind chest and action, but Weman's ideas were most frequently adopted, and a lot of old organs were rebuilt and enlarged with tubular-pneumatic action and new consoles. If the organ was considered historically important, the original slider chest would be retained, but supplemented with pneumatic-lever action. However, the wind chest and bellows were usually discarded, leaving only the case and some old stops and after such work it was difficult to recognize a previously historic instrument.

At the start of the 1950s, Dr Erici gained influence and encouraged a new approach. He did not accept that old instruments were necessarily unsuitable for service use – he saw these organs as works of art, and insisted that small classical organs were perfectly adequate, not only for liturgical but also recital use. By emphasizing the *wonderful sound* of the old instruments as the basis of selection, he took issue with those who saw the organ as exclusively subservient to the liturgy. With support from some of the younger leading organists and organ builders, Erici's ideas became more widely accepted as the basic ideology for preservation and care.

Erici worked in several ways, publishing his researches in popular articles suitable for the local press, lecturing in churches and arranging concerts featuring such organs. In this way, he was able to convince congregations that old instruments could still be serviceable, were works of art and a credit to their church. Erici advocated the same principles as Wester – that old organs should be preserved, with neither alterations nor additions, and used as living instruments, not museum pieces. Erici's approach had an impact during the 1960s and radical rebuilds and enlargements became less common, and single-manual instruments more accepted.[2]

The breakthrough for sympathetic restoration in the 1950s and 1960s was also dependent on the competence of organ builders. The careful work at the end of the 1940s by the Danish firm Frobenius was influential but other restorations, carried out by contemporary Swedish firms, were comparatively heavy-handed. The Swedish Bröderna Moberg (Moberg Brothers) dominated restoration work for over two decades and they played an important part in establishing standards of antiquarian respect. Like Frobenius, their basic principle was to preserve the organ in every detail, but with technical improvements judged necessary for silent tracker action and protection against potential damage caused by modern heating-systems. Gradually, however, there were increasing demands for extensive modifications, including modern wood screws, and extensive action bushing to eliminate noise.

Paradoxically, this insistence on technical perfection was, to some extent, a consequence of Erici's defence of old organs as suitable, or even ideal, for liturgical use. This led organists to expect the same technical perfection as a new organ, until it became almost axiomatic that a restoration must result in technical improvement in the form of silent tracker action, resistance to humidity problems and a steady wind supply. Such pursuit of perfection even presumed problems which may never have existed, such as heavy action – predicted in theory and 'solved' by unwarranted alterations.

In the middle of the 1960s a more cautious line was introduced, and care was taken to preserve the original qualities of actions by giving up bushing, preserving old wind systems and interfering as little as possible. Important moral support for this more careful approach came from an international conference in Stockholm in 1970. This included visits and on-site discussions with leading organ builders, experts and organists from various continental-European countries and contact has been maintained ever since.

We still follow the basic principles of Dr Wester and Dr Erici, that a historic organ is a musical art-object *and* a document. It should be preserved as a part of our cultural heritage, and kept as a living, playable instrument, but with the care and protection given to museum exhibits, thus preventing unnecessary alterations. Such an organ should be accepted as it stands, with its individual character and, sometimes, limited resources and used within those limitations. Restorers must bear in mind that every instrument is unique, and that every restoration requires a unique approach. This necessitates thorough documentation of the instrument, combined with archive research. Analysis of the organ as a historic document, a musical instrument, a technical mechanism and so on will indicate whether to restore to the original state or keep later additions from, say, the late-nineteenth century.

All repair or restoration has to be undertaken with the utmost respect for old material and a holistic approach to a unique musical and technical object. Every detail, from bellows and pipes to the smallest components, must be preserved. Lost parts must be replaced by exact reconstruction and, whether an action detail, a stop, or a single pipe, must follow the principle of absolute adherence to the original, in materials and workmanship. Parts which cannot be re-used should be carefully stored. Too many examples of alterations, simplifications and well-intended improvements exist, which lead to clashes of style and a lack of respect. Some ten years ago, prior to reconstruction of the lost console action of the big Schiörlin organ of 1815 in Rappestad, simplified solutions were discussed and a strict reconstruction of the rather complicated action was decided upon. As well as the best solution from the historical viewpoint, the decision to provide an action with the same properties as the original made it possible to experience the relationship between touch and music.

The same principle also applies to late romantic organs – respect for the original and preservation without alteration or additions. Some years ago, the restoration of the 1927 three-manual organ in Maria Church, Stockholm, was carried out as a repair, preserving the tubular-pneumatic action and reconstructing some lost stops. In Visby Cathedral, a restoration will reinstate the oft-rebuilt 1892 main organ, as originally constructed, reducing 70 or more stops to some 30 stops.

Such large and much-rebuilt romantic organs invite further change and additions, especially to the Swell, which often have relatively meagre specifications in the Swedish late romantic tradition. The 1998 restoration of the 1898 organ in Västerås Cathedral, with later additions, involved the reinstatement of original stops, but with the addition of several Swell stops in the English-cathedral tradition. It was very carefully done, but the Board would have preferred a restoration to the original specification, without such compromises.

Our policy today is that all historic organs, prior to 1860, should be preserved and the same applies to organs from the late romantic period, up to the 1920s – although that limit is more approximate. We have begun to consider instruments from the 1930s to the 1950s, but the great number of these organs obliges us to make a selection of the best and most representative. This is urgent, as the reaction against the instruments of the *Orgelbewegung* has already resulted in several rebuildings and revoicings and, probably, these should have been left untouched as ambitious and respected examples of this important (and now historic) period of organ building.

David Knight has already asked: 'What is a historic organ?' In Sweden we adopted the definition given in 1946, in Dr Erici's inventory of preserved classic

36

instruments: 'an organ which has kept its organ case, its wind chests and most of its original stops' and this definition applies to classical and romantic instruments. In recent decades, however, we have begun to widen this (perhaps) narrow concept and make more individual decisions. For example, many organs have lost their original chests but kept the case and pipes. An example is the Schiörlin organ in Herrberga (1799), rebuilt and provided with a new pneumatic chest, and pneumatic action in 1935. The well-preserved 1799 pipework and the beautiful case convinced us that, in spite of its ruinous state, it had to be treated as historic. Instead of building a new organ in Cavaillé-Coll style, as the adviser wanted, it was decided to restore to its original single-manual state, only adding a Subbass 16'. Since the reconstruction of the slider chest, action and bellows, this organ is one of the most inspiring of Schiörlin's organs and, within the regional inventory, we are considering whether other similar instruments should be re-assessed and become candidates for preservation or restoration.

The organ-reform movement's insistence on full implementation of the *werk* principle, and coordination of facade and instrument, often ensured the destruction of late-eighteenth- and nineteenth-century organ cases. The Central Board therefore advocated stylistic harmonization when a new instrument was placed within an existing case, and although this resulted in many old cases being preserved, until the last decade the principle of adapting the new instrument to the case has been breached more often than honoured.

In some cases ambitious reconstructions have occurred, the earliest example being the Wistenius organ in Åtvid church, reconstructed in 1957 by Bröderna Moberg in collaboration with Dr Erici. This work remains an exemplary example of consistency, technical quality and voicing. The large two-manual organ of Fredrikskyrkan, in Karlskrona, of which only the magnificent 1764 case, with its three Principals remained, was reconstructed in 1987 by Grönlunds Orgelbyggeri, with C. G. Lewenhaupt as adviser and technical designer. Absolute fidelity to the original resulted not only in a superb artistic achievement, but also in increased knowledge of eighteenth-century organ-building techniques, wind supply, scaling and voicing, and provided insights for better restoration techniques, as well as a source of inspiration for good organ building today.

Similarly, when Dr Erici defended the old organs, it was not just because of their intrinsic value, but also as a source of inspiration for new organ building, and his aim is about to be achieved. In Sweden today there is a clear tendency to turn to the classical and late romantic tradition for inspiration and solutions. Instead of wind regulators with springs, traditional wind-supply systems are used with wedge bellows; Swedish pine has replaced the oak, mahogany and aluminium associated with industrial organ building; and specifications are more cogently considered, with a desire to delve more deeply into the voicing techniques of the old masters.

Finally, let me provide some information about the GoArt project at the University of Göteborg ('*Changing processes in north European organ art*'). This started some five years ago and will be finished in about 2001. However we hope to establish a permanent centre for organ research in Göteborg.

The purpose of the project is to study the art of the organ (especially the north German school) in broad terms, including the history and technique of organ building, organ music and performance, from the baroque to the romantic and the role of the organ in the community. There is a close collaboration with the technical university of Göteborg (Chalmers) which researches, for example, classical wind-supply systems, alloys and physical structures in old pipe metal and their audible significance. Several experts on organs and organ music are attached to the project, including Harald Vogel (Germany), Jacques van Oortmerssen and the organ builder Henk van Eeken (Netherlands), Kimberly Marshall, Bill Porter and Kerala Snyder (USA) and others.

In the project's large workshop, research is followed by practical experiments with, for example, metal alloy composition, casting on sand and cloth, different ways of scraping the sheet metal, and so on. The workshop also investigates Swedish and German clavichord-making traditions.

In order to apply this research to workshop practice, GoArt has built a big four-manual organ in the north German, late-seventeenth-century style, which will be completed in 2000. It is already playable, but some stops, among them the reeds, are still missing. If you come to Sweden, I recommend a visit to this marvellous organ, constructed in the Örgryte church, Göteborg. I do not think anything like this has been done before, with such consistent application of north German organ-building techniques, from the twelve bellows, to the keys and case ornaments, and everything, materials and manufacture, is of excellent quality. If funds can be found, it is planned to build another organ in late-eighteenth-century Swedish style, and an ongoing project is the *re-restoration* of the 1604 organ from Morlanda church, rebuilt in 1715, and restored in a rough-handed way in 1952.

The project also includes the compilation of an organ database, carried out in close collaboration with corresponding projects in Britain, Germany, Italy and elsewhere, and the ongoing development of documentation methods for old organs. This includes the thorough documentation of a selection of our most valuable historic instruments, which will be published.

5

Conservation of working instruments: when to restore

Göran Grahn

Is there a right time to restore an organ? Has there ever been? These questions are likely to be asked, especially when earlier restoration and rebuilding of historic organs are reviewed. Finding an answer is sometimes difficult, since the question of preservation versus rebuild of organs is an issue that can stir up strong emotions among those involved. An organ builder once said, 'Is it not strange that a wooden box with whistles can make people so emotional?' The reason for this is probably that the greatness and splendour of the organ fascinate us. The organ can incorporate many arts, including architecture, music, history and technology. When we discuss the preservation of historic organs, we come across different terms such as repair, rebuild, renovation, restoration, reconstruction and conservation. It might therefore be good to take a look at what we mean by the terminology usually connected with such work. In Sweden in recent years, we have aimed to interpret and use these terms in the following way:[1]

Repair: to bring the organ into working condition, without the intention of changing or altering its musical and technical concept, other than exchange of damaged and worn out technical parts.

Rebuild: an intended alteration of the original concept, such as replacement of actions, change of specification, additions etc.

Renovation: to bring the organ into working order, as well as minor changes in wind supply, action and change of single stops.

Restoration: the repair and return of the organ either to its original state, or to a particular state of its history.

Reconstruction: the new construction of parts, or of an entire organ, copied from the original or a presumed original state, after research and study of preserved instruments and sources.

Conservation: halting ongoing decline and damage without any alterations, a state often used when an instrument is preserved in a museum. This state would mean that the organ is seldom playable to any great extent.

Since the word 'restore' has been used in the title of this paper, I shall henceforth use that term.

Terminology is of importance when we discuss what we are doing to historic organs. It is also important to be aware of the difference between historic organs kept in museums and those used as working instruments in churches and elsewhere. We should understand that an object in the possession of a museum should be one that is not in regular use, either on purpose or for historical reasons, and is preserved intact and as untouched as possible for future generations to study. Obvious examples from other fields of preservation might be that we do not let musicians play directly from Mozart's autographs, nor do we launch original Viking ships in order to make them sail again.

Most historic organs, however, cannot be put into this category. They are usually instruments that have been in more or less regular use ever since they were built. As living objects they represent great historical value by their survival and also reflect the history of the buildings in which they stand, as well as the fashion and function of the times of their alterations and rebuilds. To prevent our historic organs falling between ideological stools, that is to say, museum object versus function and utility, we constantly need to review our attitudes to organ restoration. It is therefore useful to take a closer look at different attitudes in this field from the late nineteenth century to the present.

Until industrial methods were introduced to organ building in the nineteenth century, constructional methods and aesthetics had not changed radically throughout the centuries. Therefore rebuilds and alterations were seen as a natural development within a continuous tradition. With the more or less industrially produced late-romantic organ came a change in aesthetics. Mass-produced, perfectly made standardized parts and pipes were assembled behind either an existing old case or a new one built in a standardized neo-gothic or eclectic style. With the growing desire to preserve historic objects in museums, historic organs were sometimes looked upon as curiosities. Some were preserved in museums and, as such, carefully treated by contemporary organ builders. A good example of this is the restoration by Cavaillé-Coll, at the end of the nineteenth century, of the seventeenth-century Compenius organ, at Fredriksborg Palace, Denmark. This can be seen as conservation rather than restoration, since the organ was preserved in more or less original condition. With instruments thought to be less prestigious, often only the case was retained as a dummy screen. This is, for instance, the situation at Riga Cathedral, Latvia, where Walcker built an entirely new organ in 1884, behind a seventeenth-century case. Other historic organs were heavily rebuilt and modernized and when they did not fall into the category of unique objects, they were usually thought to be primitive and unable to fulfil the musical demands of the time. There were of course always exceptions in places like the Netherlands, where old organs had always been prestigious objects owned by the town councils. In the British Isles, industrial methods were introduced slightly earlier to organ building than, for instance, in northern Europe, which makes the British situation somewhat different.

With the German organ-reform movement, the *Orgelbewegung* initiated by Albert Schweitzer around the turn of the century, the interest in historic organs increased. This was to a great extent a reaction against the standardized factory organ. Instruments by Silbermann and Schnitger became the basis for recreating *pure* organ sound. The aim was to give back to the organ its own sound, without imitating orchestral instruments and the movement helped save and preserve many historic organs. The step was not fully taken, however, since historic organs served as the source of inspiration for new organs, rather than as objects of detailed study and for copying. The later stages of the *Orgelbewegung* were increasingly directed by the pursuit of a *pure* organ sound. Scientific and acoustic theories and dogmas about what constituted this new sound gradually moved further away from the sound of the preserved historic organs. The result was a sharp tone quality with as much of the overtone spectra voiced into each pipe as possible.

This new perception eventually became so dominant that it was also applied to the restoration of the old instruments, and in the 1950s and 1960s there was a strong belief that modern techniques could be used to *clean* the historic organs from what was thought to be decadent romantic alterations. There were restorations where the lowering of pipe cut-ups and scraping off of original nicking from languids were standard measures. This attitude, often combined with non-existent or rudimentary historical research, unfortunately resulted in many disastrous losses of information. During this period many valuable romantic organs were scrapped when they were thought to be decadent orchestral instruments which lacked the so-called *pure* organ sound. Where there was a shortage of money, many romantic organs were altered into a more baroque specification by cutting down narrow 8' string stops to make 2' flutes, and by mixtures. Restorations were carried out not to a certain point in the history of the particular organ, but to a state which never existed. The justification for this action was often that the organ had to function in the modern musical life of the church. An often heard argument was that we must add mixtures and pedals to organs without them in order to play the music of J. S. Bach, thus ignoring the fact that Bach wrote plenty of pieces for manuals only, and is said to have preferred string stops and gravity. It would be interesting to contemplate how many valuable romantic organs have been destroyed due to a prejudiced view of the music of Bach.

This period can therefore be characterized as a time when ideology was more important than a humble attitude to the historic material dealt with. Original organ parts were used for experimentation and for the application of acoustic theories and dogmas. In many ways, especially in technical aspects, the industrial organ building prevailed, but with an ideological and aesthetic facade. In some extreme cases, alterations were so radical that the restored, or maybe we should rather say *re-stroyed* organs could be seen as newly built, but using old parts and pipe metal. In an attempt to improve reliability, modern materials, foreign to the original concept, such as plywood, plastic and aluminium, were sometimes introduced.

In the 1970s and 1980s, a counter reaction against this view came with more historically oriented organ building, where preserved old organs served as originals to be copied anew. The historic organ itself was the source of knowledge that set the agenda and inspired the revival of craftsmanship and technical aesthetics. Historic organs that had been heavily altered during the previous ideology were now re-restored as near to their original state as possible. Restorations were only carried out after thorough archival research and the archaeological examination of material in surviving instruments. Eventually this later movement also resulted in a better understanding of the historic significance of romantic and recently built instruments. The effect was often a rediscovery of the musical potential of earlier instruments, when treated with an open mind and without prejudice. We stand in this position today, where our experience of the regrettable failures of previous decades enables us to avoid repeating past mistakes.

If we look at the more technical side of organ restoration, it is interesting to compare things with the human body. A human body can be infected with a great number of illnesses and syndromes, often abbreviated in acronyms such as TB, AIDS, etc. Similarly, the protection afforded by the immune system of a historic organ can also be badly hurt by various syndromes and one of the most lethal is CORRS – the Cheap Organ Repair and Rebuild Syndrome. Let me give some examples.

A cathedral in Sweden had an eighteenth-century organ. At the end of the nineteenth century, the interior of the organ was sold to a country church near the cathedral town. The original case and case pipes remained as a screen in front of the new late romantic instrument and in the country church, the old organ was installed behind an existing case. In the 1930s the country organ was rebuilt with pneumatic action and a new free-standing console, but still keeping the old organ basically intact, except for minor alterations undertaken during the nineteenth century. In the 1960s the dominant *Orgelbewegung* ideology was that an organ with pneumatic action was automatically a bad organ, however good it sounded. Therefore a new tracker action was ordered from an organ builder, who turned out to be inexpensive and not very interested in studying the design of the original maker. He retained the keys from the pneumatic console, which had a length and balance point designed to lift the small pneumatic relays. He then connected modern standard trackers to these keys and to the fairly big pallets of the original wind chests. The organist was then left with a tracker action that was extremely heavy to play because it had the wrong proportions. After complaints by the organist, another inexpensive organ repairer was consulted to find out why the organ was so heavy to play. Obviously he thought that the heaviness must be due to big overlap (although original) of the pallets. Therefore in order to improve the touch, the original pallets had their sides planed off. These measures still did not cure the heavy touch of the wrongly constructed action and, together with harsh tuning and other alterations to the pipework, has resulted in the loss of much original information. The parish is now left with an organ far removed from its original splendour. Recently the cathedral council that originally possessed the instrument has decided to reconstruct their eighteenth-century organ. Hopefully, they will succeed in buying back the original parts and have them restored more carefully. Had the instrument remained in its pneumatic state, we would probably have had a much better notion of where to start from and avoided these (unnecessary) rebuilds.

Another example – a historic organ in another country had been in decline for many years. An organ festival planned to include a concert on this organ and it was decided to allow an inexperienced organ tuner to work on it for two weeks. First, all the pipes were taken outside and scrubbed harshly with a brush and soap and water. The wind chests were just temporarily repaired with masking tape to tighten the most obvious leaks. Since the organ had been rebuilt many times during its history, the pipes had three to four different tone markings. When returning the pipes, the organ tuner had great problems finding the correct places, especially in the mixture. Later research shows that the instrument is the only preserved example by this particular organ builder. Some of the metal pipes were damaged by oxidation after their harsh cleaning treatment. The composition of the mixture will be very difficult to determine, since the pipes have only been returned where they fit. If the next restoration is not professionally done, the organ might face final destruction.

Whatever we do to historic organs, whether we restore or not, will mean change to their original condition. If we do nothing, time is likely to change the condition for us. In order to make these changes as small and as reversible as possible, we must get to know the original organ builder and his thoughts and aesthetics. We must always undertake extensive research and documentation in order to recover all possible information. When dealing with unique organs it might occasionally be necessary to make a copy prior to restoration. This would be done in order to avoid experimenting on the valuable original. Only then will we learn enough to be able to take the right decisions and, hopefully, might come closer to knowing whether and when to restore. With these preconditions fulfilled, careful restoration work will certainly help preserve the organ for the future and ensure that the immune protection against CORRS (and other syndromes) is also increased. Remember that organs have always been expensive and valuable instruments, and should be treated as such when they are being restored. Attempts to get away with cheap solutions are likely to strike back and make even more expensive measures necessary to put things right.

When we restore, we must not forget to make sure that our own work is as well documented as possible. Every detail must be clear to those dealing with the organ next time, what work was undertaken and why. Therefore an extensive report, as well as minutes of discussions concerning the restoration, is of vital importance.

After restoring an organ, its maintenance is as important as the restoration itself. In some cases the organ might become so popular that it is used too much. In Riga Cathedral, the organ was carefully restored in 1983, but has since then been played almost day and night. Some parts are now so worn that restoration measures will soon be necessary again. In such cases, the amount of playing time should be restricted, and the use of the organ should be forbidden for learning pieces. Recently, an organ from the nineteenth century was temporarily set up in a music conservatory and used for tuition and practice. When it was dismantled, the action had obviously been worn more during a period of about five years, than during the rest of the organ's life.

To conclude, it is important that we contemplate what we expect of our historic organs. They have served their purpose for many generations and survived many fashions and organists. There will, unfortunately, always be organists and others in charge who lack understanding and many of these will not be interested in learning and would probably prefer a modern instrument. Is it then right to alter a historic organ to the desires of a particular time or for a particular organist? Would it not be fairer to be open-minded and let the historic organ teach us something that may never have occurred to us? An organ preserved in its original state will most certainly do so. Whatever is done to our historic organs today – whether we restore or not and, if so, when – the judgement of future generations on our work is most likely to be hard.

6

Conservation of old material in organs

Dominic Gwynn

This paper contrasts the ways in which organs should not be restored with the ways in which they should. The premise is that as much of the original material and construction as possible should be kept. Since it is impossible to be prescriptive about the preservation of original material in any particular instrument, it is desirable to adopt an approach which tries to preserve it.

The difficulty for any restorer, however conservative, is to deliver an organ which works well, in addition to keeping the original material. If the customer is paying for an organ which will have to be used for the next few decades, the restorer has to assess the durability of the materials for that period. On the other hand, if the organ has a character which needs to be preserved, the original materials and construction are what make that character.

This dilemma, whether to preserve or replace, is central to the craft of the restorer. An objective assessment of the restorer's skill should be based on his or her ingenuity in preserving as much of the organ as possible, still leaving a functioning musical instrument.

Various external factors will tilt the balance one way or another:

- The customer's priorities will vary; a museum will have a different approach from a busy church with organ students, frequent services and concerts. The former sees the importance of preserving the organ for its own sake. The latter is more interested in efficient execution of the organ's function.

- If the organ is not to be used a great deal, an assessment of the durability of the parts, and even of the organ's efficiency, will be different from that of a frequently used organ.

- The manner of raising the money will influence the scope of the project. If the customer is wealthy, and likely to remain wealthy, then the project might well be less complete than the case of a less-wealthy customer with a unique chance of applying funds to the organ.

- On the other hand, more money can mean that the customer has more influence over the project, for good or ill.

The conscientious restorer may well regret the influence these matters have on the project. The central dilemma, that of keeping the organ intact but functioning, is one over which such a person will agonize at every stage.

Other factors will be part of the restoration policy. These include

- the age and rarity of the organ, and its parts;
- the amount of later work to be preserved;
- the quality of the original organ-builder's work and the efficiency of its parts.

These issues are not my main subject, except that they become entangled with the preservation of old material. We may seem to be making objective decisions with pure motives, but we rarely are. Life for those coping with a restoration project really can be very complicated, as we all know.

Here we deal with the restoration project after those policy decisions have been taken. If the organ restorer has the correct approach, then the level of ingenuity in preserving the original parts, and the flexibility of approach required to assess the line between preservation and use, will follow. And at least one problem for the historic organ will have been removed.

As an example, here is a summary of what happened about five years ago to a perfectly respectable and unaltered organ built by a provincial builder in a small parish church around 1840:

> No obvious tonal changes, though it is difficult to tell from the console because the original ivory stop labels have been replaced with plastic. The front pipes have been replaced with zinc replicas, and the reed tongues and tuning wires are new. The metal pipes have been bathed in a caustic solution and mopped. The wooden pipes have been planed down and oiled, the caps removed and screwed back. The reed resonators have been slotted, and the bass tongues loaded. The pipes had already been cut down and tuning slides fitted.

> Unlike the casework, the console had not been stripped and oiled, but the ivory overlay of the naturals had been replaced with a synthetic substitute, the stop labels had been replaced, department name labels added, the organ-builder's label attached prominently on an otherwise anonymous organ, and all the switches and light fittings replaced in the latest plastic. The stop shanks were square, but the jamb holes had been enlarged and bushed with red cloth. There was a new pedalboard.

> The cloth bushings of the key action had been replaced. There were new trackers with phosphor-bronze wires and plastic buttons, the roller arms had been cut open and plastic eyes inserted. The steel rollers had been re-painted black, the rollerboard painted, for the first time, in battleship grey. The pedal action has been replaced with electro-pneumatic.

In the chest, the upper boards had all been lifted onto Schmidt seals, the bearers had been packed up with hardboard, and the sliders replaced with a synthetic substitute. There was a new bushed hole into each channel through the front rail of the bar frame. The upper board and face-board screws had been replaced. The pallets had been re-leathered, with new paper on the grid and with felt on the pallets. The springs, pull-downs, pallet eyes and pallet guide pins had been replaced with new phosphor-bronze wire with plastic inserts in the eyes. The brass pull-down strip had been replaced with nylon inserts. The inside of the pallet box had been painted red, and the outside painted brown.

The swell box had been painted black on the outside and white inside, and all the shutter cloth had been replaced. The vertical rod had been replaced with aluminium tube, and the trigger swell pedal had been replaced with a balanced one.

There was already a blower, but the re-leathering of the bellows was taken as an opportunity to remove the original feeders and pumping mechanism, and to paint all the bellows and trunking black.

This list has been conflated for effect, to convey the spirit of a thorough *restoration* of a certain sort. The work was tidy and the craftsmanship competent, but the spirit of the original organ had been completely obliterated.

It is possible that parts had to be replaced. But in this case there were few signs of environmental problems. It was an organ which had gradually subsided into decay, after about 160 years with not much more than annual maintenance. Difficult to tell now, but it felt like an organ which could have been restored intact, and with a better prospect than the organ in its present state of making it to the next restoration.

Such an approach is careless, not careless in action but careless in thought. In the process, what the organ may be able to tell us about our musical traditions, starts to disappear; it ceases to be what it purports to be. The aim of the restorer should be to do as little as possible, dismantle as little as possible, replace as little material as possible, leave as little impression of his or her own work as possible. Paradoxically that can be more time-consuming and require more time than replacing parts would.

The process should start by examining the organ to see what can be kept. It is an attitude which should start with the estimate, a time when builders are most eager to protect themselves from future embarrassments. The organ should be examined again before dismantling, when the builder's approach is better focused, and again in the workshop, when the separate parts can be looked at with greater leisure. Assessments may change through the project; it is crucial that the estimate is not treated like a government manifesto. Restorers should be able to change their minds as they get to know the organ better.

Some of the parts that are routinely replaced can easily be left alone. If we take the wind chest alterations just described, painting the pallet box (or anything else inside the organ) is pointless. Organs are made of wood, a material which reacts to and is dependent on its environment. If an organ has survived, it has presumably settled in its environment, and should continue to do so. If there are problems, then it is likely that the environment has changed, and it should be the environment which is altered. For if this paint is protecting anything, it is protecting the least critical part of the wind chest.

Metal corrosion often looks worse than it is. An oxide layer on iron pull-downs and pallet springs can provide a protective layer. Sometimes the corrosion can be the result of agents in new wood encouraging electrolytic corrosion between pull-downs and eyes of different metals. The corrosive action may have stopped a long time ago.

Pallet leather can retain its bedding qualities for centuries if it has not suffered from the airborne chemicals of gas lighting or heating, excessive exterior pollution or prolonged periods of humidity below the 50 per cent mark. If the chest does not need flooding, it can usually be left.

Cleaning may revive the material sufficiently to do its job. Under the direction of a textile conservator, we wet-cleaned some 1864 swell-shutter cloth, a process which brought back enough of its bedding quality to be useable for a few more decades.

If there were obvious faults identified when the organ was still being played, or in the workshop once dismantled, then the first option to be considered should be repair, that is, without the introduction of new material:

- Most of a restoration project will consist of minor repairs and adjustments. A key action may have evident faults which may seem tolerable once the action has been adjusted.

- If a glue joint has failed, it is usually better to re-glue it without the introduction of other materials. That is, it is better to clean and re-glue a clean, true joint, than to use screws or nails, or reinforce with thread or plastic tape, or whatever. Take a wooden pipe, where an environment alternately damp and dry has loosened the joints sufficiently for the stopper to prise it apart. If the glue can be re-activated (i.e. it is hide glue), and if the joint is not affected, glue applied on a slip of card or brass, and a heat gun, will restore the effectiveness of the joint. Joints which have in the past been screwed or nailed, or reinforced with thread or tape, are often ineffective and difficult to restore as easily. Thread and tape tends to eat into the corners of the pipe and destroy the pipe marks.

- Sometimes a repair can only be effected with new material, in which case it should be an obvious repair, of the same kind as the original work. If the pivot and balance pins of the keys are loose in their holes, there will have to be an improvement. If the pins are rusty, they could be replaced with larger pins, or slips of wood could be let into or laid on top of the slot. A less intrusive repair is achieved by widening the hole slightly and letting in a piece of wood on either side of the pin. Such repairs are best done ad hoc, piecemeal rather than wholesale, so that the originals, in this case the less-used keys, are still obvious to later repairers.

The original material can also be reinforced so that it continues to do its job with assistance:

- Damage to metal pipe feet can be caused by corrosion. In the days of gas lighting and coal fires, airborne sulphur dioxide could be deposited on the inside of the feet as dilute sulphuric acid, as the moisture in the air condensed in the cold space between upper board and rack board. The conditions for this corrosion have passed into history, so the deterioration will not get worse. It is not likely to be consistent, so most of the pipe feet can be left. The rest will be in states which require a different level of attention. Some may have broken, some become so swollen that they cannot be pulled through the rack, some are so brittle they cannot support the pipe, not to mention being porous, or with minute punctures. The approach would vary. The worst may need new feet below the rack, or sections between toe and rack level. The practicality of repair depends on the degree to which the brittle metal can be soldered. Those feet still intact but brittle could be reinforced with a resin such as *Paraloid* B72, which penetrates and polymerizes. If there is a wholesale replacement of feet, then the original toes are uniformly lost, along with valuable evidence about the sound. On the other hand, pipes with fragile feet have to be tuned with great care, if at all. The approach taken depends on circumstances, for pipes with fragile feet can suffer in other ways, and the precautions which seem obvious to its current custodians may not seem so obvious in the future.

Sometimes the original material really does have to be replaced:

- The most obvious examples are the result of the natural deterioration of leather. As leather ages, the fibres shorten, and they stop matting together. This process is accelerated if the atmosphere is dry; it cannot be retarded artificially. So a leather button which no longer grips the tracker end wire, a bellows gusset which has started to crack, or bedding leather which has became powdery will have to be replaced. Again an assessment should be made about the life left in the material. Bedding leather will do its job for much longer than gusset leather in the same condition. It may be that not all the leather needs to be replaced. If it does, the procedure of the original builder should be repeated, so that future generations can make sense of it. If there is any possibility of them confusing it with the original work, then a graffito can make the situation clear.

If material does have to be replaced it should be in a consistent style:

- Pallets should not be felted in organs where they would not have been felted originally. Very often one suspects that felt is used to allow for an uneven surface on the bar frame, which it does not do. In any event, a pallet should be leathered as it was originally, with a leather hinge, etc. Not only are there sound reasons for using the classical method, there are sound reasons for matching the dexterity and technique of the original builder. It is part of the learning process, and the finest restorers are those who have become familiar with the techniques of the builders with whose work they are dealing.

Restoration usually becomes contentious only when it involves reconstruction, i.e. when material that has already been replaced is set aside and replaced with new material closer to the original.

The tonal area is one where interpretative repairs involve the original material. It is usually clear when pipes are unaltered (though they may still be quieter than originally, through settlement of toes, dropping of languids, etc.). If they have been altered, then a thorough acquaintance with other work from the same period and in the same style has to be acquired before alterations can proceed.

There is nothing wrong with doing nothing. If the status quo is maintained, future restorers can proceed from the same basis. If there have been changes, a thorough record should be made both of the situation before the restoration and of subsequent changes. If the wind pressure has been altered, and it is agreed to change it, or if the toe holes are felt to be smaller than can be dealt with in regularizing the voicing, then future listeners should know what they are listening to.

Keeping records of the organ's building history is very important. If the player and the listener cannot be certain that the organ is an authentic representation (i.e. that it is what it purports to be), then they should at least have an idea of the influence of the alterations. It is important to have a record of the organ before and after restoration. Funds should be allocated specifically for a technical survey, especially when it is unlikely that such an organ will be restored in the near future.

Finally, a regime of use and maintenance should be established for an old organ, so that the materials in it last for as long as possible before the next restoration project. It is probably true that more damage is done to an organ when it is dismantled, transported, stored and worked on than in the years up to the restoration. It is important that those events occur as infrequently as possible. The regime will have to be tailored to each circumstance, stipulating the amount of use, tuning, monitoring of humidity, general housekeeping, etc. None of this needs to be formal, so long as it is carried on in a fairly systematic way through the generations. If a Liverpool conference in 2100 is grateful to us, it will be because we have felt our responsibilities to the organs themselves, and not simply paid lip service to the ideas they represent.

7

Archaeological research: pipework

David C. Wickens

First impressions

The first sight of the interior of an organ immediately influences your interpretation of its content: is it a jumble of off-note chests, passage boards narrowed by the addition of soundboard clamps, conveyance tubes, with pipework of many different shades of colour? Or is it a neat composition laid out like an idealized diagram or a photograph in an organ-builder's publicity leaflet, with rows of uniform pipework? It tells you about the integrity of the instrument. The latter – the neat composition – is probably the better, from a musical point of view, but the former – the chaotic jumble – is probably more interesting from an archaeological point of view.

First impressions, however, can be misleading. There are neat compositions by builders of indifferent abilities, possibly technically correct, which are musically dull; and there are chaotic conglomerations, assembled by builders of genius, that are stunningly successful. I always find it worthwhile simply to sit on a convenient passage board for several minutes, looking at the array of pipes, becoming accustomed to the lack of bright light, drinking in the atmosphere. Many people, perhaps most, may find this rather esoteric and eccentric, but if you are of the temperament that feels history oozing out of the stones of an ancient building when you stop and contemplate it, you will know what I mean!

Pipework can look old or look new; but there are no absolute standards about the look of pipes. Very dark pipework that looks as ancient as the hills may be not so old but coloured by atmospheric pollution, or incense. Bright pipework, looking as though it was fresh from the pipemaker, may be centuries old protected from the effects of light, dust and other pollution by a swell box. (Such an unlikely instance is to be found at Powderham Castle, where the pipework in the Swell is uncannily fresh-looking, and yet it dates from *c.* 1790; the swell box has been left closed for most of its life.)

It must also be remembered, of course, that what may look genuinely old may have been imported from another organ and therefore have no bearing on the origins of the instrument being investigated.

Wooden pipework often suffers by being varnished, or even painted, in relatively recent times. Varnishing can disguise wooden pipes quite radically. For instance, an organ builder had some Schulze pipes in his workshop from an organ that had been broken up. At some stage in their life they had been varnished and were barely recognizable as being the same breed as the rough, down-to-earth pipes that one encounters in Schulze's untouched work.

Pipe formations

The shape of a pipe is more informative than its superficial appearance. The shapes of pipes are, from an archaeological point of view, more important than the names on the stop heads. It is useful, therefore, to jot down a stop-list of the organ from the pipework on the soundboards before noting the console stop-list, before the stop-shield names influence what you see with your eyes.

Pipe formations have a definite history – though that history has yet to be written in anything like acceptable completeness. It tells us, for example, that a very narrow-scaled Viole d'Orchestre in an organ thought to be from the early nineteenth century cannot be original; or that the presence of a flute with inverted mouths indicates alteration to an eighteenth-century organ sometime after 1840. (I hasten to make the qualification that we are thinking of the British organ.)

We find a limited variety of pipe formations in eighteenth-century English organs: among flue stops there were open metal of moderate scale, stopped metal with soldered tops and chimneys, stopped wood with wooden stoppers. To these were added the narrow-scale open metal stops (Dulcianas – the Snetzler variety, and the later Green variety) from the 1750s; the stopped metal with soldered top but no chimneys (a Green simplification of the traditional Chimney Flute) from the 1770s.

The tapered stops that 'Father' Smith (and Gerard Smith at Whitchurch) made are not generally to be found in eighteenth-century British organ-building, but reappear with William Hill about 1847. Hill was also responsible for introducing wooden stops with inverted mouths from 1840 (though there are some earlier instances, such as by Hamilton). The narrow-scaled Keraulophon, with its distinctive long tuning slide pierced with a hole, made its widely publicized debut with Gray & Davison in 1843. There are perennial attempts to assert that this stop occurred in earlier organs, the argument almost always based on stop-lists that were written down sometime after 1843 and therefore inevitably reflecting later alterations.

There are other details of pipe formation that have definite histories: beards, bridges, the frein harmonique – all devices to assist the speech of narrow-scaled pipes; the use of cork stoppers, or bored wooden stoppers, or sliding canister tops instead of soldered tops. A problem is that these developments may have been applied to ancient pipework in modern times. It is not uncommon to find eighteenth-century ear-tuned, solid-topped flutes that have been modified with sliding canister tops, their long ears removed or replaced. Such alterations are usually easy to spot.

Materials

The materials used to make stops may give a clue to date. With metal stops it has commonly been a matter of informed guesswork: a pipe looks 'leady' or 'tinny'. The blue/grey coloration of low-tin/high-lead content contrasts with the silvery sheen of high-tin/low-lead content; and spotted metal, around the 50-50 point, is unmistakable. Handling the pipe may help to confirm the visual impression. The availability of accurate analysis in the laboratory has made it possible to be more precise about this.

Although, once again, no comprehensive history has been assembled, there are dates defining the metal composition of pipework. The common 'English' formula in the eighteenth century seems to have been around 20 per cent tin/80 per cent lead, but this can be found, I imagine, at practically every stage in the history of the British organ. Spotted metal, on the other hand, seems to have had a more particular history. Hopkins and Rimbault tell us that this composition was used by the younger Harris, Green, and Lincoln (whether John or his son H.C. is not stated), the implication being that this was unusual.[1] The spotted metal that Green produced was of at least two kinds: a rough granulated, unplaned variety used in large pipes, and a spotless planed variety used in small pipes. It is quite different from the spotted metal that appeared in the mid-nineteenth century (Willis, Lewis, etc.) that has the more familiar 'blotches'. Zinc, of course, appears in the mid-nineteenth century with Hill's invention of a zinc-rolling machine. It is not unknown for one to be told that the front pipes of an organ are original eighteenth century and then find that could not be as they are made of zinc! Paint can cover up much indiscretion!

The different kinds of wood used for pipes at different periods in history can be informative. For instance, oak for pipe bodies gave way to pine; yellow pine and red pine appear to have been favoured at particular times.

Mouths

The mouth of a pipe – the very centre of its function – may reveal much about its history, though because of its importance it is particularly vulnerable to alteration. Upper lip flatting with parallel scribe lines seems to be a feature of pre-nineteenth-century pipework, but I cannot give any dates relating to this. Thin languids with acute bevels (say, 60 per cent) are general up to the middle of the nineteenth century when thicker languids and moderate bevels (say, 45 per cent) became more usual; but there are a lot of subtle differences that need to be noted (for instance counterfaces found by Goetze & Gwynn on pipework by Richard Bridge).[2] High cut-ups are frequently an indication of alteration, usually associated with the raising of wind pressures, but often the original pipe-maker's cut-up can be discerned from the side of the mouth. Nicking is also commonly compromised by later alterations, but sparsely placed light incisions on a thin languid are almost certainly original in eighteenth-century pipework. Heavy cuts, making the languid look like the blade of a hack-saw, are certainly late Victorian or twentieth century.

Because of its vulnerability the mouth is probably less likely to provide secure information about the history of a pipe.

Compass

Much can be gained by examining the compass of a rank of pipes. It is useful to identify the original top note of the rank. The top note of the compass has a definite history. In its simplest form, taking 1660 as a starting point, this may be described as follows (where c^3 is two octaves above middle C, 'c in altissimo' in old parlance):

c^3 to *c.* 1710;

d^3 to *c.* 1750;

e^3 from *c.* 1750 to *c.* 1800;

f^3 in chamber organs from *c.* 1750, and in church organs from *c.* 1790 to 1850s;

g^3 from *c.* 1850;

a^3 from *c.* 1860;

c^4 in concert organs from *c.* 1860, somewhat later generally.

There are, of course, certain exceptional organs with increased compasses one way or the other, but in general, organ builders conformed to a standard formula. An instance of the usefulness of detecting the upper compass of a stop is to be found at St Helen, Abingdon. Here, some internal pipework has been described as by Jordan in 1726, from which date the case survives. The organ was rebuilt or renewed in 1780 by Byfield, England and Russell. The old pipework can be shown to belong to the later date because of the presence of some e^3 pipes original to the particular stops. Jordan's upper compass was d^3.

Pipe markings

Finally, we come to pipe markings. Metal pipes are usually marked at the start of the making-up process. The marks are etched onto the flat sheet to identify what is being made. Because the foot and pipe-body are cut out separately they each have a mark. It is usual to find, therefore, at least two marks on a pipe – though Samuel Green, for instance, did not mark his pipe feet. If pipes are subsequently transposed or used in a different role from that originally intended, they usually carry additional marks signifying the change. If a pipe has been used in a variety of different situations it may carry several marks.

The original mark is usually dull in appearance. After the mark has been scratched onto the flat metal and the pipe has been made up it is washed to remove the excess size around the soldered joints. This washing process fills the scratches with sediment, giving them a dull appearance. Subsequent pipe marks will usually appear fresh and bright. The marking on the foot will be the original mark; it is rare that any re-marking is done other than on the body of the pipe.

The marking on the body will consist of a sounding note and often a stop name and/or the division to which the stop belongs – in abbreviation. Mutations may be marked according to the keyboard or according to actual sound. Mixture pipes are usually given a rank number.

The style of the script can often give a clue as to the authorship of the pipes, or the identity of the person who altered them. There are distinctive alphabets in the seventeenth and eighteenth centuries, but the further one proceeds into the nineteenth century the less distinctive they become as standard handwriting and factory methods take hold. In the early days it was the master organ builder who marked out the pipes, using his own scale rod or chart. Later, there would be a staff of pipe-makers using standard scale rods. Later still, many pipe-makers used die-stamps.

Certain conventional signs changed over the years. The 'secretarial' script used by Smith disappeared after his School had terminated – though there are scripts that show the use of an inverted 'L' for 'C' well into the nineteenth century (Richard Jackson, for instance). Early scripts used 'H' for B natural, and 'B' for B flat/A sharp; this gave way to using 'B' and 'A#' respectively. The dividing line is not clear – though A# seems rarely to have been used before the end of the eighteenth century. Up to about 1770 a sharp was signified by the addition of a squiggle to the letter name; the sharp sign as such seems not to have been used until late in the eighteenth century, but a clear exception is, for instance, the Griffin pipework from 1742 at St Helen, Bishopsgate.

The pipe markings will show clearly how a stop has been transposed or re-scaled, or moved to a different department.

The markings on wooden pipes are less instructive. There are usually no markings on the feet, and there are many stops that were not marked in the first place. The scripts are less distinctive, and are vulnerable to being varnished or painted over. If altered, the originals are often rubbed out first.

General comment

It is important to understand that any one of these observations is insufficient on its own to provide a certain history of a pipe. When these different observations are used in combination, there is a good chance of discovering a reasonably true picture.

8

Archaeological research: casework and other woodwork

Martin Goetze

Over the past 20 years, the archaeological research of the organ-building firm of Goetze & Gwynn has developed in a reasonably continuous fashion, and we have built up a respectable corpus of information about the older types of British organ through examination, restoration and conservation. I would like to outline how our researches have developed, how we carry them out, and examine ways in which we could improve, both for others and ourselves.

From a background of building *Orgelbewegung* instruments made of glass, steel, aluminium and chipboard, it came as something of a revelation to visit Poland in 1976, and be taken to visit some of its most interesting historic organs. Some had been maintained and were in use, but many were in ruins, awaiting restoration. However, the state department for organ restoration had instigated a documentation project to record details of every historic organ in the country. From their initial listing of 2,000 instruments, certain organs had been selected for restoration, and further, more detailed examination had been carried out. On the basis of this study, the organs could be restored, and a specialist workshop had recently been set up in Kracow. It is fortunate that the documentation was so well organized, because an alarming number of instruments seem to have gone up in smoke since my visit.[1]

Goetze & Gwynn's first instrument was, supposedly, an early-seventeenth-century-type English table-organ rather like the one now at Smithfield, Virginia, which was the subject of a colloquium in 1999 (see Figure 9.4). That it displays a few characteristics of the originals is more by accident than research, since we had not looked in detail at any English instruments of this type before we made it. Our quest for the old style led us to early seventeenth-century organs with square metal pipes, round wooden ones, and an exquisite positive organ, entirely composed of paper pipes.

From the start we have tried to document each organ, and where there is sufficient information, make it available to others in the form of monographs. The most important element of these publications is the technical detail that is presented in the form of measured drawings and pipe measurements. In trying to recreate styles this is essential information, but its value as the documentation of historic material is really of greater importance and, as the number of organ restorations and monographs grows, the more convincing and scholarly each project becomes (in theory).[2]

Photography forms a very important aspect of documentation. Although not normally useable for deriving measurements, it can show information which is impossible to draw or quantify. Photographs usually tell no lies, and we consult them constantly for many purposes. The rule is that however many are taken, there are not enough. The *Harley Monographs* are reproduced by photocopying, as the market for them does not justify the expense of printing, but this does result in poorer reproduction of photographs. However, as we make more use of computers we hope presentation will improve.

It is to be expected that all British organs built until recent times (and some even today) were measured in feet, inches and, except for items like wire or reed-tongue thicknesses, fractions of an inch. Nevertheless, we use millimetres (mm.) when measuring for two particular reasons:

1. because it is tempting for the measurer to misinterpret imperial measurements to dimensions it is believed the organ builder intended;

2. it is easy to train the eye to estimate metric measurements to 0.1 mm. accuracy. The equivalent in imperial fractions of an inch is $^1/_{256}{}^{th}$.

My eyes are not what they used to be, and I find that I am making increasing use of headband magnifiers. This makes me look a little odd, but there is an amazing increase in the number of things that can be spotted. I find them particularly useful in the examination and measurement of pipes where, for example, a multitude of pipe marks can be more readily sorted out.

Computers play a central role in our documentation process, but we (Goetze & Gwynn) have yet to develop a satisfactory technique in computer-aided design (CAD), because there are problems in efficiently drawing the decidedly unstraight lines of old organ parts. However, the techniques and technology are developing so rapidly that it is a system that is bound to become more used. Taking pipe measurements is more easily and accurately carried out with the aid of a computer. One person does the measuring, the other person types in the figures (though, with voice recognition programs, this can now be a one person job). With ranks laid out on the bench, the measurer can concentrate on one job, which leads to greater accuracy and consistency, and fewer mistakes.

Restoration or conservation always provides a unique opportunity for the close examination and measurement of parts that are not normally reached. Measured drawings of important parts can be useful for future research; rubbings of rack boards, upper boards, sliders and table are quite easily done and, provided care is taken, can be very accurate. Problems can occur if there is movement of the paper, or if a scale is not used. A problem is that research and documentation are seldom included in the budget, and clients frequently think them an unnecessary luxury. Where this happens, we still try to find time to collect a minimum of information and, of course, take several rolls of film.

The archaeological study of the substance of the organ is something of a specialist subject, and requires knowledge and discipline not usually needed by most builders. However, it falls to many organ builders to carry out work on historic instruments, and then interesting things go unnoticed. This is where consultants and training such as that given by the University of Reading's organ historiography course should, perhaps, be better used.

Background information of an organ's history and other references have formed an increasingly important part of archaeological research. Although it is important that drawings and measurements record the instrument in its present state, the history can inform observation, giving clues about, for example, the dates of alterations.

It is very important that the historical survey should be carried out as part of the preliminary work in any restoration project, in case this indicates changes in the nature of the work proposal. It is interesting to note that in a good number of our restorations, we made the historical discoveries during or even after the course of the project. One example followed the restoration of the 1743 Griffin organ at St Helen, Bishopsgate, which had survived with original case, soundboards, building frame and much pipework, but not those in the prospect. Dominic Gwynn, one of my partners, was asked to look at the organ in St Paul, Deptford, and discovered that it was virtually a twin to St Helen, with casework and unaltered front pipes, though sadly nothing original inside. The scaling, voicing, order of the front pipes and the console door details would have been very useful to our work at St Helen's.

Scientific analysis is increasingly used to provide a more certain basis for history. This has been standard practice in other conservation areas for many years, but is still regarded with suspicion by organ builders who feel that they can neither afford nor understand it usefully. For a number of years we have routinely carried out a metal analysis on any pipework that we restored.[3] More recently we have taken advantage of other types of analysis, depending on what is considered to be most useful. Dendrochronology and X-ray were very useful in the study of two early sixteenth-century soundboards that were discovered recently in Suffolk. Dendrochronology is the dating of timber by tree ring analysis: the growth of species varies from year to year depending on the climatic conditions, and patterns emerge which can identify the years in which a tree was growing. Much work has been carried out on European oak, particularly in the dating of panels used in painting, and the oak of the Wetheringsett soundboard could be identified with some certainty as of east European origin, and was felled in about 1525. The Wingfield soundboard has the remains of sliders, and the X-rays showed that one had at some stage been put back under the wrong upper board. X-rays were also used for checking drawing details: any iron objects showed up very well, and hole sizes and positions could be checked with adjustments for parallax. Of more general use is paint and varnish analysis. Too often casework is given only a visual examination, and opinions can be formed which lead to inappropriate treatment. There are old cases still being restored by stripping and re-polishing in spite of having the surviving original finish.

Turning to particular examples of documentation, a recent project was the restoration of the 1826 Elliot organ at Belton House, Lincolnshire. This is a Great and short-compass-Swell organ with pedal pull-downs. There is a pumping handle at the treble-end and, working towards the bass-end, a hitch-down swell pedal and, just to the left of the pedalboard, the double-sided shifting-movement pedal – push one side to bring the desired stops on, push the other to take them off. It had become unplayable over a number of years, in large part due to corrosion inside the pipe feet. Sample pipes were sent to Dr Nigel Seeley, Surveyor of Conservation to the National Trust. Having established that the corrosion was not progressive, the organ was left until the closed winter season of 1997–8, when funds allowed for restoration. Another problem was that part of the table of the soundboard had come away from the bar frame, a common occurrence with this type of construction. With only minor mechanical problems, the organ was found to be very little altered from its original condition and it was decided that if a satisfactory method of conserving the metal pipework could be devised, restoration to playing condition would be desirable.

Once the pipes were in the workshop they were examined individually and measurements of all the pipes were taken as work on each rank progressed (Figure 8.1). An inventory was made of the dents, deformation and corrosion, that also listed the treatment given to each pipe. Such documentation is relatively easy to carry out and serves as a reference for future care: in this case it is important to be aware of changes in the condition of the pipes, and to know what treatment each one has had (Figure 8.2). After considering various treatments, it was decided to follow three lines of action:

1. Where there was very little or no corrosion, the pipes were repaired and no further treatment given.
2. Where there was moderate corrosion, but the feet remained mechanically sound after cleaning, pipes were put into a container of 5 per cent solution of *Paraloid* B72[4] in toluene in order to consolidate loose matter.
3. Some pipe feet had become so brittle that parts had fallen off. It was not possible to solder at this point, so the feet were cut off at the lowest solderable point, and new lower sections were made and re-joined.

Other damage also followed a pattern:

4. Where the largest pipe feet had settled into the upper board holes and become deformed. This settling also pinched the pipe feet in the rack board and, in the worst cases, or where the pipe showed signs of falling over, the feet were cut apart, re-formed with a ring of solder placed on the inside, and the parts re-soldered.
5. Minor dents and tears in the metal, mainly caused through tuning, rough handling and accidents. The inventory listed damage and treatment given. Repairing the damaged pipes was sufficient, in most cases, for the pipes to need no further voicing work. With all the pipes placed back in the organ, each was tested for speech and then for regularity of volume. Where there was a marked difference with neighbouring pipes, flue thickness and toe-hole sizes were checked using the measurement sheets (i.e. using the measurements

Sw Dulciana

Note	Body length	Circum- ference	Mouth width	Mouth height	Flue	Nicks	Toe hole
f	905.0	162.0	38.8	10.2	65/70	27	4.8
f#	863.0	155.2	37.0	9.8	55/60		5.6
g	806.0	149.1	34.5	9.0	60/65	26	4.3
g#	774.5	141.5	33.0	8.6	50/60		4.5
a	720.0	133.4	31.6	8.1	52/55		4.4
a#	674.0	128.9	30.5	8.1	35/45		4.5
b	645.0	122.2	29.3	7.6	45/55		4.6
c^1	597.0	117.6	28.0	7.3	35/40	23	3.7
c#	573.5	113.0	27.3	7.2	40		3.6
d	537.5	108.6	25.6	6.7	35/45		3.4
d#	502.0	101.4	24.4	6.3	30/40		3.4
e	478.0	97.3	22.8	6.5	45		3.5
f	445.0	93.3	21.8	5.7	40/45		3.4
f#	424.0	89.3	20.6	5.7	40/45		3.4
g	402.0	86.5	20.4	5.5	30/40	20	3.3
g#	377.0	83.1	19.2	5.6	48		3.1
a	356.0	79.9	18.8	5.2	30/40		3.0
a#	331.0	77.7	17.9	5.0	35		3.1
b	315.0	75.0	17.2	4.9	30/35		2.9
c^2	295.0	71.1	16.6	4.8	33	16	2.9
c#	277.0	69.6	16.3	4.6	30/40		2.6
d	261.0	68.4	14.7	4.3	40		3.1
d#	245.0	64.0	14.3	4.3	30		2.8
e	235.0	61.8	13.4	4.1	25		2.9
f	217.0	59.8	13.2	4.0	25		3.0
f#	206.0	58.0	12.8	3.7	35		2.7
g	194.0	55.1	12.2	3.7	30	14	2.7
g#	182.0	53.0	11.6	3.4	35		2.6
a	173.0	50.8	10.9	3.3	30/35		2.4
a#	162.0	49.0	10.8	3.2	25/30		2.4
b	152.0	46.9	9.8	2.7	30/35		2.2
c^3	142.0	45.9	9.7	2.8	30/35	13	2.1
c#	136.0	43.3	9.7	2.7	30		2.3
d	127.0	41.5	9.0	2.5	25		2.1
d#	120.0	40.5	8.7	2.3	25		2.0
e	112.0	38.9	7.9	2.5	40		1.9
f	106.0	36.9	7.7	2.3	25	10	1.9

Figure 8.1 Belton House, Lincolnshire. Measurement table of the Swell Dulciana, accompanied in the restoration report by photographs and a detailed description of the stop.

taken before any conservation was carried out), and in nearly all cases the toe size was adjusted to match the others. Before any alteration of sizes was made, all other parts of the voicing were looked at – alignment of upper and lower lips, straightness (or otherwise) of the lips and languid, and height of the languid.

KEY: l = light damage   m = medium   e = extensive   p = paraloid treatment
      c = cut apart   o = solder ring   n = new piece   r = re-formed

Note	Body							Foot					Other	
	dents	tears at top	coning damage	rounding out	flatting damage	folding at mth	upper lip	deformed flue	flatting damage	deformed toe	rackb/d pinching	dents	corrosion	treatment
GG	l			l						ecor				
AA	l			l						ecor				
AA#	l			l						ecor				
BB	l			l						ecor	mcor			
C	l			l						ecor				
C#	l			l						ecor				
D	l			l						ecor				
D#				l										
E				l										
F				l										
F#				l										
G				l	l									
G#				l									l	p
A				l									l	p
A#				l									l	p
B				l									m	p
c				l										
c#													l	p
d														
d#														
e														
f														
f#														
g													m	p
g#														
a														
a#														
b													l	p
c¹													l	p
c#													m	p
d													m	p
d#													m	p
e													l	p
f													e	p
f#													e	p
g													e	p
g#													e	p

Figure 8.2 Belton House, Lincolnshire. Example of a damage schedule prepared for the restoration of the organ.

The project was shortlisted for a conservation award in 1998, and I am sure that the documentation played a crucial role for the selection panel.

Whereas the Belton House organ was a concise project lasting just a few months, the documentation of the organ at Stanford-on-Avon, Northamptonshire, appears to be never ending. We began taking measurements in 1976, but it was many years before the results of occasional day visits could be assembled into a monograph. Drawings of internal parts were made full size; the keyboard drawing shows the surviving keys, centre pivoted but with holes in the ends, where they were formerly hinged, and eyes where the action was suspended. The back rail, now used for backfall guide pins, has holes for the original pivot pins. The soundboard drawing was compiled by using a combination of measurements, rubbings and photographs, and shows a rather confusing amount of information – rack boards, upper boards, sliders and, in part, the table (see Figure 8.3).

The instrument was originally made around 1630 by Thomas and Robert Dallam as a two-manual organ for Magdalen College, Oxford. It was taken down and stored around 1730 and, when Swarbrick installed his new organ in the chapel, the main case was sold to the

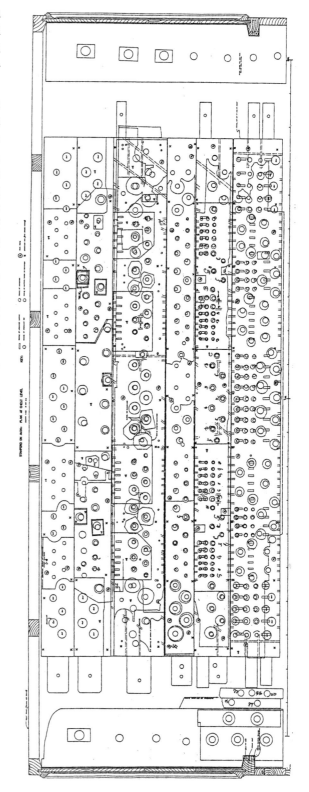

Figure 8.3 Stanford-on-Avon. Northamptonshire, Soundboard plan.

parishioners of Tewkesbury Abbey in 1737. It could be that the old chair organ was then converted by Swarbrick into a single-manual organ for use in the college chapel until his new instrument was ready. At any rate, the conversion involved a change of stop-list, with alterations using small blocks, placed on top of the original upper boards, and an entirely new upper board, at the back, for the Trumpet and Cornet bass. The survival of the roller board made it possible to find the present note order, and it is also possible to draw up an original note order.

It is distressing that in the time that I have been measuring this relic, there has been a noticeable deterioration in its condition; wood pipes have virtually crumbled to dust, mouldings and carvings have dropped off, and some pipe metal appears to have been sawn off one of the front pipes. It is clearly an organ that should not be restored to playing condition, but its current state of preservation is less than it deserves.

The interior of many old cases can reveal signs of earlier states, for instance Finedon, Northamptonshire. Built by a Smith, that is 'Father' Smith or one of his family around 1700, it was altered by Holdich in the middle of the last century by installing new chromatic soundboards, set at a right-angle to the case-front. However, the slings for the old chests are still there, as is the opening for the old keyboards with stop knob holes and many of the old labels. On the back of the upper case there are slings to show where the old choir chests were supported. Numbering on the pipework shows that the soundboard layout followed the front pipe order, even on the choir chest.[5]

As the Finedon organ was thought to be made in 1717 by Gerard Smith, our investigations formed part of research into the organ we were restoring at St Lawrence, Whitchurch, Edgware, known to be by that builder. Comparison between the two organs of the casework panels showed them to be rather differently constructed and, although not in itself sufficient evidence to point to different builders, might make one suspicious.

Photogrammetry can be a useful form of documenting casework, having been used for recording architecture and archaeological remains. The technique involves photographs taken with survey cameras, with a built-in grid plate mounted in front of the film plane. As the camera position is known, precise measurements can be calculated. The drawing shown here is finished by hand, but other systems make more use of computers, which can generate three-dimensional models allowing layering, dimensioning, etc. Modern techniques can involve CAD but, even though it is a supposedly cost-efficient method of documentation, the cost, so far as most organ builders are concerned, is prohibitive (Figure 8.5).

One of the aims of this conference is to explore current practices and see what can be learned from others, but it is something of the deficiencies with which I close.

GREAT SOUNDBOARD: CROSS SECTION

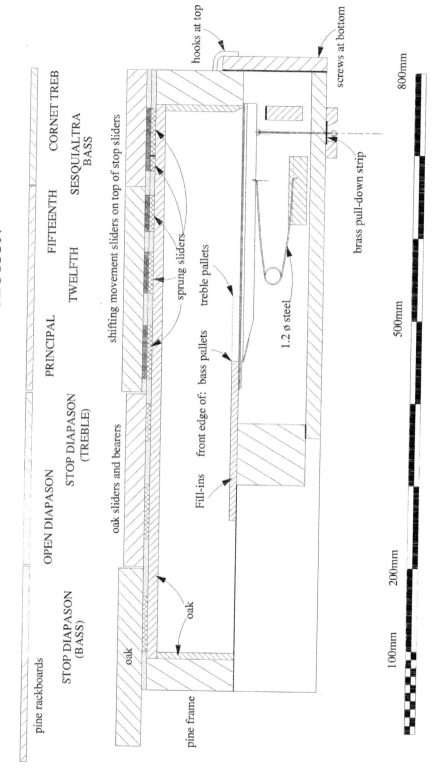

Figure 8.4 Belton House, Lincolnshire. Cross section of the Great soundboard in the Elliot organ.

Space for Organ
Console (modern)

FRONT ELEVATION

Figure 8.5 St Peter's Chapel, Tower of London. Detail from a photogrammetric record, commissioned by the Historic Royal Palaces, showing the Smith casework.

The Dutch system of organ restoration, having been established for many years, is worth looking at. I know there are many differences from the situation in this country but, in organ building as in other disciplines, you can always find interesting things in someone else's workshop. In all restoration projects in Holland, the role of the adviser is central. They are paid as a percentage of the restoration costs, and are a good deal more involved than advisers in this country. They carry out complete archival work, make a technical survey (including all pipe marks and other details), formulate the restoration policy and draw up the specification for restoration, before any builder has been approached. The advisers obviously need to be well qualified in order to carry out these duties convincingly and in a country which has developed a reputation for the highest standards of restoration workmanship, there are sometimes conflicts, when a good builder disagrees with the adviser.

In Britain, it is co-operation between experts which needs to be developed, especially among organ builders who have neither the time nor experience to document comprehensively themselves. There is much information available if you know where to obtain it. We spent many years struggling to find information on our own, as 'a good organ builder should be able to do everything' was the motto of our training years. Now I am more likely to think 'who can help me with this job?', since I feel we waste time and effort on matters with which others can better assist.

I ask advisers, who are in many cases better able to carry out documentation than organ builders, to take a more active part in this process, if only to record basic details and, most importantly, take more photographs than they think we need.

9

Performance standards meet museum standards: the conservation of pipe organs

John R. Watson

Performance standards – meaning the restorer's standards for historic organs – may seem an odd companion to the standards by which conservators treat museum objects. At first glance, the two may appear to come separately from the land of the living and the land of the dead, since the popular wisdom equates museum instruments with an imposed, cadaverous silence. In a way, such a metaphysical allusion may have a surprising element of truth. While the discipline of the organ restorer is indeed to ensure the present vitality of ancient organs, the discipline of the conservator exists for the organ's eternal life – or at least for its longest possible life. Thus, the roles of organ restorer and museum conservator are far more closely allied than one might first assume, and the potential for combining insights represents a bright promise for historic organs.

There has been, however, little such combining of insights between conservation professionals and organ restorers. The major impediment to meaningful collaboration has to do with the cultural gap between them. A culture can be defined as a people distinguished by its particular customs, language, values and religion. Inasmuch as we see in our two groups different customs, different language, different values, and even devotion to different masters, yes, we have a distinct culture of the workshop and of the laboratory.

Therefore, the conference and this volume contain a meeting of cultures and I thought it might be useful to take the opportunity to do some cultural anthropology. I guess I've spent most of my life being a kind of amateur cultural anthropologist. Yes, to spin out the first of several metaphors, I've devoted a lifetime crossing cultural lines to study indigenous peoples. I've lived among the church musicians as one of them, even acquiring a university degree in music and taking employment as a professional church musician. I've also lived among the instrument builders as one of them. I have made 32 keyboard instruments – mostly harpsichords and spinets, a piano and a regal. I re-leathered two church organs and performed traditional restoration on nearly 20 old keyboard instruments. I also live among the organologists as one of them, and speak their language. Most of my publications – more than a dozen articles and a book in progress – have been in the keyboard-organology field.

A decade ago, with my cultural anthropology hat on, I crossed a great sea to live among the peculiar peoples of a radically different culture – the culture of museum conservators. I assimilated the cultural values fairly quickly. In time I analysed and came to understand the religion, and I can see the point of their customs. The language is a stretch, but it is coming. I've lived among the conservators long enough now, I think, to come back to my own people and give a report of what I found and it is absolutely fascinating.

Before we talk about the characteristics of the two cultures, first let us look at a phenomenon in the medical profession that might be illuminating. Gradually over the last century or so, medical researchers discovered that the symptoms of illness could be understood by observing microscopic evidence. The medical profession thus developed highly sophisticated methods of diagnosing human illness by looking into microscopes, and treating illnesses with micro-engineered medications. If the problem is at the level of living cell, then the cure must operate on the same micro-level. The trend to micro-perspective continues today with genome research, which looks not at a single cell, but at a much smaller single molecule – mapping the DNA.

This 'microscopic perspective' has brought about a revolution in medicine (as it has in forensic science, biology, botany and all the physical sciences). However, in medicine, we have begun to notice that it is possible for the human being to be lost in the micro-details. In recent years, the medical profession has responded to the problem by expanding the other way too, reaffirming the relevance of such macroscopic considerations as the patient's general diet, lifestyle, and mental outlook – even these play a part in healing. In the past couple of decades, the medical profession has begun to re-incorporate the macro view. It relies neither on a microscopic view, nor on a macroscopic view, but on both.

Now back to our two professions – restorers and conservators. Are there any parallels? Since conservators and restorers have a common ancestry, our stories begin together as recently as the third quarter of the twentieth century, and it is there that we shall start. Like the early medical profession, we all beheld historic objects with a macroscopic view. Scraping old paint off some casework, washing ancient wooden surfaces with soapy water, and polishing old ivory seemed like a good idea; we simply were not looking closely enough at historical objects to see the physical records of the past that we were scrubbing away. This state of affairs remained generally true through the first half of the twentieth century or so, and claims a few souls even today.

In the third quarter of the twentieth century, the new conservation profession reached adolescence, and the microscopic view came to the museum. Working in a laboratory environment and equipped with scientific gizmos, this new breed discovered the usefulness of re-examining the material patrimony in terms of organic chemistry and micro-structures. It is not leather, it is collagen fibre tissue composed of polypeptides. It is not shellac, it is low molecular weight polymers formed by the esterification of polyhydroxy carboxylic acids. It is not oak wood, it is cellulose in the form of a ring-porous deciduous wood distinguished by large multiseriate rays – and watch out for the acetic acid that is volatilizing out of it!

Besides the usual visual inspection of objects, material science relies on minute structural characteristics of materials as revealed in microscopy. Even more minute observations are possible through chemical analysis which reveals information about historical material in terms of the structure and behaviour of atoms. The conservation profession used the micro-perspective to understand the chemistry of ageing and also to develop means of stabilizing the attrition of historic materials, again using chemistry in an approach similar to that used by the medical profession.

An important implication of this similarity between conservation and medicine has to do with the two levels at which they both can be administered. In medical terms, these are called 'over-the-counter' and 'prescription'. Medicines that are predictable and mild enough are eventually approved for use by anyone, even without any advanced medical training. However, many of the drugs on which physicians and hospitals rely are highly specific to a particular patient in a particular situation. They must be chosen with a scientific understanding of the biochemical interactions that will take place. Likewise, restorers can do many conservation treatments themselves, while leaving some specialized treatments to be administered by conservators having the necessary training in materials science. In other words, one cannot safely regard all conservation laboratory treatments as restoration 'shop tips'.

The microscopic perspective reveals the agents of destruction and measures their effect on historic materials. Examining the layers of finish coatings reveals detailed historical stratification embedded on an ancient surface. Spectrometric analysis reveals volumes of information about historic objects. X-radiography, infrared, ultraviolet, and fluorescence spectroscopy allow us to see through the skin of an object, to see ghosts of past states, or the otherwise-invisible markings of the original maker.

Now that does get interesting! The microscopic perspective teaches an axiom that a few builders of historically informed instruments have begun to appreciate: the closer one looks at the historic instrument, the better one sees the workshop that produced it.

Museums are becoming research centres for the developing field of historical-technology research. This is partly because museums increasingly have conservation laboratories with special equipment for revealing and recording the micro-evidence. Scientific analysis of materials can identify with growing precision wood species, metal alloys, textile fibres, leather tanning agents, coatings, and historic accretions.

One of the most revealing but under-used methods of analysis is visual inspection using controlled raking light with or without magnification. As Figure 9.1 shows, these sometimes micro-striations, cuts and imprints reveal to the knowing eye a complete language that tells clearly not only what tools were used in the

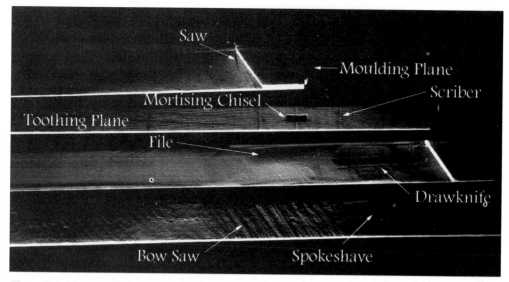

Figure 9.1 These eighteenth-century key-levers from a harpsichord by Jacob Kirkman contain a voluminous record of the tools used in the historical worshop. The photograph is part of a detailed study that pieced together the steps to produce this set of keyboards.

historical workshop, but the order of steps in the construction process. With careful interpretation, they even reveal the maker's attitudes about the relative importance of each step, and record his priorities.[1] My own laboratory has contributed a methodology of analysing number stamps often used on old keyboards. Because pre-industrial-revolution metal stamps were hand-filed, no two sets are exactly alike. The distinguishing characteristics of a set of number stamps can be objectively catalogued, and constitute no less than a maker's identifying fingerprint.

Such information takes up where other documentary information leaves off, and records the detail that would not have been thought important enough in its day to write down for posterity.[2] Yet to a skilled reader of this language, historic surfaces contain so much information about everyday practice in the historic workshop, that it is like going back in time to watch the Dallams, Snetzler or Green at the bench. Today, such physical evidence is our direct link with the original instrument builder and his craft. It is no wonder that the people who have learned to read this kind of evidence are some of the most outspoken about conservation ethics.[3] We are talking about a vast archive of historical information that is concentrated in the top half-millimetre of the surface of a historic instrument. Even cleaning that abrades the surface and swells old wood fibres or dissolves historic deposits can scrub away pages of the document.

So, the microscopic focus of conservation has a great deal to offer all of us who care about the preservation of historical organs. Yet, such a focus on micro-evidence sets up the same criticism that was eventually levelled at the medical profession; preoccupation with micro-details can make us forget that we must also step back and see the whole patient.

By the end of the 1980s, a trend began in the conservation field that re-affirmed the value of the macroscopic view. A few forward-thinking conservators realized that many of their peers responsible for historical collections had become preoccupied with the physical state of such objects and had lost sight of their aesthetic state; historical integrity had become physical integrity. But around the beginning of the 1990s, conservators began to talk about the role of connoisseurship in the conservation laboratory. The new code of conservation ethics adopted by the American Institute for Conservation in 1994 called the conservation professional to respect not only the physical aspect of cultural property, but also its 'unique character and significance'. Treatments are increasingly designed to preserve the 'aesthetic [and the] conceptual' characteristics of historic objects, not just the historic material.[4]

The microscopic view is as important today as ever, it is just not enough on its own. Put another way, the conservation profession is turning down the same path already being travelled by the medical profession, expanding their approach to be more comprehensive in both their understanding and treatment of artefacts.

We will leave conservators there for a moment. What have organ specialists been doing all this time? It would appear that they have continued an impressive growth towards deeper and deeper understanding of historic organs. They have clearly not lost track of the macroscopic view. On the contrary, they have continued to develop it to a staggering quality. In recent years, they have mined archives and undertaken comparative studies of hundreds of historic organs, all to learn more about the form and function of their noble instrument. They found new ways to put the artistic meaning of organs first. They have continued to rediscover the secrets of period tonal design and the mysteries of historic temperaments, even turning to musicological evidence in organ scores. They have done their research, to get into the mind of the artists who first made these instruments, and they are constantly rediscovering the principles from which historic organs were made in the first place – especially the aesthetic principles. It is indeed an impressive track record.

Just as the winds of change are blowing in the medical and conservation professions, so something new is going on among the practitioners of organ restoration. With increasing regularity, they are using the word 'conservation'. Its meaning seems to vary widely, but generally is intended to connote a respect for the historical aspect of old organs. I doubt this conference could have occurred quite this way a few short years ago. In this last year of the twentieth century, two English-language conferences on the conservation of organs have occurred, each with speakers representing museum conservation, and speakers representing organ restoration; the other conference was in Virginia in January 1999. I am starting to hear organ restorers pronounce a restoration to be up to 'museum standards'. It is clear that at least some of them are not quite sure what museum standards actually are, but at least they aspire. Clearly, there is growing respect for the cultural value of organs in their historic form and these are encouraging signs.

So the restoration of organs has made remarkable progress over the last quarter of a century or so, but on two separate tracks. The macroscopic perspective continued to mature in the workshops of organ builders while the microscopic view developed in the laboratories of museum conservators. In the last couple of years, the stars seem to have come into correct alignment for us to realize that our attentions should not be exclusively microscopic nor macroscopic, but both. Organs deserve a comprehensive approach to treatment. You do not have to sacrifice the music and you do not have to sacrifice the historical record. They are both important and worthy of preservation.

The separate disciplines of organ restorer and conservator have advanced the prospects for historic organs on separate, equally valid, equally essential tracks. But like railway tracks, they remain separate, parallel and interdependent – a circumstance I hope to demonstrate is a good thing if we are careful to handle it correctly.

Leaving anthropology for a moment, we come to an exercise in epistemology. Epistemology is the philosophy and study of knowledge itself. How did we come to have different philosophies, different perspectives, different points of view about restoration?

Let me use the 'window metaphor' as a tool to analyse the two perspectives.[5] The following conversation between the two people in Figure 9.2 demonstrates the metaphor.

Figure 9.2 A pictogram illustrating the window metaphor. How will the two people reconcile their different views of the reality on the other side of the window?

Mr B: That's a fine summer scene!

Mr A: Yes, the leaves are so green and the hedge is trimmed perfectly!

Mr B: Indeed, and I think the house is freshly painted.

Mr A: Oh, is there a painted house too? How splendid. All I see is an unpainted brick house.

Mr B: Oh no, there is no brick house, only a painted house.

Mr A: . . . and a brick house.

Mr B: I beg your pardon, but there is no brick house, only a white one, and it has a white well.

Mr A: Oh, I quite believe you, but you must believe me there is a brick house too. You just can't see it because of your view through the window.

Mr B: (incredulously) Window! I say you are confused! That's not a window, it's a photograph!

Mr A: I'm quite sure it is a window and everything we both see is really out there.

Mr B: This discussion is getting nowhere. Good day, Mr A!

The window metaphor is based on the epistemological assumption that every person has a more or less unique 'point of view'. Their place in the 'room of life' determines the reality they see. Where they are in the room, and thus their particular perspective, is determined and limited by their education, experience, and genetics, the particular combination of which is unique to each individual. Because they are human, everyone in the room has biases that limit their vision. Each person's place in the room is fixed by these biases – their vision is forever limited even though their knowledge need not be as limited. Whoever knows it is a window will ask others about the view they each see in order to increase his or her own knowledge. The most important of the many implications of the window metaphor is that everyone has a unique set of insights and most of the time reality exists not in 'either/ or' but in 'both/ and'.

Applying the window metaphor to organs will combine epistemology with cultural anthropology. Imagine a room, shown schematically in Figure 9.6, page 80. The room has a window and on its other side is a historic pipe organ. For present purposes, we will give the organ a verbal representation: 'A historic organ is a material legacy with a musical function'. In the room are an open-minded organ restorer and an open-minded conservator. Each of the two has special insights depending on their position in the room. Because of training and personal experiences, each of them has particular understanding of certain things on the other side of the window. This is about insights and not blind spots; each has particular insight into one side of the equation. Because we assume our two people understand it is a window (and not a photograph), then they are both interested in the other person's insights. A few of those insights follow.

Cultural anthropologists are guided by the truism that 'one must first observe differences in order to discover attributes'.[6] Thus it is in a spirit of deeper cross-cultural appreciation that we seek the contrasting characteristics of conservators and organ restorers. Again, a culture is made distinct by its religion, its language, its customs, and its values. My own notes catalogue several pages of issues organized under headings that distinguish the unique insights of our two specialists. We will sample just a few of them; first, religion. Well, not religion *per se*, but the particular light that illuminates their world. What 'world view' does each hold? Needless to say, both of our specialists are equally interested in the historic organ's condition. But how do they each understand 'condition' based on their perspective through the window?

I will start with a little story from American mythology. General George Washington presided over the American Revolution, and was a much-glorified founding father of the United States. Every American school child learned the concept of honesty by hearing the story of George Washington as a child. One day, young George foolishly cut down a cherry tree. His father questioned him about it, and young George is reported to have said, 'I cannot tell a lie, I cut down the cherry tree.' A joke about the implement he used circulated a few years ago. Have you heard about George Washington's axe? It *still exists*. The handle was replaced in 1831 and the head was replaced in 1867.

Always one to take things a bit too seriously, I decided to analyse George Washington's axe from a condition standpoint. Using the graph in Figure 9.3, the X-axis marks the passage of time, and the Y-axis measures condition. Thus, when the object is new, its condition graph would always start in the upper left corner. A horizontal line in the middle of the graph indicates the minimum condition below which the object can no longer fulfil its function.

Italic text tells the social history of the object, marking the famous moment when young George cut down the cherry tree, and then his death in 1799. Any acts of restoration are labelled. The solid line, indicating the functional condition of the axe, generally slopes downward illustrating that the axe continuously suffered from wear-and-tear and ageing. By 1831, the handle had cracked and was replaced. The line shoots almost to the top, as the axe was like new again. Then the head became deformed from so much sharpening, and rusty. It was replaced in 1867 and the functional condition again jumped to near perfect. The process continued with half of the axe being replaced every couple of generations, resulting in this characteristic saw-tooth line.

Why is this absurd? Obviously, there is more to a historic object than its functional condition. The historical evidence embedded in the surface of an object speaks volumes about how the object was made, how it was used and all kinds of information about its maker and first users. The functional condition of the axe is fine, but what has become of its condition as a historical document? If we see a scratch in this artefact, we want at least the possibility that we are seeing evidence of young George Washington. We expect to see what an eighteenth-century axe looks like, and we want to inspect *his* axe, not a restorer's replacement parts. So the artefact has a functional condition which is distinct from its documentary condition.

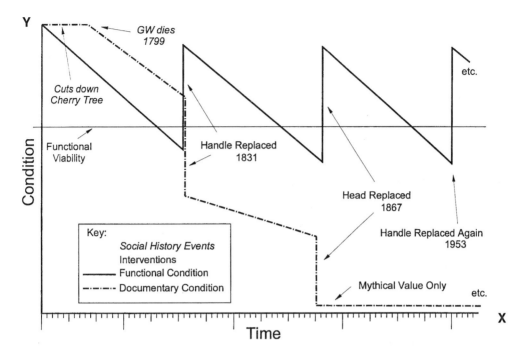

Figure 9.3 The solid line in this graph illustrates the vicissitudes of George Washington's mythical axe as it deteriorates and is repeatedly restored. The dash-dot line follows the condition of the axe as a historical 'document'.

If we record the documentary condition of George's axe, it might look like the dash-dot line in Figure 9.3. At the top left, the line is horizontal; there is no loss of historical information during this early period, since the axe is accumulating the information that most interests us. Then comes the normal attrition of time, similar to the functional attrition we saw before. When the handle of the axe was replaced in 1831, which way did the line go? Not up, but down! Suddenly we lost fully half of the documentary evidence in the artefact. Then in 1867, when the other half of the axe was replaced, the condition of the axe as a physical, historical document, dropped to near zero. I stopped short of absolute zero, since there are a few people who still think it is pretty neat to see 'George Washington's Axe' (which we must now, of course, put in quotes).

It is axiomatic that documentary condition can only go down-hill following the historical period for which the artefact is important. Of course, if another American hero, like Abraham Lincoln had later owned and used the axe, the documentary condition would seem to increase again. However, the principle remains that documentary condition can only go down-hill from the historical period or periods for which the artefact is important. There is no saw-tooth line here. You cannot turn back the clock.

So you might say the axe has two lives: functional and documentary. Both lines record condition, yet they move in this paradoxical, contrary motion. I will call this *restoration's paradox of contrary motion*. Thus the documentary content of an artefact erodes in direct reaction to the thoroughness of restoration.

Figure 9.4 This c. 1630 chamber organ originally stood in Hunstanton Hall, Norfolk, where house musician John Jenkins and the LeStrange family were noted for their music making. Now owned by Historic St Luke's Resoration in Smithfield, Virginia, USA, this rare organ tests our understanding of preservation and restoration.

Our example here is very simplistic and exaggerated, but the principle is universal and provable. The restoration paradox has bedevilled both professions for years. Conservation circles used to use the term 'reversible'. If we choose treatments that are 'reversible', then there is no permanent impact on the documentary content of the object. Over the past decade or so, the doctrine of reversibility has come under fire, most conservators now admitting that all treatments leave some permanent mark on the artefact. Conservators now prefer to call their treatments 'minimally intrusive'.

We will leave the simple world of mythical axes for the far more complex world of the historic organ. The early seventeenth-century English chamber organ illustrated in Figure 9.4 was originally from Hunstanton Hall, Norfolk. It served as a backdrop for a colloquium in January 1999 on the same topic that we are considering and, following that event, two organ specialists, Dominic Gwynn and Barbara Owen, and two conservators, myself and Robert Barclay, examined the instrument in some detail.[7] From the information derived from that examination, and from other documentary information, I have recorded the organ's functional condition through time in the graph in Figure 9.5. Some of this is, of course, conjectural.

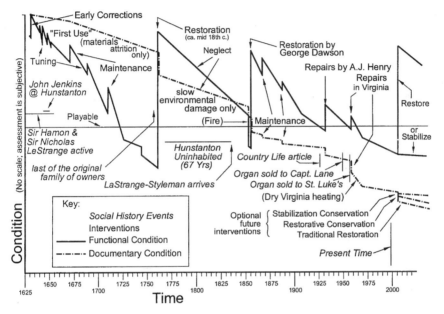

Figure 9.5 A graph of the functional condition (solid line) and documentary condition (dash-dot line) of the Hunstanton Hall organ. The vicissitudes of functional condition through deterioration and restoration can be seen in relation to the gradual erosion of documentary condition. Three possible futures are also shown.

The organ appears to have been made in 1630 for the LeStrange family of Hunstanton Hall.[8] The social history of the organ is recorded in our chart in italics. The LeStranges were champions of music. Most interestingly, the house musician at Hunstanton during the late 1640s was none other than John Jenkins, a composer whose music enjoys great popularity even today. It would appear we have an organ with a stellar past. The solid line on the graph shows the vicissitudes of the organ's functional condition. In the important early period, when the organ had its greatest stylistic currency, it received fairly heavy use and undoubtedly regular tuning and maintenance. Each time the organ received maintenance, its condition, of course, improved.

Evidence inside the organ that emerged during the recent examination showed that sometime in the mid-eighteenth century, the organ was restored. It received all new pallets, some new leather and parchment and, possibly then, the pipes were fitted with tuning flaps. Later, the house organ received little use, especially for a 67-year period during which the Hall was vacant. We do not know for sure if a mid-nineteenth-century fire at Hunstanton damaged the organ, but very soon after (in 1855), the organ was substantially restored by George Dawson, who provided a new wind system. More repairs came in 1932 by A. J. Henry.

More than three centuries after first coming to Hunstanton, the organ was removed to the collection of Captain Lane and then, in 1957, it went to St Luke's, an early seventeenth-century church in Smithfield, Virginia. On its arrival, a local handy-man fitted the organ with a vacuum cleaner for wind, and replaced some of the stopper leather with foam rubber. If that indignity was not enough, the organ was rendered completely unplayable by an over-exuberant heating system that caused cracks and distortions. In the last five years or so, the instrument was rediscovered by the organ and viol worlds, and the stage set for more change.

So far, we have been talking about the organ's functional condition. Now, how would we graph its documentary condition? Remember, the historical information contained in an artefact can only degrade following that time period for which it is important. Therefore, we know our graph cannot have any upward swings.[9] Also, a functional restoration always involves changes to at least some of the historic materials, causing some erosion of the historic information in that information-rich but fragile top layer of tool marks and historic deposits. Some cleaning, some leather replacement, re-gluing – every intervention of even the most stringent conservation treatment will cause greater or lesser loss of historical evidence.

The documentary condition of the organ is represented in Figure 9.5 by a dash-dot line. On the upper left, the graph is almost level during its historic association with John Jenkins and the LeStranges. If the organ received any heavy-handed maintenance during that time, our graph shows no corresponding attrition, since that is part of the early history we most value. Just a little attrition from ageing of materials is indicated by a slightly sloping line. Then in the mid-eighteenth century, the organ got its first real campaign of restoration. Notice that the graph line actually drops rather noticeably at that time. After all, during the two or three restorations, the organ lost all the original pallets, some leather, and parchment. The pipes were also cut down, destroying the Jenkins-period pitch and temperament. In the 1855 restoration, the organ further lost the winding system, and with it a significant technical and musical aspect of the organ. Inexpert repairs in the 1950s resulted in more loss. Of course, it may be because of all these changes that this rare instrument so miraculously survives. However, there is not a person among us who would not like to examine and hear this early seventeenth-century organ exactly as it existed when John Jenkins sat at its keyboard. We all want to preserve as much historical information as possible.

This week the St Luke's Organ Committee is meeting again to discuss the next chapter in the life of the Hunstanton organ. What will it be? The next intervention will fall into one of three categories, graphically illustrated on the right of

Figure 9.5. If preservation of historical material is considered of principal importance, as it is in many other museum artefacts, the organ might be stabilized in its present form. The functional and documentary condition both become more stable somewhere near their current, non-functional level. The graph shows that stabilization conservation designed to save historical information still involves very small erosion of documentary information. Far more typical of the organs in our care is the restoration option. In restoration, the functional condition perks right back up and we have an excellent musical instrument again, but the graph of documentary condition takes a more or less hard hit. If we do a state-of-the-art restoration using the best that modern conservation and restoration methods offer, the attrition is a little worse than stabilization alone, but is not too bad. Some unserviceable materials get replaced, including more of the original leather. Some erosion of surface evidence must occur during cleaning, and old parchment must be patched here and there. The restorer may give in to just a tweak here and there of the voicing; after all, if we don't restore the musical quality of the organ, we will have wasted our time. We coax the organ into some conformity with our standards of what constitutes a good musical instrument. Yes, we are used to thinking that a little more loss of documentary evidence is a small price to pay.

The lowest dash-dot line is traditional restoration – the kind that is uninformed by the best of modern conservation. If we fail to exploit current advances in conservation science then fewer historic materials and less surface evidence can be salvaged. Notice the sloping of the three dash-dot lines. Both of the restoration options mean the organ will attract a great deal of interest: more playing, more maintenance, more tuning, and all the kinds of handling that replace old surface evidence with new. However much the cost may be worth for the musical benefits, we fool ourselves if we forget altogether that there are, in fact, documentary losses.

Now we can return to our anthropological analysis of conservation and restoration. We started with the main belief system of our two protagonists. What masters do they serve? The functional condition and documentary condition graphs can serve as visual symbols of their separate world views (see Figure 9.6). Our organ builder sees the organ as renewable – we can 'put it back the way it was'. The conservator, on the other hand, sees the historic organ as a non-renewable historical resource. You cannot restore historical evidence once it is lost; only by our best efforts can we slow its decay over time. Do we have the makings for an intractable disagreement? To use the terms of the window metaphor – if either one of our specialists thought he was looking at a photograph on the wall, yes, there would be either some argument, or a cold silence. We will assume, however, that our protagonists both understand it is a window, and although each continues to have special insights, both have useful things to contribute towards the preservation of both musical function and historical integrity.

Figure 9.6 The pictogram shows a conservator and an organ builder each guided by the implications of their own unique insight about historic organs. The graphs behind them show their respective concepts of condition. For the organ builder, condition is primarily a rise and fall of decay and restoration, while the conservator understands condition to be the objects non-renewable historic dimension, which should be protected.

The following are a few basic questions to pose to our imaginary specialists. Notice how the answers are informed by the separate perspectives, and are quite different without being irreconcilable. Restoration can proceed with sensitivity to both agendas.

1. WHAT IS THIS OBJECT WE SEE THROUGH THE WINDOW AND FOR WHOM DOES IT EXIST?

Organ builder:

> Whatever else it may be this is, most importantly, a musical instrument. Its destiny is to make music. It exists for church musicians and musical congregations, music lovers, organ enthusiasts, and all people who appreciate organ music. My obligation to future generations is fulfilled when they inherit the organ in better condition than it was when it came to us.

Conservator:

> The object is a historic artefact full of information about the past. Its destiny is to inform us and future investigators about the people who made it and used it. Because it is historic it is a legacy of the past for the future. Therefore, the present generation shares ownership with the future. That makes us like trustees, trying to preserve the

document for not only the next generation, but for the ten generations after that. Because it is much more than a musical instrument, I want to preserve it for all kinds of historians and researchers interested not only in musical history, but also art history, technological history, local history, church history, and family history. It exists for everyone who can learn from it about the past, including people of this and future generations.

Without either one of them having to abandon their loyalties, the two specialists can agree that the organ has value and meaning to several constituencies. Whatever treatment either of them proposes for the organ can be accountable to both perspectives. The organ is both a musical instrument and a historical document.

2. WHAT IS YOUR RESPONSIBILITY TOWARDS THE INSTRUMENT?

Conservator:

My work is to preserve the document from deterioration. My training and experience equip me to employ the best of modern science and technology to protect historical information for the future.

Organ builder:

My job is to restore the organ to its original musical glory. My training and experience equip me to make of it an excellent musical instrument.

In the discussion, the restorer and conservator agree that restoration to good musical functionality can be either more damaging or less damaging to the historical document, depending on the method of the work. Thus, the organ specialist knows what needs to be accomplished in a musical restoration, and the conservator can contribute some modern methods that allow the work to proceed with minimum loss of historical document. Together they can devise treatments that reach musical goals in the most minimally intrusive way.

3. WHAT IS THE ROLE OF ARTISTIC INTUITION?

The third question is actually a cluster of related questions. What is the role of artistic intuition in organ restoration? For example, if the wooden back of a chamber organ is missing, should it be replaced? If so, how much should we trust our own artistic intuition to tell us how to design the replacement? Finally, should we match our materials and construction to that of the original maker?

Organ builder:

I would make a new back for the organ case. The back panel is very important to the acoustic effect of the organ. I would also try to conform my work and materials as closely as possible to the original maker's. After all, if I am restoring the instrument to its former state, then the closer it can come to its original form, the more successful I will have been. That is what non-intrusiveness is to me. Now, about intuition: first I study the particular maker's usual practice, and if that is not enough to answer all questions, I use what I've learned from period organ building in general. Then if there's still ambiguity about the missing detail, I exercise my own judgement as an organ builder. If I remove all artistic judgement in my restoration, the result will be a musically unsuccessful instrument. In order to restore the musical soul of the instrument, I have to take an artistic leap of faith, using historical knowledge as far as it goes, but then my own artistic intuition. After all, I work within the same unbroken craft tradition as the original maker. If this restoration is to result in a worthy musical instrument then, ultimately, the original builder and I are professional and artistic peers.

Conservator:

Replacing missing details can potentially confuse the historical integrity of the document. It is especially dangerous to use materials and construction techniques that match the original. Imitating period work can falsify the historical content of the entire artefact; when an investigator is not sure whether he or she is looking at period work or a restorer's work, then the whole artefact becomes questionable. Moreover, we should not trust our intuition. Adding old-style material to a historic object can greatly confuse the historical record. Our own ideas can always turn out to be incorrect – especially aesthetic judgements, since our aesthetic sense is unavoidably shaped by current fashion. I would prefer to leave this organ case without a back, and if I had to add a protective back, I might just make it out of perspex (acrylic) sheet.

Our conservator and restorer have a lot to talk about here. You can see why the path of least resistance might simply be to give up talking. It might seem easier for one of them to win the contract, and do it their own way. But then we would have forgotten that reality exists in the combined perspectives. If we integrate the two sets of insights, then we will gain a perspective that is more informed than any one person's inevitably limited point of view.

As far apart as the two points of view may seem, there is actually a fairly simple synthesis of both views, and no real compromise is needed on either side. The two agree that filling in the gaps, sometimes relying on research and more or less on intuition, is often a necessary step in restoration. The organ builder's proposal to reconstruct the organ's back is perfectly agreeable to the conservator with a single, palatable caveat. Preservation of the historical record will remain clear to the extent that our intrusions are detectable, documented, and removable. Where we add materials, we can leave clear evidence of our authorship, both through physical evidence and through documentation. What makes this intervention either an unconscionable falsification or a legitimate treatment is in documenting the work and making it detectable and removable. If future scholarship shows us to be wrong, our work can be removed and replaced. If experience tells us anything, we can be almost sure that future scholarship will, indeed, find us to be wrong far more often than we expect.

4. THESE DAYS, EVERYONE AGREES THAT DOCUMENTATION IS IMPORTANT. WHAT EXACTLY ARE WE DOCUMENTING?

Conservator:

Most of my documentation falls into three categories. First are analytical reports on scientific identification of materials, coatings, corrosion products, pollutants, and all other scientific analysis. Second is documentation of condition, including the structural stability, and the current condition of all parts broken down by mat-erial. The report identifies the causes of condition problems and reports whether they are actively degrading or stable. Third and most important is the treatment report that records in detail my treatment interventions. These reports are for future investigators and conservators who should know precisely the changes that I made to the object.

Organ builder:

I document the things that contribute to the organ's musical character. This includes specifications, like the stop-list, keyboards, compass, couplers, key action, stop action, and wind specifications. Pipe details are recorded, including scales, mouth dimensions, toe-hole diameters, and that sort of thing. I also document tonal characteristics of each section of the organ, and whatever history of alterations that can be observed. The value of this documentation is to inform the restoration of similar organs, and to benefit us in the making of new organs.

Again our two window-watchers have seen very different realities. The two spheres of documentation are different, but in no way contradictory; again, it is not 'either/ or', but 'both/ and'.

These are four questions out of dozens from my own anthropological notes on these two allied yet, perhaps, estranged cultures. Having lived among the peoples of both groups, I am quite convinced that it was inevitable that conservation and restoration split into separate tracks. That is not a bad thing as long as they continue to discover just how interdependent they are. The two disciplines are two halves of an essential whole. If we take seriously the complexity of organ restoration on the one hand, and the complexity of conservation on the other, we will see that both disciplines are unlikely to reside in a single person. And if we accept the fundamental difference of perspective that is endemic to conservators and organ specialists, again we should question whether one person can serve two masters that are so different. We can only hope that through conferences like this, conservators and restorers will begin to develop new collaborative relationships.

10

A USA perspective: 2

Jonathan Ambrosino

Readers of this paper's first instalment will surely be curious as to whether any preservation or restoration is practised in America. Regard for our organ heritage may be at an all time high, but acting on that regard has been slow in coming. Efforts at preservation and restoration have been sporadic, but occasionally of high quality and great sensitivity.

The 1970s saw an equal resurgence in the sensitive restoration of both tracker and electric-action organs. In that decade, the Andover Organ Company, the primary rebuilder of so many old tracker organs, undertook a proper restoration of the 1850s Hook organ in Old South Church, Newburyport, Massachusetts. The most notable change was the fitting of tuning slides to the flue pipes. Around the same time Andover also restored a Hutchings-Plaisted that had been Eugene Thayer's practice organ, again of great historical significance and deemed worthy of true restoration, given Thayer's tremendous influence on organ music and pedagogy, and his German training.

The tracker builder George Bozeman also had an early hand in true restoration work during the 1970s by restoring the GG-compass 1840s Stevens organ in Belfast, Maine. Action, wind system and specification remained unchanged. Tuning was an issue; though the pipes remained cone-tuned, the unequal temperament was not reinstated. Bozeman continued this approach in Bangor, Maine with a three-manual 1860 Hook. Missing pipes were re-created following the originals, and the action repaired as necessary using parts in the style of the original. Compass, not pitch, reared its head here: the 25-note pedal compass was extended to 27, and the slide for a prepared-for Pedal 'Cello was used to install a replica Hook Trombone with wooden resonators. If not precisely restoration, these jobs signalled at last a degree of sensitivity in the reconsideration of an old tracker organ uncommon up to that point in all but the most routine cleaning and overhaul jobs where funds limited ambition.

This period came to a benchmark moment with Fritz Noack's restoration of the Mechanics Hall, Worcester, Hook organ of 1864, essentially America's first town-hall-type concert organ. It was the re-trackerization for which all the others had been test cases, and the evidence was easy to establish. The Mechanics Hall organ had been rebuilt, electrified and enlarged only once, by Hutchings. Essentially all the original material remained, and Mr Noack was charged with re-trackerizing the instrument, building a new Barker machine and replicating the console, the last aspect being done particularly well. The job was not without complications, stemming mostly from difficulties making the Barker machine do its job. The rest of the work was carried out to a high standard of European restoration: all new or replica work was done in a modern style distinctly apart from the old, so as to leave no question where old left off and new began.

By and large the organ has been a great success, with a big public following. What is equally clear is that the spirit of this restoration was the clear answer for its time. The love for old tracker organs may have begun 20 years before, but it took two decades for respect to catch up with regard.

Respect and regard started up more concurrently with the first major Skinner restorations in the mid-1970s, since the organs themselves had been strongly derided up to that point. It should be remembered that this was a horrible time for most electric-action organs: Perflex, the thought-to-be marvellous plastic substitute for leather, was turning out to be a first-class disaster. In large urban organs, Perflex was replacing thin, brown vegetable-tanned leather that had in no way held up to big-city pollution. Upon Perflex's failure, purses were once again being replaced with leather that might last only ten to twelve years. Faced with such an expensive future, many churches were replacing their organs outright, or switching out pitman soundboards for traditional slider soundboards, or fitting all-electric valves inside hollowed-out soundboard shells – all fates both costly and inconsistent with any preservation stance. Luckily the Perflex chapter was a short, if painful one, to be fully vilified by research into chrome-tanned leathers, the chemical proof of their longevity, and their widespread availability. Without the availability of durable rubber cloth and leather, the prudence of much electro-pneumatic organ restoration would have come into strong question long ago.

The first noteworthy and publicized Skinner restoration was the entirely vintage Skinner organ of 1926 in Jefferson Avenue Presbyterian Church, Detroit, Michigan, carried out by Ken and Dorothy Holden in 1976. Mrs Holden is the author of a biography of Skinner published by the OHS in 1984. Nothing about the organ was changed, due to a reverence for this particular instrument, the innate conservatism of the restorers, and the fact that the organ was in excellent restorable condition.

A year later the A. Thompson-Allen Company of Yale finished their first Skinner restoration, the 1928 three-manual in First Presbyterian Church, Wilmington, North Carolina. Again, no changes. In the following year Nelson Barden of Boston completed a restoration of a 1936 Kimball at the First Church of Christ (Scientist) in Cambridge, Massachusetts, an even less popular sort of instrument (in this period, a Skinner would be saved but all other electric-action organs were to be considered highly suspicious). Although a consultant forced a mixture to be added to the Great, the organ otherwise remains tonally and mechanically intact. This job won for Barden a large body of mechanical restoration work at the Church of the Advent in Boston and a burgeoning reputation.

As the 1980s and 1990s progressed, the work of Barden, Thompson-Allen and Edward Stout in San Francisco dominated the top-echelon scene of rehabilitating better-quality early twentieth-century electro-pneumatic organs. In the 1990s more builders absorbed and perfected techniques for making success of this sort of work. In 1996, Barden, Stout and Thompson-Allen co-hosted a seminar for the topic, sponsored by the American Institute of Organbuilders (AIO); with 38 in attendance, it was the best-attended seminar in AIO history.

Reverence for Skinner, however, was slow in coming, and many more organs were subject to rebuilds of the traditional variety. Even in the early 1990s, when Skinner reverence had reached a certain high pitch, some of his earliest work was being rebuilt under the notion that it was not equal to his later efforts (again, according to this bizarre premise, since it doesn't represent the best, it cannot be worthy of restoration, since there is no bad history?) I quote from a pamphlet issued by St Andrew's Episcopal Church in Pittsburgh, which had a four-manual Ernest M. Skinner organ of 1913 – before its alteration, the oldest completely unaltered four-manual Skinner organ. (Of note is that Edwin Lemare's wife Charlotte was organist here for a time.) Unlike the Casavant fiction (see Chapter 3), there is no doublespeak here – the writer is at once more honest and more clever.

> Pipe organs in Europe have been rebuilt more frequently than discarded. Many famous European organs contain pipes or parts from previous organs in the same church. Thankfully, this attitude of conservation is now being practised in this country by all of the finest builders. In addition, the approach of historic restoration is beginning to appear for historical rather than economic reasons. (The cost of historic restoration can often exceed the price of a new instrument!)

> St Andrew's organ was a candidate for either rebuilding or historic restoration. There is much to be commended to the historic restoration movement. However, the preservation of the idiosyncrasies of the developing mechanism and electrical systems at the turn of the century can limit the practicality and usefulness of the instrument. One might draw an analogy to owning an antique car – a worthy and viable transportation source for a Sunday drive, but problematic as transportation to work in bad weather.

> The Vestry at St Andrew's chose to rebuild (as opposed to restore) the Skinner organ, preserving as much as was feasible of the mechanics of the organ. Contracts were signed in 1990 for the replacement of the console and rebuilding of the entire organ. All of the electrical components of the organ are new, including solid-state relays and new wiring. All leather has been replaced on the reservoirs (bellows) and in the wind chests. Additionally, the wind chests have been fitted with new magnets and primary valve cases.

> A chronology of the work of E. M. Skinner reveals the evolution of the tonal design he pursued. In his early years (of which the St Andrew's organ is representative), Skinner's knowledge of tonal design was based on other American organs. In the early twenties, Skinner travelled to England and met the famous English organ builder Henry Willis, who built the organ at St Paul's Cathedral in London and Liverpool Cathedral among others. Skinner was much impressed with the English tonal ensemble, which was much brighter and clearer than he was accustomed to. All of his subsequent organs began to bear a closer resemblance to the English Cathedral sound. Skinner's magnum opus is to be found at Washington National Cathedral, although this instrument has been substantially altered since.

> The tonal design of St Andrew's organ now much more closely resembles the sound of the English cathedral organs. Additional stops were carefully scaled and voiced to meet this aesthetic.

It is commendable that the writer does not try to fool his audience into thinking that restoration, rebuilding and drastic change all fall together under one happy roof, even though he gets some of his facts wrong. But the larger truth here is that we continue to struggle to justify our actions when often the only reason we change anything is simply because we want to. Shouldn't we just admit it from the outset and save everyone's time? In Pittsburgh, the desire to restore is clearly absent, nor is it articulated. Blithely implied is the desire for more pistons, more mixtures and more modern tonal resources.

The true and shining example of twentieth-century organ conservation is all the more shocking because it exists in one of America's largest and most regularly used organs: the Newberry Memorial Organ in Woolsey Hall, Yale University, New Haven. This is a one-of-a-kind instrument built in 1903 by Hutchings-Votey, rebuilt with an entirely new chassis in 1915 by the Steere Organ Company, and then almost doubled in size with a new console in 1928–9 by the Skinner Organ Company. It poses many interesting restoration issues.

First of all, there has never been any notion that the organ should be returned to either its Steere or its Hutchings state; the organ's fame rests on its Skinner incarnation, in which it is roundly hailed as perhaps one of the two or three finest ultra-romantic organs ever built. In this context one would no more suggest a restorative re-creation than propose that Saint-Sulpice be returned to its Clicquot disposition. Although tonal revisions were once considered for Woolsey Hall in the 1950s, lack of funds prevented anything other than routine cleaning; and even re-leathering work was put off for funding reasons until the 1970s.

Under the careful guidance of the Thompson-Allen Company and a supportive and sympathetic university faculty, this organ has become a living shrine to the fact that an organ can serve 60 hours a week in term time, 14 students and an active concert schedule, all while being in almost every respect precisely as the

Skinner Company left it in 1929. Changes have been extraordinarily few, so few that they are worth recording. Long ago Aubrey Thompson-Allen rewired the Pedal second Diapason to borrow from a metal, not a wood rank; the original Choir 'Cello was replaced with a Hook & Hastings set for tuning stability; one stop that was traded out in 1931 has been reinstated (the unique Solo Orchestral Trombone stop on 25 inches wind pressure), retaining its replacement, the Trumpet Harmonique. That's it. The electrical system, combination action, console, wiring, chests, wind system, and every pneumatic action: all operate as originally designed and built. Perishable materials have been renewed; the twin blowers have been rewound and re-balanced. This is not a museum piece. Rather, it is a living instrument and a great testament to the reality of most good organ building: it is built to be rebuilt.

Of the Barden, Stout, Thompson-Allen trio, the Thompson-Allen Company is the most sensitive to the aesthetic of keeping electric-action organs entirely original. They have never electrified a console, they have never solid-stated any organ, and they have restored all kinds of electric-action organs with success, including bothersome ones. To date, they have restored ten Skinner and Aeolian-Skinner organs in 20 years, as well as others; their current project is a 1930 Kimball organ in Western Pennsylvania. Here is a clear ethic of restoration.

But, is it also an ethic of conservation? Strictly speaking, the answer must be no; nor, it must be pointed out, has it ever intended to be. When a client is a church or a university – not a museum – daily use and an expectation of reliability must of necessity inform the nature of restoration. Therefore, it is only natural that, even with this most preservation-minded of firms, some of what they do goes against the strict grain of conservation. For example, new tuning slides are fitted to slide-tuned pipes; certain cone-tuned pipes are trimmed and sleeved also. (Certainly, and sadly, there are many more rough-handed tuners than pristine cone-tuned pipes in American organs: to sleeve a cone-tuned pipe is often its best means of preservation.)

Also, the Yale restorers re-finish pipes and wooden surfaces, duplicating original techniques and applications. Some surfaces that received minimal finish (such as walkboards and perchboards) are re-finished and sealed in varnish. In the interest of tuning stability and tonal regularity, reed stops have occasionally been fitted with new tongues of a different thickness schedule and with a different style and schedule of weighting. The Thompson-Allen people do this only where reeds have proven themselves highly unstable or in other ways unreliable; moreover, original tongues are always preserved on-site.

The conservator might choose to view this work – by far the most conservative of any American electric-action organ restoration shop – as a well-intentioned confusion between the aims of restoration and the modern expectation that an old organ behave like a new one. That would be an unfair judgement, since it is a conscious and painfully-arrived-at code devised by people who know that one of the modern burdens of historic objects is that they look after their own future welfare. And it must be remembered that this firm does not advertise itself as a conservation laboratory, but a restoration shop, with no decision idly arrived at. In the words of Joseph Dzeda:

> The organ restorer, as with any other restoration artisan, must confront a basic issue, namely knowing when to stop. On the one hand it would be possible to do the scrimpy minimum to return the instrument to duty, eschewing all but the most unavoidable tasks in the name of (misplaced) historicity, (false) economy, or simply good old-fashioned laziness. Organs restored to these standards tend to look not fully refreshed, like someone who shows up for work bleary-eyed and having slept in yesterday's clothes. At the other extreme one could strip and refinish every square inch of woodwork, replace every scrap of felt, and generally indulge in every imaginable exercise of gratuitous restoration in an attempt to make the result look like it was made yesterday. Taking our cue from the techniques used to conserve antiques, we advocate a more moderate approach, seeking to preserve the undeniable patina of the past, while generally freshening up the organ's chassis and pipework to give the impression not of a new instrument, but rather of one which has been respectfully cared for over the years.

Having achieved such incredible levels at high-end restoration, one new direction for certain organs may be to apply conservation-informed techniques in place of now-traditional restoration techniques, towards a result that leaves more of the original finish, appearance and ambience intact – again, as the instrument's condition, and its environment and owner, will allow. In America some recent tracker restorations point the way in this regard. In a twentieth-century organ a particularly striking example of this newer type of approach is Columbia Organ Works' restoration in 1991 of the 1931 Steinmeyer organ imported from Germany to Altoona, Pennsylvania, and installed there in the Roman Catholic Cathedral of the Blessed Sacrament. If you don't know of this organ, you ought to: it pretends to be a neo-classical organ of its time but really ends up being a big late ultra-romantic German organ of considerable impact, curiosity and interest. It is set in a gloriously rolling acoustic, and can be heard on a superb Raven recording by Peter Sykes called *Maximum Reger*.

Columbia's work on this organ was plagued with challenge, mostly related to the curious individual square-pneumatic note action with ventil stop action. Many experiments were required to get things right; certain mechanisms had to be done over twice, thickness and porosity of leather and paper regularly re-evaluated. And, because of an uninformed consultant (who died midway through the project), one unfortunate change was inflicted upon the process: the fitting of solenoid units to the otherwise action-less register tablets on the console in order to provide a modern solid-state combination action. However, through rods and squares, these solenoids have been fitted in such a way as to be entirely removable, as have the additional key-slips. All new porcelain indicators to accommodate this system were supplied by Laukhuff, who are thought to have built the original console, and the new match the old (Laukhuff have never stopped making them in this particular style), so it is hard to know what is new and what is old. The original free-combination system remains untouched and in perfect working order.

Playing this organ, and inspecting its interior, the work of the restorer is transparent. The organ has been wiped clean, otherwise it looks its age. Surfaces that look nice have perhaps been buffed a little harder to invigorate and refresh the original polish: an interpretative touch that ensures that the donors have gained something for their money. The same basic idea applies to the sound of the organ; egregious speech, timbral and power issues have obviously been corrected, but no attempt has been made to make this into any other than how it has been handed down.

So, the news has grown both better and worse. The shameless rebuild has mellowed into the sympathetic updating, which is just the same thing in a fancy new guise. Come 2025 we may have only a handful of original electro-pneumatic consoles left. And philosophies are changing, on the one hand towards less intrusive restoration practices and, on the other hand, towards less idealistic and possibly more realistic notions of how we should be approaching old organs whose fate is far from obvious. I close with one fascinating situation, to stimulate thought.

The E. and G. G. Hook organ built in 1863 for Boston's Church of the Immaculate Conception is now considered to be probably the finest nineteenth-century American organ, easily standing on a par with any other organ of the world in its day. It was installed under intense artistic pressure, in the light of the completion of the famous Boston Music Hall organ by Walcker, whose construction began in 1857 and was completed in the year of the Immaculate Conception organ.

Evidence is sketchy, but initial research seems to indicate that the Immaculate Conception was no overnight success. In the very first year a systematic loudening began. By the 1880s, the Great reeds had been moved to the Swell, and a new set of parallel shallot reeds had been installed in the Great. The organ was prepared for several stops in 1863, some of which were installed in subsequent decades. The remainder, including a Cymbale VII on the Great, along with electrification, several very stylistically consistent additions, a highly elegant terrace-jamb console, a new Solo organ, and re-pitching, occurred in a major rebuild of 1902 by Hook & Hastings, Hook's successor firm, not even 40 years after the organ's completion.

Nothing else occurred until the 1970s, when the Lahaise brothers of Boston Perflexed the pneumatic pull-down actions and fitted a new setterboard combination action to the console. In this state the organ remains, and poses numerous questions.

1. To what point in history should this instrument be restored?
2. Is it possible to pinpoint any state of the organ prior to 1902 with any accuracy?
3. In adding to and completing the organ in 1902, did the rebuilders fulfil a long-time wish of the original builders that no restoration should erase?
4. If Mechanics Hall was re-trackerized and its size reduced back to its 1864 specification, why would we not unhesitatingly do so here?
5. If the organ has been in its present state for 97 years, and existed in something like its original for only 39, which historical continuum takes precedent in restoration philosophy?
6. And, finally, in an organ like this, what is restoration?

Restoration is a discipline that will always pose more questions than it answers. Only when we highlight the issues and study the past will we find, if not concrete answers, at least clues to how we can be as sensitive as possible in the consideration of old instruments. Although in theory it should be the simplest thing possible to leave something alone, it does not seem easy for most of us to accept. We would do well to ponder why.

11

Training opportunities in organ restoration

John Mander

It has to be admitted from the outset that training opportunities in this field are limited and inadequate which, to put it mildly, is sad. This is an area that desperately needs more attention and resources and this paper deals essentially with practical training and not college- or museum-based training courses.

First, I would like to look at the training opportunities in organ building as a whole, as that would seem to be a prerequisite for any sort of restoration training. Traditionally, the larger firms here and abroad offered so-called apprenticeships. Unfortunately, these apprenticeships were often little more than a source for cheap labour to be exploited by the firms as long as possible. In addition, journeymen frequently had an in-built reluctance to train others as they always seemed to fear that if they trained a youngster, he would in time take the journeyman's job. This ingrained attitude continued until well after the Second World War, both here and to some extent abroad as well.

With the general decline in the organ-building industry in the United Kingdom (I would guess it is about half the size it was before the Second World War, but I have not researched the figures) the opportunity for apprentices, such as it was, declined as well. In essence, you 'served your time' as an apprentice and picked up as much as you could without appearing too inquisitive. It was not really formal, even if it called itself a formal apprenticeship. We now have a situation where there is very little ground-up training actually taking place. I think I am right in saying that it is probably only Harrison & Harrison and Manders who still have apprentices undergoing training. The situation is even worse than it seems as (I think to some extent understandably) we are keener to train apprentices who we think will stay with the company than those who will want to learn and move on. That is probably the worst aspect of the training dilemma as it precludes any sort of mobility and exchange of skills within the trade. Manders' apprentices are encouraged and assisted to take courses outside the works in cabinet making and associated trades, or even to go to Ludwigsburg.

Most people are aware of what is sometimes called the organ-building school at Ludwigsburg, Germany, but few really appreciate what it is all about. It is not an organ-building school at all, but an apprentices' school, a large complex providing training on a sandwich-course basis for everything from dentists' assistants, mechanics, bakers, butchers and sales assistants, through organ building, flute, brass, lute, violin and piano making. This is not a system unique to Germany either. There are similar schools in Austria and Switzerland. One has to be an apprentice with a company and attendance at the Musical Instrument Manufacturers' School (as it is roughly translated), which forms part of the vast complex at Ludwigsburg, is for six visits, each of six weeks, during the apprenticeship. The facilities are shared with other trades, but most of the instructors are specific to instrument making, if not organ building, and it aims to complement training in the workshop. There is a practical side, but it is relatively minor. There are absolutely no stylistic elements at all. The subjects cover everything from the German language to mathematics, materials theory, tool technology, history and music, and even foreign languages. The German authorities are very generous with the use of these facilities. Three of our apprentices have been allowed to attend the courses and take the exams, which they all passed, and Bill Drake and I were able to complete the Masters' course which they offer every two years. Knowledge of the German language is an advantage of course, and two of our apprentices who attended learned German first. The system in Germany is based on a continuation of education beyond the end of schooling and offers the so-called second-education track, which can lead to university. It is indicative of the importance education is given in Germany in general.

It is this basic form of training that is completely lacking in this country. An assembly-line worker at the nearby Ford factory, remains just that, but at Ford's German works, they can become engineers. Most of course do not, but all have a better understanding of what it is all about than a similar worker here. There was a time when it looked as if we might get something similar here with the advent of the Industrial Training Boards, but it needed a political and economic commitment it was never to get. In the organ-building field, the scheme was in part under the auspices of the Federation of Master Organbuilders and one of their members attempted to convince the authorities that only organ builders could undertake this training. The list of tools that were claimed to be used in organ building was so long that I honestly believe I only knew the name and purpose of 10 per cent of them. It was effectively sabotaged and too many people in the trade thought it was an expensive waste of time, so that opportunity was lost, probably forever. The importance of education in society, particularly for its economic well-being, seems totally misunderstood here. The communists understood it a lot better than we do.

The IBO has, as one of its aims, improvement in the area of training, but it is questionable whether that will ever happen, much as it is to be encouraged. It is unrealistic to expect a small industry like ours to fund such a scheme, in terms of time and money. If I took three to six months off, I could set up a training scheme on paper – having been through the process, I know what is needed – but who would pay for it and who would run the business while I was away? Is there a capable person who might have the time? Where would the training take place if the scheme was established and how would it be funded? However, the IBO is trying to do something and that is well worth encouraging. Who knows, we may just manage it.

I fear I have wandered from my brief, but an understanding of the background is necessary to know where we stand and how poor the opportunities really are. Even on a worldwide basis there is little opportunity for training in organ conservation and restoration. As far as I know, there is still no restoration or conservation element in the training of apprentices in Germany, at least on a formal basis.

What might be possible?

Fortunately, there are firms engaged in restoration and conservation and I suspect that the best way to gain experience at the moment is to join one of those companies and work on such projects for a year or two, assuming they had sufficient restoration work on their books. A fairly solid foundation in organ building itself is pretty well essential before one can graduate to such work. Some of our best restorers are small companies of just three or four people who may not have the space or resources to take on more employees. The larger companies might do nothing but new work for long periods, which was our situation a few years back. Of course, there are companies abroad one might approach, but the economic situation is so dire in many parts of Continental Europe at the moment that they too might be reluctant to take on such applicants. One possible exception is the former East Germany, where there is much which needs to be done. Most of it is being directed to firms in the region, in an effort to overcome the high unemployment, but here funding is more limited than it might have been. While the Church in eastern Germany thrived under the old communist rule (it was seen as a form of passive resistance to attend church), since the fall of the wall attendance has dropped dramatically and, with it, funding.

The other possibility is to go to firms specializing in art restoration, such as Plowden & Smith, to gain experience in conservation at a more general level, having first gained general organ-building experience. I have to say that I do not know what such possibilities are and their work on organs is non-existent, of course, but their skills in other areas may make it worthwhile. Similarly, more general instruction (I hesitate to use the word education) in furniture restoration is offered by some of the universities and technical colleges.

Although not offering training, the Crafts Council did start to produce information in a series of books for conservators entitled *Science for Conservators*. Three volumes were published: *Introduction to Materials*, *Cleaning* and *Adhesives and Coatings*. I never received notification of the three books that were supposed to follow and, anyway, they were highly scientific and not aimed at practitioner level.

Some things have happened which, at one stage, looked as if they might improve matters. The first light at the end of the tunnel was the setting up of the Heritage Lottery Fund. Here was a possibility to regulate (at least) restoration work. Funds were only to be made available to those bodies wanting to undertake proper restoration, with personnel who had a track record, and the work was to be monitored to ensure good practice. But first (it seems to me at least), it was clogged up by bureaucracy and just as it got going, the present government decided to use the funds for things which in the past had been funded out of tax-payers' money, thereby covertly milking the fund in an effort to save money from their own coffers. In addition, when English Heritage got involved (in the Joint Grant Scheme for Churches and other places of worship), the agenda was changed so radically that organs essentially got written out of the equation completely, at least for the time being. Secondly, the IBO has encouraged firms to educate themselves by introducing the accreditation scheme for its business members actively investigating the ability and the attitudes and concepts of would-be members in and to restoration. But all this is a filtration process rather than development – traffic lights rather than a new road. At best it might prevent the wrong thing being done, but it is not really advancing the cause very much and is still not training.

Sadly, the bottom line is that there is not as much opportunity for training in restoration and conservation work in organ building as is needed, especially in the present economic climate, where the funds available are so limited. In a slightly bizarre way, the lack of funding for restoration and preservation is matched by the lack of training possibilities and I suggest that the two are connected. There is, without doubt, plenty of work to be done and, if this can be encouraged, the situation would change. It is true to say that it is ultimately the government and English Heritage who have that under their control. The first needs to have its knuckles rapped for pilfering funds which were originally ear-marked for that purpose and English Heritage needs to be shaken to its roots and provided with a pair of glasses so that it can recognize projects which can set an example. A little more finance and a couple of restorations which could act as flagships (an English Jakobikirche or Berliner Dom for example) might start to move things in the right direction.

Are there any volunteers to do the rapping and shaking?[1]

12

Towards historically informed advisers

Christopher Kent

A perfect organ historian would have the skills of a musician, a crafts-
man, a palaeographer and an archaeologist as well as having general
interests in antiquarian, ecclesiological and architectural study.

Stephen Bicknell

The first of these conferences that I attended was at Sherborne in 1987 – on that
occasion I was a guest contributor invited to talk on the work of BIOS, being its
recently elected, somewhat zealous, if not a shade arrogant, Honorary Secretary.
Shortly afterwards, by a process which still seemed to be mysteriously opaque,
and seems sometimes to remain so, like some other aspects of the mysterious
administrative machinery of the Church of England, I was invited to become one
of the organ advisers to the Diocese of Oxford. It was made clear to me, very soon,
that I was merely an adviser and would remain on the fringe of the Diocesan
Advisory Committee, whose meetings I was welcome to attend, but without
voting rights. Although the Diocese has generously supported my cost of being
here, being denied DAC membership makes me feel uneasy, not personally, but
on account of the inadequate regard it seems to bestow on the organ. Particularly
as it is often among the most complex and costly items that a Diocesan Advisory
Committee is required to deliberate upon. It is therefore crucial that those who
serve as advisers should aspire to many of the laudable attributes that Stephen
Bicknell believes an ideal organ historian should possess.

When comparing Bicknell's set of requirements with my remarks made twelve
years ago in Sherborne, I find that there is only one point of variance; indeed it
is a significant point of omission. In common with other fields of scholarly
research, organ historians, before exercising their skills in palaeography or archaeology in relation to an instrument, it is crucial that they first bring to bear their
skills in bibliographical research. It follows that such *complete bibliographical
control* is also a crucial prerequisite for the organ adviser or consultant preparing
reports for churches or other clients. It is also my belief that any code of ethics
for conservation should be founded on a similar prerequisite, and any who
formulate and seek to practise and promulgate such a code of principles should
also be historically informed in the broadest possible sense.

When I stipulated this to be a sine qua non in the still somewhat laissez-faire
and complacent conduct of organ advice in 1987 – a time when BIOS still had

something of an *enfant terrible* image – there were reactions ranging from respectful smiles to 'fine, as long as we're not too extreme' to goldfish-like gawps of disbelief. We have come some way since then, but there is still a considerable distance to go before we can meet the best practices of our European colleagues. Yet one can still read reports where advisers' lack of bibliographical rigour has given rise to questionable conclusions or recommendations. Although it is necessary for archaeological, conservatorial, bibliographical and musical skills to be interactive, sometimes this is not a reasonable prospect for a single adviser, particularly when the futures of large instruments, or those with complex histories and antiquities are under review. Although it may be ideal for the individual adviser or consultant to be a historical, musical, technical and architectural polymath within his or her field, it is becoming increasingly clear that in the cases of instruments with long and complex histories and equally difficult situations from the viewpoints of liturgy and repertoire, this is a task that should not be set upon the shoulders of one adviser or consultant, but should be shared by a panel of three appropriately equipped specialists who would assume collective responsibility.

For the core of this short paper, let me present an overall view of the challenges and responsibilities that we must address if we wish to be better organ historians and morally qualified to follow the code of conservation ethics that this conference seeks to identify, since such a code must surely be built on the broadest of historically informed foundations. Some of the following observations stem from the contributions of my colleagues (particularly James Wallman) who participated in a round-table session on organographical issues held during the conference 'The Organ in the New Millennium' in April 1999 at the Pacific Lutheran University at Tacoma, near Seattle, USA.

The consensus was that the attributes of the *perfect* organ historian would include:

- a knowledge of the general history of music from the medieval period to the present day, including the history of the repertoire of the organ;
- an awareness of related histories, in particular church history, liturgy, technology, art, general history and politics, economics, archaeology, architecture, palaeography, conservation theory and practice;
- practical ability as an organist who has had international experience of playing repertoires on historically and stylistically appropriate instruments;
- a technical and historical understanding of actions, wind chest designs, blowing systems, pipe formations, scaling practices and philosophies;
- an acquaintance with the major European treatises and histories of the organ by Zwolle, Schlick, Antegnati, Praetorius, Werckmeister, Bedos, Adlung, Seidel, Hopkins & Rimbault, Töpfer, Audsley, Klotz, Andersen, Vente, Perrot, Williams and Van Biezen, *et al.*;
- being a reader of current periodicals: *The Organ Yearbook, Journal of the British Institute of Organ Studies, Ars Organi, Acta Organologica, L' Orgue, Tribune de l' Orgue, Het Orgel, L' Organo, The Tracker*, etc.;
- good ears, and an ability to assess tone qualities objectively;

- an acquaintance with relevant archival resources: County Record Offices, Public Record Office, National Monuments Record, Society of Antiquaries, British Organ Archive, National Pipe Organ Register;
- an acquaintance with relevant bibliographical resources: *RILM Abstracts*, Warman, Williams & Owen (*New Grove*), etc.

A few days ago I celebrated my half-century with a short recital for a few friends on a Scudamore-type instrument by Bates & Son of the early 1860s in Wiltshire. It has one manual, three stops: two at 8' and one at 4' pitch and no pedals. This has been ethically conserved (with lottery funding) since:

- it is tonally very good;
- its construction is good;
- it is aesthetically pleasing, both in its own terms and in its interaction with its surroundings;
- it responds well to a diverse cross section of the repertoire, far beyond its intended role as a functional instrument for hymn accompaniment.

To further general understanding in this field, an M.Mus. degree course in Organ Historiography was established at the University of Reading in 1993 and has attracted a steady stream of full- and part-time students. Organ historiography is now a flourishing part of the research programme of the Department of Music at staff and senior postgraduate levels. Contacts are maintained with universities with similar interests in Austria, Germany, the Netherlands and Sweden. As well as its ongoing commitment to research into the British organ, the Department is affiliated to the (IAOD) and has recently become the United Kingdom representative for the European Organ Database. In 1997 the status of the course was changed to MA in order to accommodate a wider range of student backgrounds and to facilitate the availability of related M.Phil. and Diploma courses. The Reading courses attempt to address all aspects of our opening statement, with the exception of the craftwork – restoration and conservation skills are not taught, only the related historical philosophies. In respect of the craft skills, I would stress that the degree does not carry any implication of superiority in the organ builder's workshop – it is primarily a literary course.

Let me end with some words of Sir Thomas More (slightly adapted):

> Learning, study, reading, and the preservation of books are all integral to the ethics of organ conservation [spiritual practice]. We get into trouble when we give up any of these: when beauty turns into sentimentality or propaganda, when architecture and the others are unconscious or considered secondary, when we forget the importance of ongoing, lifelong learning in all areas as support for the work of the organ adviser, historian or conservator [spiritual life], and especially when we make [spiritual] advisory practice the project of creating a certain kind of self.

And as Albert Schweitzer stated: 'We work for the future. May we do so in the right spirit.'

13

Association of Independent Organ Advisers (AIOA)

John Norman

Because organs are so long-lasting, work is only needed infrequently. When it is required however, such work is a major project. Those responsible for organs then find themselves in a position where they would benefit from independent expert advice on what is, for the commissioning body, virtually a one-off exercise. The question is – to whom should they turn?

The most influential organ adviser in the history of the British organ was Dr Henry Gauntlett, the hymn writer. In the 1830s and 1840s Gauntlett took a great interest in organ design and strongly influenced William Hill, the leading London organ builder of the day. Together they championed the introduction of the 'German' compass to C in the bass, the inclusion of 16' stops on the manuals and the provision of a proper Pedal organ. This change killed off the old GG compass and led to the rebuilding of almost all pre-1840 organs in Britain.

Not all musician advisers took such an intelligent interest, however. At the turn of the twentieth century, one cathedral organist advised churches seeking new organs to go to one of three organ builders (recommending each builder in turn). He then took no further interest in the matter except to demand a 5 per cent commission from the organ builder he had recommended!

It is clearly vital that those who offer advice should have wide knowledge of the musical, technical, acoustical, architectural and historical questions that will arise. Advisers should be impartial yet should also be acquainted with the recent achievements of different organ builders and be aware of their particular skills and experience.

Fortunately, the agreement whereby the Church of England used its faculty system as a form of self-regulation to avoid secular listed-building controls has led to the appointment of diocesan organ advisers. There is no doubt that the advice of the diocesan organ adviser has been of great benefit to parishes and has some-times (though not always) helped to avoid the despoliation or destruction of valuable instruments.

In addition, organs in Roman Catholic, Methodist, United Reformed and Baptist churches in England and Wales now come under the control systems of those denominations. Organs in secular buildings such as concert halls and town halls, in churches of other denominations and organs in university and school chapels are, however, only controlled by the secular system administered by local government. Work on these instruments is unregulated unless they stand in buildings that are themselves listed as historic. The secular system takes advice from English Heritage (or Historic Scotland or CADW in Wales). However, English Heritage now has no staff specializing in organs and, in practice, is only interested in organ cases, not their contents.

Legally, the role of the diocesan organ adviser (DOA) in the Church of England is only to advise the DAC and the Chancellor whether a faculty should be granted for the work proposed and to help applicants to prepare schemes of work that will gain approval. Nothing more. It is *not* the job of the DOA to choose which organ builder a church should employ – although some DOAs do advise churches informally about unsatisfactory organ builders. More importantly, it is not the job of the DOA to monitor work, authorize payments or certify completion. In the London Diocese alone that would be a full-time job for two people. However, DOAs are unpaid. Most are musicians with an interest in organ design. The only training provided is in the form of optional attendance at the annual DOA conference.

Clearly there is a need for professional advice that goes into greater depth than can possibly be provided by a system manned solely by volunteers. It should not compete with the DOA system but supplement it in difficult cases. There is also a need for advice on organs in other buildings, such as school chapels and town halls which are outside the ecclesiastical systems.

In the last 20 years a few individuals have started to practise as professional organ consultants. The trustees of independent schools looked for outside advice on the organs in their school chapels and the recent advent of lottery funds, which expect organ work to be professionally supervised like any other project, has accelerated the demand. Until the formation of the AIOA it was difficult for those wishing to commission new organs or restore existing ones to identify an appropriate adviser for their project. Sadly, there have been a few cases where musicians who did not know much about the inside of organs acted as professional consultants, with dire results.

The AIOA was started in 1997 to identify qualified professional advisers/consultants. It currently has ten members who each agreed to have one project examined by another member before accreditation. Of the members, two are experienced former organ builders (no longer connected with their old companies), three are professional musicians (one of whom formerly worked for an organ builder), one an architect who formerly worked for English Heritage, one a priest with a doctorate in the history of English organ building, one a retired physicist and amateur organist and two are university academics (one of whom runs organ history courses).

There is no formal procedure for work by AIOA members but advice may be given about:

- the drawing up of an initial brief for the organ, in consultation with the client and in relation to architecture, acoustics, liturgical function (where applicable), musical requirements and future maintenance;
- conservation issues that may arise in connection with the restoration, renovation, reconstruction or replacement of an existing organ and/or its case;
- the choice of organ builder;
- the obtaining of initial quotations;
- the relative merits of tenders received;
- where applicable, the design and layout of the organ;
- aspects of the detailed design, contractual arrangements between client and organ builder and work schedules;
- the progress of work by the selected builder in the workshop and on site;
- acceptance of the completed organ;
- the continuing maintenance and insurance of the organ.

The adviser undertakes to act with impartiality and without any financial or commercial interest in any organ-building firm.

Hopefully, as the availability of professional advisers becomes better known, they will be able to help improve the quality of organ advice, and thus of organ building itself. Prospective clients are welcome to seek help from the association in selecting a suitable adviser. The membership list is available from the Administrator (see Appendix 1, p. 123).

14

From the organ bench

Gordon Stewart

When Dame Gillian Weir presented a series of programmes some years ago for the BBC, visiting some of the finest organs in Europe and the British Isles, she went first to Haarlem. Few of us had any problem with her choice. It was, as she said, 'the Mecca for organists'. I wonder now if the St Bavo organ would still be our first port of call? With its 1960s action, new mixtures, and re-voiced choruses, does it feel quite right now, 30 years on? Might we start now instead at Alkmaar, with its perfectly restored action and 16' mixtures? Certainly with my organ teacher's hat on, I find this a better starting point. The feel, look and sound of the organ are as one. Certainly it is more difficult to play, and makes you think about the attack and release of every note; but it is a whole. A wonderful, musical whole. Incidentally, when I mentioned this organ to Dame Gillian, she said that being locked in that church playing the organ as a student had been one of the inspirations of her early years.

Why has our taste changed in this way? I believe that it is because we have learned so much from the early music revival. We have become like the string players who find what they may have thought of as limitations of old instruments the very things which allow them the freedom to play the music as they wish. So one sits at the Alkmaar console, finding the imposed all-toe pedalling somehow liberating, and the sensitivity of the opening and closing of the pallets, first frightening, then the very musical vehicle one has been seeking since becoming interested in early performance practice. It is that feeling of musical cohesion; the case, specification, sound, position of stop knobs, keyboards and pedals, all exactly as they were when the organ was completed in 1726, that makes the Alkmaar experience different from the Haarlem one, wonderful as it is in its own way.

So I approach this conference as a player and teacher. One who has reached the conclusion that a good organ is probably going to feel and sound best if it is left as the builder made it. That is not to say that all organs are to be museum pieces. Changes of use in church organs may well lead to changes in the instrument. What I do believe is that any changes should be made only after careful consideration of the importance of the organ both locally and nationally. Some British organs, such as that of St George's Hall here in Liverpool, have a worldwide importance and should only be altered following the most careful consideration by a panel of consultants.

What I find worrying is how we communicate this to an amateur local organist who wants a 2' stop added to the Great Organ of the church's small two-manual instrument in order to give a better lead in the hymns. The thought of the might of BIOS and its experts descending upon him or her ready to do a careful archaeological survey is enough to frighten the organist off altogether. But as the one who plays the organ most often, he or she may be right. The organ should perhaps have had a 2' from the start!

The cathedral organ loft is not a good place to learn about organ preservation, any more than the town hall. Both cathedral organs and town hall organs are now used to play music for which they were not designed. Yet, if they are not equipped to play that music, then whole sections of the repertoire will not be heard in live performance in that area. In my own case for instance, the organ at Blackburn Cathedral sounded wonderful in the music of Messiaen and Naji Hakim, but it was only after the installation of a new capture system to replace the four generals and their attendant rows of switches, that performance of the music became possible. At Blackburn I had no problem with the idea of restoring the console and fitting new pistons to match the old ones, but what of an older organ with an original console? Does there need to be compromise here, a realization that the organ is not in a museum, and that like a listed building, it has to be made able to do the job it needs to do? Exciting as it would be to hear the Huddersfield Town Hall organ sounding as 'Father' Willis built it, one would have to admit that the original pitch and loss of many stops, not least the 32' pedal, would make it unsuitable for many of the things it does now when it plays with large choirs and orchestras. Indeed the loss of the mutations on the 1980 choir would very much restrict the repertoire for lunchtime concerts!

So do I speak with forked tongue? In a way I do. I realize that many of the working organs in this country, and certainly all the cathedral organs, have been changed just so that they could keep up with the increasing demands put on them. No 'Father' Willis organ was built to play the range of repertoire which cathedrals now perform in both solo music and accompaniments. The advances in console control have made composers view the organ in new ways, with many more stop changes than were possible before multi-level systems. Modern French composers are quick to admit that their music is not playable on a standard Cavaillé-Coll organ without two stop assistants. Cathedral organists and touring recitalists seldom have such helpers, and in any case they are not part of the British tradition! So I will keep my 128 levels of generals and my advancer. They have become part of the town hall organ, at least for now!

Having been lucky enough to play in the Netherlands and Germany and been able to watch the teaching of the finest teachers, I realize that there is much to do with educating all levels of organists in this country. But where to start? All the major conservatoires are teaching on modern mechanical action organs, and producing, it seems to me, students who believe that if they can play a late twentieth-century action they can play anywhere. And they are so insular. Teaching in London one day I asked a postgraduate student playing some Vierne if he had ever played a Cavaillé-Coll organ. He had not. Had he seen a Cavaillé-Coll console? He had not. Had he heard a Cavaillé-Coll organ? He had not. Indeed he had never been to France and really could not see the point, as he really wanted to get ready for a concert in Westminster Abbey. We have a long way to go.

Perhaps we need to look to the Royal College of Organists (RCO) and the Royal School of Church Music (RSCM) for help. Perhaps all FRCO candidates need to attend a conference in the Netherlands as part of their examination preparation and all the new RSCM courses need to include classes in organ preservation. But I do not hold out much hope. The FRCO exams are held on modern mechanical action organs and the students seem to believe that these organs are the ideal for huge chunks of the repertoire from Frescobaldi to Howells. And parish church music is in such a mess that the ability to play hymns and keep on the right side of the clergy will certainly be considered more important than knowledge of organ preservation.

One could be more hopeful if one felt that influence would come from the early music audience, but the organ has somehow kept itself separate from this world. Certainly small organs appear as continuo, but such works as the Vivaldi organ concertos have never really found their way into the repertoire, and solo organ concerts of Baroque music still attract small organ-specialist audiences. To get a large audience you need to play to the gallery with huge varied programmes including transcriptions. Just the sort of programmes which call for sequencers and much altered organs!

New concert hall organs with two consoles do not help either. Most of the players at the Bridgewater Hall in Manchester choose to use the electric console as it allows them to hear the instrument. What the audience sees is that there cannot be much difference between mechanical- and electric-action if the world-famous players choose the electric.

Add to this the shame of the state of the organs in St George's Hall, Liverpool, and Manchester Town Hall, let alone hundreds of lesser instruments crying out for attention, and you get the picture.

What Britain needs is an educated organ world; teachers, students, performers and audience. BIOS, the Royal College of Organists, the Incorporated Association of Organists (IAO), the Royal School of Church Music and IBO must work together to inform at all levels, so that great organs of all ages are preserved and wonderful new organs are built.

15

Instruments and repertoire: concert use

John Kitchen

The end of the twentieth century is as good a time as any, I suppose, to survey the present state of the organ world. We all recognize the extraordinary stylistic diversity of instruments – of organs old and new, of varying views on design and so on. The range of organ types readily to hand in, for example, the city of Edinburgh is remarkable and I think this reflects the nationwide picture. Does such diversity reflect a lack of focus, a lack of confidence, a confusion as to the purposes, nature and function of the organ? Or does it indicate a healthy, enquiring and adventurous spirit? (One might draw parallels with the stylistic diversity of contemporary musical composition, but that is another story.)

My brief is to discuss concert organs and their repertoire and I will attempt to address two questions:

- How best can we use them today?
- What do they teach us?

Many of our town and city halls contain remarkable instruments, indicative of civic pride in their day, of confidence in the future, but which reflect values rather different from our own. Many were, and still are, astounding both musically (aurally?) and technologically. Most were built in the second half of the nineteenth century, although the first great civic organ was built in Birmingham Town Hall as early as 1834; and some date from the early decades of the twentieth century, such as the restored 1923 Harrison in the Caird Hall, Dundee, and the about-to-be-restored 1914 Norman & Beard in Edinburgh's Usher Hall.

Many of these instruments languished in the 1960s and 1970s at a time when their style was out of favour, but it is encouraging, in the last ten or twenty years, to observe an upturn in the fortunes of at least some of them, with quite a few notable restorations. But having restored them, what do we play on them? How do we justify the expense of the restoration? One might first look to the main purposes for which they were built: to accompany oratorio and large-scale choral works, either playing the organ part along with the orchestra (or indeed substituting for the orchestra) and to give solo recitals. The first of these purposes still applies, even if oratorio performances are nowadays less numerous than they were in the instruments' heyday and even if we now wish to perform Handel (probably the most popular composer in the nineteenth century) in a rather different style. What, though, of solo recitals?

Well, one can play much of the standard organ repertory on these organs; most romantic and modern music will sound pretty well, and some earlier music will be quite acceptable. Of course one can play Bach, as nineteenth-century players certainly did; the music is of such integrity that it sounds well (if not historically accurate) played on almost anything. Peter Williams has observed that successive generations of organists, playing totally different styles of organs, have in turn been convinced that theirs was 'ideal for Bach' (as Schweitzer, perhaps surprisingly, said about Cavaillé-Coll instruments). This of course says much more about Bach's music than about any type of organ.

It is well known that nineteenth-century organ programmes, such as those of W. T. Best at St George's Hall, Liverpool, consisted mainly of transcriptions of orchestral, chamber and choral music, with only a few original organ works. This is what these instruments were primarily built to do; their tone colours, the increasing interest in the provision of registration aids, aspects of the style of voicing and so on all reflect this desire to be 'orchestral'. We can readily acknowledge the fact that great music was thus brought to those who would otherwise have had no chance of hearing it. Reflecting the philanthropic views of the time, Best himself said, 'In endeavouring to raise the tastes of the humbler classes, the municipal authorities of our large towns did not intend their concert organs to be restricted to the performance of preludes and fugues and somewhat dry sonatas . . .'[1] This is all very well, but such a justification does not apply today. What justification can we have, then, for playing transcriptions?

Relf Clark has argued persuasively in favour of transcriptions,[2] and an increasing number of organ recitalists now include them in their programmes. Audiences patently enjoy them (perhaps this is a good enough reason for playing them) and I suspect that many organists rather enjoy playing them, and are even prepared to admit it. I believe that this is a healthy and legitimate development, since it shows off our great civic organs to full advantage, and uses them as they were intended to be used.

Many musicians today are interested in studying performance styles of the past; this even extends to a consideration of how successive generations performed music of the past. (I seem to recall reading about a recent attempt to recreate Mendelssohn's 1829 performance of the *St Matthew Passion*.) Now, playing Handel transcriptions in St George's Hall will not tell us much about performance practices of Handel's day; but it might say something about Handelian styles in Best's day, and that should interest us. The link between music and appropriate instruments is paramount – each informs the other. We (some of us) are now interested in finding out about the particular instruments on which individuals played regularly, and for which they conceived their music. We want to hear Buxtehude on a Schnitger and Bach on a Silbermann; when considering Franck, we study not just Cavaillé-Coll organs in general, but those in St-Clothilde and the Trocadéro in particular; we are interested in hearing Liszt played at Merseburg and Reger played on a turn-of-the-century Sauer, like the splendidly restored 1905 113-stop instrument in Berlin Cathedral.

But in nineteenth-century Britain there was no school of organ composition equivalent to the French or German; transcriptions ruled. This is not the place to ponder reasons for this phenomenon; simply to record it. Therefore, if we want to study nineteenth-century performance practices with regard to the British organ, we must consider – and play – transcriptions; only in this way will we fully understand the instruments. In order to do so, we must preserve and maintain these instruments, as far as possible in their original state.

What sort of things do the instruments tell us? First of all, the experience simply of sitting at a particular console can be most informative; this is true of organs of any period. Consoles of different styles have a *feel* which is often difficult to define, but is nonetheless real. Presiding at a large Cavaillé-Coll reversed console, surveying a large church from a unique vantage point high in the west-end organ gallery, will help us understand the music of Vierne and Widor. (I recall playing the Lemmens' *Final* in D at the Cavaillé-Coll-style organ by Pierre Schyven in the west gallery of Antwerp Cathedral; the position, the acoustic, and the stately *feel* of the instrument seemed to bestow dignity and grandeur on a piece which is arguably rather trite.) I experience a similar sensation when playing the great 1906 Lewis concert organ in Kelvingrove Art Gallery in Glasgow; its exalted position, amid the opulence of the building, influences the way we think about the music. It also encourages showmanship!

There are many specific aspects about which we can learn from nineteenth-century concert organs, for example, how the type of action influences the player. Most large concert organs had either pneumatic assistance to a mechanical action, or were tubular-pneumatic; recent restorations of original actions have enabled us to experience the particular type of responsiveness of such actions and this can be influential. Matters such as console dimensions, distance between the manuals, style of the pedalboard and its relationship to the manuals, layout of stop-jambs, and even the manner in which the stops are positioned – at Kelvingrove, where the console is unaltered, the horizontal rows of 8's seem to encourage the use of several at once.

Perhaps most significant, in terms of organ management, is the provision – or absence – of registrational aids, that aspect of organ building which has caused, and continues to cause, so much ingenuity, agonizing and argument. British instrument makers had always liked devices and gadgets – one thinks of machine stops on eighteenth-century harpsichords and shifting movements on chamber organs, both designed to add or subtract registers – but there is no doubt that increasing attention was given to such matters from the 1850s onwards (more so in Britain than in Europe). Willis took out a patent in 1851 for thumb pistons, an action which was to have far-reaching consequences, and which provided greater scope for stop-changing than composition pedals (which continued to be standard on many organs).

Old organs often tell us that we want to change stops too often, that kaleidoscopically changing colour, however attractive or ingenious, was not part of the original conception of much romantic music, let alone earlier repertoire. Having said that, the detailed and often complicated registrations specified in many of Best's editions, particularly his transcriptions, could not have been carried out without quite sophisticated registrational devices. Even so, he must have been remarkably adept at hand-registering, so numerous are the changes. We are told that he eschewed the services of either a stop-puller or page-turner! (What would he have thought of a sequencer?!)

A study of original piston arrangements (and original settings where these are available) is of immense interest from a performance-practice point of view. One can experience this at Kelvingrove, for example, where the Lewis console, pistons and indeed settings have all been carefully preserved. Here Lewis used 'liquorice all-sorts' placed at the back of the keyboard to which they applied – to be different from Willis and his thumb pistons? Registrational practices of the time are reflected in the piston settings which build up masses of 8' tone before adding upperwork, where chorus reeds are added before mixtures and so on; all this evidence is valuable.

Among many other aspects that could be mentioned is the nature of the voicing. Most of the music played on such organs was homophonic rather than contrapuntal; the voicing of many concert organs reflects this by building in a gentle but perceptible crescendo as one goes up the scale. Willis did this, and I have noticed it especially when playing the music of Alfred Hollins on the Caird Hall organ, which Hollins designed. His great thick chords, with a tune on the top, can sound pretty nonsensical on certain organs, but the textures (whether we like them or not) make perfect sense with Harrison's 1923 voicing.

There is no doubt, then, that a historic organ from whatever period will inform the receptive player in all sorts of ways; but the player must be *receptive* and allow the instrument to dictate to a certain extent. There will always be tension, I think, between performers and strict conservationists; recent debates and the correspondence columns in organists' journals are testament to that. Many organists regard rigorous conservation as unduly restricting, and there are cases where I believe this can be so. But far too many organists sit down at a console with preconceived ideas of what they want to do. Such an approach is certainly restricting.

16

The conservation of concert organs

Nicholas Thistlethwaite

The conservation of concert organs presents particular problems which are either peculiar to instruments in secular public halls or pose, in an exaggerated form, difficulties already familiar from the church organ sphere. They may be grouped under five headings.

First, environment. Concert organs are subjected to extremes of temperature and humidity which, over an extended period, can impose a significant strain on natural timbers, leather, adhesives and other materials. Church organs, of course, also suffer in this respect, but few churches experience such frequent variations in temperature and humidity as a busy concert hall. Modern organs are built to withstand these conditions, as far as possible. Not so old organs, and with the up-grading of so many public halls in recent years they are being subjected to novel heating regimes and atmospheric conditions. In these circumstances, an old instrument will deteriorate more rapidly than a new one.

Frequent use also generates more dust pollution. Halls with large capacities and comfortable seats might have seven or eight audiences in and out of the audit-orium during the course of a week. Smaller, more traditional halls (Kidderminster Town Hall, for example) continue to thrive on a programme of jumble sales, horticultural shows, trade exhibitions, Scouts and Guides use, concert extrava-ganzas, dances and discos, and all these varied activities (and all the furniture moving they require) create dust which deposits itself in, among other places, the organ. As a result, it is probably true to say that concert organs need more frequent cleaning than the average church organ: there is consequently more intervention with the instrument and more opportunities for alteration – inten-tional or otherwise.

To this add the physical vulnerability of the organ, located as it is in a building through which the public pass in large numbers, plus the seemingly endless programme of building work required by constantly changing Health and Safety regulations, plus the tendency of local authorities to re-paint their concert halls every year or two, and in the process to re-paint the organ case, pipes and swell boxes without consulting the organ builders, and one begins to understand why (in general) concert organs deteriorate more rapidly than church organs. (As an aside, and as an example of the dangers to which organs are subject in multi-purpose halls, I might mention the historic dent in one of the front pipes at Birmingham Town Hall. It was apparently caused at a political meeting around the time of the First World War when a protester hurled a brick at Lloyd George. Unfortunately – and I assure you I am not making a political point – it missed its target and struck the organ instead.)

I have mentioned local authorities, so I might move on to the second problem impeding the conservation of concert organs in this country, and that is the ambivalent attitude of their custodians.

The majority of our concert organs are, directly or indirectly, the responsibility of local authorities. Birmingham, Liverpool, Leeds, Belfast, Leicester, Lancaster: they, and a good many others, are civic organs (town hall organs), dependent on the whim of local councillors and civil servants. Unfortunately, there are few votes to be had for supporting the retention of a historic concert organ. An instructive example occurred a few years ago, when there was a move to have a large concert organ restored. (The instrument in question is effectively unplayable.) One political party in a 'hung' council supported the proposal and tenders were sought. But then political control changed in the local elections, and the project was shelved as being 'elitist' and not apt for 'Cool Britannia'. Something similar nearly happened at Reading, where the proposal to restore the wonderful 'Father' Willis organ became for many years a political football in the town.

Of course, if one can sound a note of local pride in having a remarkable musical instrument, and if this is then reinforced by people further afield taking an interest or (even better) giving money to help conserve the instrument, then councillors may sit up and take notice – or, at any rate, credit. But without a statutory listing system to concentrate the minds of those in authority, it is altogether more likely that Councillor Smartjack will want to 'modernize' the organ to make it more adaptable to the varied functions which take place in the hall, while Councillor Pursestrings will propose selling it to America.

None of this is very edifying. But then it is hardly reasonable to expect politicians to be organ enthusiasts. If they have any sense they will seek advice. And that (as you may have guessed) brings us to the third problem.

Concert organs are vulnerable to physical damage. But they are also vulnerable to changes of fashion in repertoire and performance practice. This is, of course, true of church organs, too, but not (I think) to the same extent. Their *raison d'être* is the accompaniment of liturgy, while the role of the concert organ is entertainment – of a more or less serious nature, depending on your point of view. On the whole, liturgy changes gradually. In much of the Church of England, for example, the part the organ plays has changed little for 150 years. Fashions in concert programming, however, change all the time, repertoire too. The changes in repertoire since the 1920s have been staggering. Leading recitalists expect instruments that can cope with a vast range of styles and periods, and they are often in a position to effect the outcome of any rebuilding. For reasons that are understandable, their priority will be an instrument that meets their professional needs rather than an instrument of historical integrity.

It was ever thus. In 1932, G. D. Cunningham planned what he regarded as a conservative reconstruction of the Birmingham Town Hall organ. Typically of the period there was no thought that the console or actions might be of any historical interest. Hill's 1890 console was dismissed as 'old-fashioned and out of date', and the key and pedal actions were electrified. The Choir and Solo Organs were enclosed for the first time (the Solo had been partly enclosed in 1890) thus rendering them 'much more useful and expressive', as Cunningham put it, and superficially modest but actually highly significant changes were made to the tonal scheme: wind pressures were raised throughout the organ, chorus reeds were replaced or re-voiced, and a number of Henry Willis III's specialities appeared (Flute Couverte, Triangular Flute, French Horn, Choir mutations and various strings). Cunningham acknowledged the organ's historical importance when he refused to allow Willis to discard the Tuba, but in most other respects his priority was to modernize the instrument, making it more like a 1930s concert organ, and less like a Victorian town hall organ.

Today, the discussion tends to revolve around compasses, sequencers, memory levels, general pistons, mutations, pedalboards and swell pedals. Recitalists' objectives are not necessarily misconceived in themselves, but they may be mistaken in the context of an existing instrument of pronounced character. But try telling that to the 'big name' recitalist who has a recital in Manchester today, one in Stuttgart tomorrow, and whose assistant is even now programming the console in Mexico City for a recital the day after that.

So much for the organ in its solo role. The fourth obstacle to conservation is its use in conjunction with other musical forces. Reading Town Hall (once again) provides an example of the sort of problems to which this can give rise. Like many organs built towards the end of the last century, the Reading organ had a sharp pitch (approximately $c^2 = 540$ Hz). In 1947 the pitch was lowered to something approximating to the present standard of 523.3 Hz. The work was done crudely. Most of the fluework and closed reeds were transposed one pipe, and new bottom notes of varying quality were provided. The open reeds were lengthened by fitting extension sleeves to the resonators. This is not an easy operation, and some of the sleeves fitted badly.

We therefore had to decide what course of action to take. Conservation demanded a return to the original sharp pitch and a reversal of the alterations made in 1947 to restore the organ's physical and tonal integrity. Contemporary use pleaded for the retention of the 1947 pitch so that it might be readily used with other instruments – an entirely legitimate use for a modern concert organ.

However, it isn't a modern concert organ. It is the only concert organ by 'Father' Willis now left in something very close to its original condition. So despite the furore raised by those who felt that this was an unbelievably obscurantist approach, it has been finally agreed to return to the original sharp pitch. In these special circumstances, it was right that conservation should take priority over one particular contemporary use.

The type of discussion that took place around the issue of pitch at Reading is always going to be difficult because people approach it with a different list of priorities. Each case has to be considered on its merits. The underlying philosophy at Birmingham Town Hall when we came to consider the future of that instrument in 1982–4 was to return the organ's tonal scheme to its 1890 form. But this was not a restoration in the fullest sense of that word and it was therefore reasonable to concede the request for a Bombarde division to fulfil the perceived contemporary need for more volume to support large orchestral and choral forces.

The final problem I want to mention is common to virtually all restoration projects, but there are historical circumstances which make it particularly acute in the case of concert organs. It is the problem of where to draw the line. Every old organ has a history. It may be uneventful, or it may be 'crowded with incident', to use Oscar Wilde's phrase. We have seen that even so apparently unaltered an instrument as the Willis in Reading Town Hall has a history. So what is to be conserved? What is 'history' and what is not 'history'?

The problem is made more intractable in the case of some concert organs because they were pioneering instruments and were frequently worked on (they would have said, 'improved') by their builder and others over many years. St George's Hall, Liverpool, is a prime example.

The 1855 organ was a remarkable achievement, but both common sense and contemporary reports remind us that it was not perfect. So, in 1867 Willis was glad of an opportunity to make small but significant changes, introducing celestes, modern strings and flutes, equalizing the temperament, adding four heavy-pressure reeds and probably doing a good deal more work of which we know nothing. Then, in 1898, he was back, and this time an extensive reconstruction took place, with a new console, new actions and much tonal revision. No doubt he died happy in the knowledge that he had 'perfected' his Liverpool organ, but would we accept that judgement, or would we want, if we could, to return it to 1867 or even 1855?

There is a whole catalogue of fascinating but flawed innovations and gadgets tried out by Victorian and later builders in their exhibition and concert organs. Pneumatic actions of fiendish ingenuity by people like Brindley, all manner of relief pallets, steam engines to blow large concert organs, multiple-fronted swell boxes, various designs of adjustable piston, sforzando pedals, crescendo pedals, Willis's 'cigarette-holder' swell control, and so on. Tonal innovations, too. Perhaps one day some earnest conservationist will wish to reinstate replicas of the Rochesson reeds at the Royal Festival Hall.

Again, every case has to be considered on its merits. Sometimes it will be appropriate to retain and conserve a historical core of material and create a sympathetic musical instrument around it (which is what we tried to do at Birmingham). Sometimes it will be possible to pursue a much more rigorous and exacting restoration, as at Reading. Even better, perhaps one day state funding will be available to enable us to build an exact replica of St George's Hall as it was in 1855, and inside it an exact replica of the Willis organ as it was when Dr Wesley gave the opening recital. I can't wait.

Today, the survival of a representative body of British concert organs hangs in the balance. The Forster & Andrews in West Bromwich Town Hall, the Binns in Nottingham's Albert Hall, the Taylor organ in De Montfort Hall, Leicester, the Harrison in the Caird Hall, Dundee, and soon the Willis in Reading Town Hall have been (or will have been) restored. The Hill organs in Kidderminster and Middlesborough, the Cavaillé-Coll in Manchester Town Hall and the Harrison organ in Newcastle City Hall are among other important survivals awaiting restoration. Elsewhere (St George's Hall, Liverpool and the Royal Albert Hall, London) one must hope for an imaginative approach to instruments retaining large quantities of historical material. For the reasons discussed earlier, the survival of these organs can by no means be assured.

17

Monitoring of conservation work and quinquennial inspections

John Norman

The Newman report to Her Majesty's Government on the workings of the Ecclesiastical Exemption from listed-building controls commented that 'the execution of works without . . . approval . . . is a very serious matter . . . However, it is not clear that there are effective procedures in place for monitoring that permissions have been correctly implemented . . . or even that refusals have been respected.' The report goes on to recommend that all exempt denominations review their monitoring arrangements.

These statements clearly identify two areas of concern – work which is unauthorized, and work that is not properly carried out. I am sure that many Diocesan Organ Advisers have experience of being called in to a church where the organ is in trouble following low-grade work, perhaps by an amateur. On further enquiry one is told 'Oh, we didn't think there was any need to get a faculty for *that*.'

As for the supervision of work, the role of the DAC, as defined by statute, is to advise the chancellor whether a faculty should be granted for the work proposed and to advise and assist parishes to prepare faculty applications. It is *not* the duty of the DAC or its members to monitor the execution of faculties. The work of organ advisers in many continental countries includes inspection of work in progress and approval of completed work. Of course, vigilance about both unauthorized work and proper execution is much easier when the money is coming from public funds. It is noticeable that publicly funded bodies insist on professional supervision to help protect their own reputations against accusations of funding unsatisfactory work.

In the Church of England, monitoring is part of the archdeacon's triennial inspection. However, few archdeacons know much about organs (or bells or archaeology). They really need some form of technically qualified assistance. When this problem was aired recently in the London DAC, it was pointed out that the monitoring of listed-building consents by local authorities was itself distinctly patchy. There was some suggestion that English Heritage might be able to help with problems of archaeology but, where organs are concerned, English Heritage no longer employ any staff with relevant qualifications.

One way of discouraging unapproved work on buildings is by the statutory quinquennial inspections. This also has the important benefit of alerting church

115

councils to impending requirements. Although the inspecting architect's remit includes all furnishings, his report normally glosses over the organ because he has neither the training nor the experience to do anything else. Indeed, it is a rare architect who has a detailed knowledge of acoustics.

Ideally, of course, the DOA would have both the training and the time to inspect every organ in the diocese every five years. Assuming that, with travelling, one could do two a day, this would involve approximately 1,500 working-days a year for the Church of England alone – a full-time professional job for seven people!

The way out seems to be to tackle the problem in a more focused way. The problem of unauthorized work can be addressed by requiring churchwardens to complete a form listing work done and faculties granted. If the form includes a return of the stop-list somewhere, this may also reveal unauthorized changes. At the same time, the architect can be asked to certify the structure surrounding the instrument and other security issues. Finally, a short section enabling the organ tuner to comment on the instrument's condition will help parishes receive early warning of problems. We are asking tuners to give perhaps five minutes of their time (for which the parish is in any case paying) in the knowledge that this sort of report will do their business more good than harm. However, this section cannot be detailed. The tuner will know the organ better than anyone else but will not be a master organ designer and one cannot expect anything beyond the most general outline. It is, of course, also important that the form should be simple enough to allow an archdeacon to scan a completed quinquennial report quickly, and spot trouble on the horizon. In London the archdeacons helped us to resist calls for unnecessary detail.

Both London and St Albans Dioceses have now been operating organ quinquennial schemes for over a year now. Initial take-up has inevitably been low; in London only 20 per cent of quinquennial reports have so far included the organ appendix, although the take-up appears to be improving and hopefully a reminder system will soon be in place. Of the London reports so far received, only 28 per cent reported all parts of the organ as in good condition, 39 per cent sounded a warning that some part of the instrument would need attention within five years and an alarming 33 per cent – one third – reported that some part of the instrument was failing now. In St Albans Diocese it is reported that the process of filling in the report has brought the organ's existence to the consciousness of the parish with beneficial effects. The tuner's comment has been eye-opening in some cases, although a few were unnecessarily damning. The quinquennial can be helpful in reminding constantly changing church officers of the need to insure the organ realistically, of the need to report on it to church committees and, sometimes, of past undertakings to the chancellor to keep an organ properly maintained or to build up a fund to fulfil a time-limited faculty condition. Certainly the early warning feature of a quinquennial should help to reduce the number of organs decaying to the point where no one wants to play them – at which point the instrument is effectively dead.

In both dioceses, the reports should be increasingly useful in the second five-year cycle, when comparison with the report originating in the first cycle should help to reveal unauthorized work. The St Albans form includes a log of organ work through each year of the quinquennium. The London DAC office is highly computerized.[1] Stop-lists given in the returns can be transferred to the diocese's organs database to build up the information needed to compile the list of historic organs required by the Newman report. Then we can ensure that the quinquennials for such instruments receive special attention. I do recommend that organ quinquennials be introduced in other dioceses. Information is power!

18

Conservation plans[1]

John Clare

Those responsible for the care and conservation of historic organs might find it helpful to adopt the concept of *conservation plans* as a fundamental (and ongoing) aid to good management.

Conservation plans are *not* specifications for major repairs, let alone substantial alterations. Indeed, it can be unwise to prepare conservation plans with specific proposals in mind, because those proposals will inevitably influence what should otherwise be a strictly objective task. For any instrument, and particularly one of historic, aesthetic or artistic importance, it is worth preparing a conservation plan even if there is no immediate intention of calling in an organ builder. Nevertheless, conservation plans are not an academic exercise. Although their preparation requires a certain amount of intellectual rigour, they have great practical value. A conservation plan:

- should bring together in a single document not so much everything that is known about an instrument (which for a big historic organ could be tediously cumbersome) but it should certainly set out the key issues relating to its physical conservation;
- might identify (and justify) the need for major repairs;
- should inform those called in to advise on, or undertake, such repairs and, in particular, it should determine the nature of their work;
- should certainly summarize the scope of routine maintenance;
- should above all be 'owned' and regularly consulted by those who are responsible for the instrument. It should therefore be updated as new facts emerge, or to take account of changing circumstances (including major repairs and/or alterations).

Conservation plans should be public documents. For any organ, there should be copies in the local public library, the denominational or other archives, and the British Organ Archive. For important organs (which would merit listing) there should also be a copy in one of the copyright libraries.

Conservation plans are being prepared for many buildings of architectural and historic significance, including churches and other buildings in which there might be organs. However, even if an organ is a fixture, it will be relatively self-contained and, in particular, might be repaired and/or altered without there being any changes to the building. Conservation plans for buildings are structured so that each of their significant elements is considered separately. It would therefore be more appropriate to prepare a separate plan for a historic organ, which could be referred to or incorporated, at least in part, in a conservation plan for the building.

The objectives of a conservation plan for an organ may be summarized as:

- an assessment of the cultural and historic significance of an instrument;
- a description of the policies required to manage and conserve the physical attributes of the instrument which contribute to that significance.

In practice, this means that a conservation plan should cover – in the following order – four quite distinct areas:

A sensibly accurate description

This should be strictly factual. It should so far as possible be based on primary sources: original documents; direct observations and measurements; *in situ* drawings; photographs, and recordings. If there has to be any reliance on secondary sources (i.e. articles and books) the source should be cited. Detailed material can be summarized in the text and quoted in full in one or more annexes. However, if any information is not already available, the organ should only be dismantled if it is already obvious that repairs must be carried out fairly urgently, and the information is required to specify those repairs. Otherwise, a conservation plan should flag up the desirability of obtaining such information in due course, and certainly before or during a conservation programme, and explain how it can be obtained.

Significance

This should explain how, and in what way, different aspects of the organ are important: e.g. the first and subsequent builders; the architecture of the case; the action; the age, extent and condition of surviving original material; its musical qualities, and its associations with notable musicians. It is in effect a listing description. While age should be almost automatically significant, neither youth nor bad taste (as currently perceived) should exclude an instrument from a more considered assessment.

Threats

The nature, likelihood and effect of the risks to which the organ is subject. Such threats are not necessarily physical; they may be financial, and redundancy is the ultimate threat. Risks can to some extent be identified and assessed against a checklist drawn up on the basis of experience, but the process also requires a certain amount of intuition and brainstorming with, for example, the architect responsible for the building.

Policies to reduce or eliminate those threats, and maintain or enhance the organ's significance

These can only be drafted once the threats have been identified and assessed. Active or serious threats should have priority. Moreover, even if the organ is not how it was left by the original builder, it may not be a good idea to attempt to reinstate their work. Most organs contain work of different periods; a subsequent builder's work might also be significant, and restoration (as opposed to conservation) is inevitably conjectural. Any work that is carried out should be carefully documented and, so far as possible, reversible.

Two commonly asked questions:

How long should a conservation plan be?

As long as it takes to cover the four areas set out above. In practice, it will entirely depend on the size, importance and sophistication of the instrument. A conservation plan for a small one-manual tracker instrument in a well-maintained village church might well be written on one side of A4. A cathedral organ with substantial remains of the original case, chests, action and pipework, in a large building which itself has structural and financial problems may require a substantial loose-leaf document, with several annexes.

Who should prepare a conservation plan?

In technical terms, it should be a team effort, involving (possibly through consultation on successive drafts) all those concerned with the use and maintenance of the organ and the building in which it stands. But it should not be so technical that it cannot be read by people who know nothing about organs. In practice, therefore, it may best be edited/coordinated by someone who can write clearly but is not involved with the instrument on a day-to-day basis; who knows which questions to ask about organs (and buildings); and whether the answers are credible. To ensure that it *is* read, it should be professionally presented and illustrated.

In short:

Fix the leaking roof before reinstating the Great mixture!

Appendices

Appendix 1

Relevant organizations

Association of Independent Organ Advisers (AIOA) maintains a list of accredited independent organ advisers possessing the necessary qualifications and the list is open for consultation. Prospective clients are welcome to seek help from the Association in selecting a suitable adviser.

Contact: Mrs José Hopkins, Administrator, Lime Tree Cottage, 39 Church Street, Haslingfield, Cambridge CB3 7JE. Tel and fax: (01223) 872190.

British Institute of Organ Studies (BIOS) is a registered charity and the amenity society for the British organ. It publishes a substantial annual *Journal* and the quarterly *Reporter*; organizes regular day and residential conferences; administers the British Organ Archive, the National Pipe Organ Register and the Historic Organs Certificate Scheme (see below) and undertakes casework in support of its aims.

Aims of BIOS (1976 and amended 1998):

To promote objective, scholarly research into the history of the organ and its music in all its aspects, and, in particular, into the organ and its music in Britain.

To conserve the sources and materials for the history of the organ in Britain, and to make them accessible to scholars.

To work for the preservation, and, where necessary, the faithful restoration of historic organs in Britain.

To encourage an exchange of scholarship with similar bodies and individuals abroad, and to promote, in Britain, a greater appreciation of historical overseas schools of organ building.

Contact: Kerr Jamieson, Membership Secretary, 17 Jordanhill Drive, Glasgow G13 1RZ. Tel: (0141) 959 5232; email: Kerr.Jamieson@strath.ac.uk.; web:www.bios.org.uk.

British Organ Archive (BOA) is contained within the Birmingham City Archive which contains other specialist photographic, manuscript and drawings collections, such as the papers of James Watt and Matthew Boulton. BIOS benefits from the facilities and specialist care of the Archive staff.

The BOA was established as a core activity of BIOS when it was founded in 1976. It contains a wide range of primary and secondary material concerning the (mainly British) organ. These are represented by many order-books, drawings, correspondence and other commercial and personal papers related to those who have commissioned, designed, constructed or used the organ. Much of the most-used material in the collection is quickly accessible by microfilm or microfiche. The index is also connected to the society's National Pipe Organ Register (NPOR), available through the BIOS web site (www.bios.org.uk), a powerful search facility in its own right. A useful, readily available, specialist library complements the collection and the wider library building in which the archive is housed contains, in its various reference sections, an outstanding collection of related and easily accessed material, especially from the nineteenth and twentieth centuries – architectural, ecclesiological, historical, science, social and technology. The City Archive staff will accept enquiries in writing or by phone (limited by the time they have available).

Contact: British Organ Archive, Birmingham City Archives, Central Library, Chamberlain Square, Birmingham B3 3HQ. *Enquiries*: tel.: (0121) 303 4217. Open 0900–1700, except Wednesdays and Sundays.

CCC, *see Council for the Care of Churches, below.*

CIMCIM, *see International Committee of Musical Instrument Museums and Collections, below.*

Conservation Centre, Whitechapel, Liverpool L1 6HZ (a short walk from Lime Street station) is open Monday to Saturday 1000–1700, Sunday 1200–1700. There is an admission charge to the *Caught in Time* display.

Information desk: tel: (0151) 484 4999; 24 hour hotline: tel: (0151) 478 4747; web site: www.connect.org.uk/merseyworld/AandE/museums.

Council for the Care of Churches (CCC). The Church of England has over 16,000 churches and 42 cathedrals in England, as well as others in mainland Europe, and 13,000 of these are listed as being of special architectural or historic interest. Some 40 per cent of Grade I listed buildings (i.e. the most valuable historic buildings in the country) are churches, and most of these are Church of England churches and cathedrals. The Council's principal aim is to help parishes carry out their functions of mission and worship through the faithful stewardship of the Church's built heritage.

The Council works to promote best practice in the care of church buildings at every level through a programme of publications; research into methods of conservation, repair and redevelopment of church buildings through a programme of professional seminars; a ministry to tourists; the use of their library of some 12,000 titles on church architecture, history and liturgy and of the unique collection of survey files relating to individual parish churches; the creative commissioning of contemporary art in churches. They hold a central register to help parishes find the right artist or craftsperson.

The Church of England cares for its buildings under the faculty jurisdiction system, the ecclesiastical equivalent of secular planning processes, and the responsibility for looking after churches lies mainly with the local church communities. They are advised in this by their local archdeacon and bodies known as **Diocesan Advisory Committees for the Care of Churches**

(DACs), who have their own specialist advisers. Before a parish can alter its church building or its contents (including organs), it must apply to the chancellor of the diocese for a faculty, and the chancellor is advised in this task by the DACs, who may refer an application to the CCC for further advice.

Through its eight specialist committees, the Council is able to offer expert advice on conservation matters. There are thirteen full-time staff, and members and staff have, between them, specialist knowledge of architecture, archaeology, art history, conservation, liturgy and ecclesiastical law. They also administer grants from charitable foundations for the care and conservation of church furnishings and works of art of all periods. In 1999 grants were awarded totalling over £200,000 from various sources, and from 2000 it will have over £300,000 available per annum for such work. Churches in England, Scotland and Wales, whether Anglican or not, are now eligible for these grants.

The Council advises and assists parishes, architects, dioceses, the Archbishops' Council, other denominations and Government departments, amenity societies and other secular bodies, which the Council actively lobbies on issues which concern the built heritage.

Contact: The Council for the Care of Churches, Fielden House, 13 Little College Street, London SW1P 3SH. Tel: (020) 7898 1866; fax: (020) 7898 1881; email: enquiries@ccc.c-of-e.org.uk.

Diocesan Advisory Committee for the Care of Churches (DAC), *see Council for the Care of Churches (CCC), above.*

Historic Organs Certificate Scheme (HOCS). Certificates for instruments of established value are awarded by BIOS who set up this scheme as a step towards a proposed introduction of a statutory listing process to protect our organ heritage. It hopes to identify instruments of importance, initially concentrating on less well-known instruments – useful when a certificate can help a diocesan adviser prevent inexpert alteration, alert a parish to a historic organ in its care, support an application for a grant, or make known rare survivals of technological innovation. Nominations are welcomed and details are available from the Administrator: Dr Michael Sayer, 23 St John's Hill, Shrewsbury SY1 1JJ. Tel: (01743) 246826.

ICOM, *see International Council of Museums, below.*

ICOMOS UK, *see International Council on Monuments and Sites UK, below.*

Institute of British Organ Building (IBO) is the recognized body representing organ-building firms and individual professional organ builders in the UK. It was established in December 1995 to represent, inform, serve and assist organ builders and their suppliers, and to encourage by all practical means the improvement of skills and standards within the craft. At the time of writing, over 200 companies or individuals have become IBO members of various categories, including over 70 businesses. Applicants who wish to become Business Members are asked to submit their workshops and examples of their work for examination before acceptance. The IBO publishes annually a *Register of Accredited Business*

Members containing details of members' workshop facilities, numbers of staff and scope of work. This register is also available on-line on the IBO web site: www.ibo.co.uk.

Meetings are held in different centres throughout Britain. In addition, members can attend courses in various organ-building and business skills and acquire formal recognition of their achievements. Newsletters are published four times a year containing a variety of articles, technical information, reviews of new products, news, letters and also advertisements for employment and products of interest to members. *The Organbuilder*, founded in 1983, while independently edited by John Norman and published annually by Positif Press, has become the official journal of the IBO since 1998.

Contact: Didier Grassin, Administrator and Secretary, 63 Colebrook Row, Islington, London N1 8AB. Tel and fax: (020) 7689 4650; email: administrator@ibo.co.uk.

International Committee of Musical Instrument Museums and Collections (CIMCIM), the acronym for *Comité International des Museés et Collections d'Instruments de Musique*, one of 25 international committees of ICOM. CIMCIM aims to promote high professional standards in the use and conservation of musical instruments in museums and collections. It meets every three years during the ICOM General Conferences and, in each of the other two years, organizes a special meeting which usually includes symposium papers and museum visits. Meetings are held in different countries and issues are discussed in detail in CIMCIM's Working Groups, which are set up as needs arise. The deliberations of Working Groups are usually published as CIMCIM publications. Membership is personal and open to individual and institutional members of ICOM, and benefits include invitations to annual meetings, the *CIMCIM Bulletin* (issued several times each year), voting rights at business meetings (held during the annual meetings), and the opportunity to participate in Working Groups. Services offered to members and non-members alike include a series of publications and CIMCIM-L, an email discussion forum devoted to topics of relevance to the use and care of musical instruments in museums.

Contact: Arnold Myers, coordinator, Edinburgh University Collection of Historic Musical Instruments, Reid Concert Hall, Bristo Square, Edinburgh EH8 9AG; email: Arnold_Myers@ed.ac.uk.

International Council of Museums (ICOM) was created in 1946 as a professional organization concerned with the development of museums and the museum profession worldwide and has around 15,000 members in 147 countries. It is a non-governmental organization maintaining formal relations with UNESCO and has a consultative status to the United Nations' Economic and Social Council. Membership is open to individuals and institutions working in the cultural field and its structure is based on national committees. There are committees that represent types of museums (e.g. art, science, literature) or particular disciplines (e.g. conservation, education, documentation).

Contact: ICOM Secretariat, Maison de l'UNESCO, 1, rue Miollis, 75732 Paris Cedex 15, France. Tel: 00 33 1 47 34 05 00; email: secretariat@icom.org. The ICOM UK Honorary Secretary is: Elaine Sansom, Director, Southern Region, South Eastern Museums Service Garden Room, Historic Dockyard, Chatham, Kent ME4 4TE. Tel: (01634) 405031; email: ElaineS@semssouth.freeserve.co.uk; web site: www.icom.org/organization.html (*See also International Committee of Musical Instrument Museums and Collections* (CIMCIM), *above.*)

International Council on Monuments and Sites UK (ICOMOS UK), an international non-governmental body of people professionally concerned with conservation, with separate arms in 94 countries. It sets the standards in conservation philosophy and techniques throughout the world, keeping them up to date through its 14 specialist and scientific committees. Since the Venice Charter of 1964, its formal statements have enshrined universal conservation principles. It is the official adviser to UNESCO on cultural World Heritage Sites.

Contact: 10 Barley Mow Passage, London W4 4PH. Tel: (020) 8994 6477; fax: (020) 8747 8464; email: icomos-uk@icomos.org; web site: www.icomos.org/uk.

National Pipe Organ Register (NPOR) offers information on instruments, accessible in many forms (by builder, location, size, date, etc.). It is designed eventually to contain details of all British pipe organs. It provides a basis for future scholarship and historic listing, and is available on-line through the BIOS web site (or at: lehuray.csi.ac.uk/npor.html).

Correspondence to: NPOR, Computer Laboratory, New Museums Site, Pembroke Street, Cambridge CB2 3QG. *Director*: Dr Michael Sayers, email: MDS11@cam.ac.uk. Manager: Paul Houghton, email: pgh1000@cam.ac.uk. *Editor*: David Atkinson, tel: (01462) 435880.

Organ Historical Society (OHS), USA. The society promotes musical and historical interest in American organ building through collection, preservation, and publication of historical information, and through recordings and public concerts. Members receive the quarterly magazine *The Tracker*, the annual *Organ Handbook*, catalogues of hundreds of organ and choral recordings, meet others who share a love for the organ and its music, and may attend the annual national convention of the society.

Contact: William T. Van Pelt, Executive Director, Organ Historical Society, PO Box 26811, Richmond VA 23261, USA. Tel: 00 1 804 353 9226; fax: 00 1 804 353 9266; email: mail@organsociety.org; web sites: www.organsociety.org (institutional); www.ohscatalog.org (online catalogue of 1,700-plus books, CDs, sheet music, videos about the organ).

Membership also supports the OHS American Organ Archives, the largest organ research college in the world, founded in 1961 and, in 1984, moved to Westminster Choir College, the Music School of Rider University.

Contact: Talbott Library, Westminster Choir College, Rider University, Hamilton at Walnut Avenue, Princeton, New Jersey 08540, USA. Tel: 00 1 609 921 7100; email: Spinel@worldnet.att.net.

Organ Historical Trust of Australia (OHTA) was founded in 1977 and incorporated in 1978 as a national organization under the Victoria Companies Act. Its aims are to preserve historic pipe organs and organ-building records; stimulate public interest in pipe organs of national or local importance; and encourage scholarly research into the history of the organ, its musical use and organ music. The Trust has held an annual conference since 1978, has carried out the technical and historical documentation of almost 350 significant organs in Australia and New Zealand, publishes a quarterly journal, *OHTA News*, and is listing all known pipe organs in Australia in gazetteer form. With about 250 members throughout Australia and overseas, OHTA has a close working relationship with government heritage bodies and the National Trust, and enjoys a high reputation in Australia's conservation and musical communities.

Contact: OHTA, PO Box 200, Camberwell, Victoria 3124, Australia; web site: www.vicnet.net.au/~ohta.

University of Reading, Department of Music. An M. Mus. degree course in Organ Historiography was established in 1993 and has attracted a steady stream of full- and part-time students. A number of them have proceeded to further postgraduate study, or have entered employment in areas relevant to the course, including organ building. Organ Historiography is now a flourishing part of the research programme of the department at staff and senior postgraduate levels, and contacts have been made with universities with similiar interests in Germany, the Netherlands and Sweden. In 1997 the status of the course was changed to MA in order to accomodate a wider range of student backgrounds. The course consists of four units and may be taken over one year full-time, two years part-time, or in a fully modular pattern over a maximum of four years. Students may transfer to an M.Phil. couse on completing Units 1–3 satisfactorily, a Diploma in Organ Historiography is also available. Contact: Dr Christopher Kent, Department of Music, University of Reading, 35 Upper Redlands Road, Reading RG1 5JE. Tel: (0118) 9318411; email: C.J.Kent@reading.ac.uk.

Appendix 2

The Burra Charter

(The Australia ICOMOS Charter for Places of Cultural Significance)

Note: Words in italics are defined in Article 1.

Preamble

Considering the International Charter for the Conservation and Restoration of Monuments and Sites (Venice 1964), and the Resolutions of the 5th General Assembly of the International Council on Monuments and Sites (ICOMOS) (Moscow 1978), the Burra Charter was adopted by Australia ICOMOS (the Australian National Committee of ICOMOS) on 19 August 1979 at Burra, South Australia. Revisions were adopted on 23 February 1981, 23 April 1988 and 26 November 1999.

The Burra Charter provides guidance for the conservation and management of places of cultural significance (cultural heritage places), and is based on the knowledge and experience of Australia ICOMOS members.

Conservation is an integral part of the management of places of cultural significance and is an ongoing responsibility.

Who is the Charter for?

The Charter sets a standard of practice for those who provide advice, make decisions about, or undertake works to places of cultural significance, including owners, managers and custodians.

Using the Charter

The Charter should be read as a whole. Many articles are interdependent. Articles in the Conservation Principles section are often further developed in the Conservation Processes and Conservation Practice sections. Headings have been included for ease of reading but do not form part of the Charter.

The Charter is self-contained, but aspects of its use and application are further explained in the following Australia ICOMOS documents:

- Guidelines to the Burra Charter: Cultural Significance;
- Guidelines to the Burra Charter: Conservation Policy;
- Guidelines to the Burra Charter: Procedures for Undertaking Studies and Reports;
- Code on the Ethics of Coexistence in Conserving Significant Places.

What places does the Charter apply to?

The Charter can be applied to all types of places of cultural significance including natural, indigenous and historic places with cultural values.

The standards of other organisations may also be relevant. These include the Australian Natural Heritage Charter and the Draft Guidelines for the Protection, Management and Use of Aboriginal and Torres Strait Islander Cultural Heritage Places.

Why conserve?

Places of cultural significance enrich people's lives, often providing a deep and inspirational sense of connection to community and landscape, to the past and to lived experiences. They are historical records, that are important as tangible expressions of Australian identity and experience. Places of cultural significance reflect the diversity of our communities, telling us about who we are and the past that has formed us and the Australian landscape. They are irreplaceable and precious.

These places of cultural significance must be conserved for present and future generations.

The Burra Charter advocates a cautious approach to change: do as much as necessary to care for the place and to make it useable, but otherwise change it as little as possible so that its cultural significance is retained.

Articles	Explanatory Notes

Article 1. Definitions

For the purposes of this Charter:

1.1 *Place* means site, area, land, landscape, building or other work, group of buildings or other works, and may include components, contents, spaces and views.

The concept of place should be broadly interpreted. The elements described in Article 1.1 may include memorials, trees, gardens, parks, places of historical events, urban areas, towns, industrial places, archaeological sites and spiritual and religious places.

1.2 *Cultural significance* means aesthetic, historic, scientific, social or spiritual value for past, present or future generations.

Cultural significance is embodied in the *place* itself, its *fabric, setting, use, associations, meanings,* records, *related places* and *related objects.*

Places may have a range of values for different individuals or groups.

The term cultural significance is synonymous with heritage significance and cultural heritage value.

Cultural significance may change as a result of the continuing history of the place.

Understanding of cultural significance may change as a result of new information.

1.3 *Fabric* means all the physical material of the *place* including components, fixtures, contents, and objects.

Fabric includes building interiors and subsurface remains, as well as excavated material.

Fabric may define spaces and these may be important elements of the significance of the place.

1.4 *Conservation* means all the processes of looking after a *place* so as to retain its *cultural significance*.

1.5 *Maintenance* means the continuous protective care of the *fabric* and *setting* of a *place*, and is to be distinguished from repair. Repair involves *restoration* or *reconstruction*.

The distinctions referred to, for example in relation to roof gutters, are:

- maintenance – regular inspection and cleaning of gutters;
- repair involving restoration – returning of dislodged gutters;
- repair involving reconstruction – replacing decayed gutters.

1.6 *Preservation* means maintaining the *fabric* of a *place* in its existing state and retarding deterioration.

It is recognised that all places and their components change over time at varying rates.

1.7 *Restoration* means returning the existing *fabric* of a *place* to a known earlier state by removing accretions or by reassembling existing components without the introduction of new material.

1.8 *Reconstruction* means returning a *place* to a known earlier state and is distinguished from *restoration* by the introduction of new material into the *fabric*.

New material may include recycled material salvaged from other places. This should not be to the detriment of any place of cultural significance.

1.9 *Adaptation* means modifying a *place* to suit the existing *use* or a proposed use.

1.10 *Use* means the functions of a place, as well as the activities and practices that may occur at the place.

1.11 *Compatible use* means a *use* which respects the *cultural significance* of a *place*. Such a use involves no, or minimal, impact on cultural significance.

1.12 *Setting* means the area around a *place*, which may include the visual catchment.

1.13 *Related place* means a *place* that contributes to the *cultural significance* of another place.

1.14 *Related object* means an object that contributes to the *cultural significance* of a *place* but is not at the place.

1.15 *Associations* mean the special connections that exist between people and a *place*.

Associations may include social or spiritual values and cultural responsibilities for a place.

1.16 *Meanings* denote what a *place* signifies, indicates, evokes or expresses.

Meanings generally relate to intangible aspects such as symbolic qualities and memories.

1.17 *Interpretation* means all the ways of presenting the *cultural significance* of a *place*.

Interpretation may be a combination of the treatment of the fabric (e.g. maintenance, restoration, reconstruction); the use of and activities at the place; and the use of introduced explanatory material.

Conservation Principles

Article 2. Conservation and management

2.1 *Places* of *cultural significance* should be conserved.

2.2 The aim of *conservation* is to retain the *cultural significance* of a *place*.

2.3 *Conservation* is an integral part of good management of *places* of *cultural significance*.

2.4 *Places* of *cultural significance* should be safeguarded and not put at risk or left in a vulnerable state.

Article 3. Cautious approach

3.1 *Conservation* is based on a respect for the existing *fabric, use, associations* and *meanings*. It requires a cautious approach of changing as much as necessary but as little as possible.

The traces of additions, alterations and earlier treatments to the fabric of a place are evidence of its history and uses which may be part of its significance. Conservation action should assist and not impede their understanding.

3.2 Changes to a *place* should not distort the physical or other evidence it provides, nor be based on conjecture.

Article 4. Knowledge, skills and techniques

4.1 *Conservation* should make use of all the knowledge, skills and disciplines which can contribute to the study and care of the *place*.

4.2 Traditional techniques and materials are preferred for the *conservation* of significant *fabric*. In some circumstances modern techniques and materials which offer substantial *conservation* benefits may be appropriate.

The use of modern materials and techniques must be supported by firm scientific evidence or by a body of experience.

Article 5. Values

5.1 *Conservation* of a *place* should identify and take into consideration all aspects of cultural and natural significance without unwarranted emphasis on any one value at the expense of others.

Conservation of places with natural significance is explained in the Australian Natural Heritage Charter. This Charter defines natural significance to mean the importance of ecosystems, biological diversity and geodiversity for their existence value, or for present or future generations in terms of their scientific, social, aesthetic and life-support value.

5.2 Relative degrees of *cultural significance* may lead to different *conservation* actions at a place.

A cautious approach is needed, as understanding of cultural significance may change. This article should not be used to justify actions which do not retain cultural significance.

Article 6. Burra Charter Process

6.1 The *cultural significance* of a *place* and other issues affecting its future are best understood by a sequence of collecting and analysing information before making decisions. Understanding cultural significance comes first, then development of policy and finally management of the place in accordance with the policy.

The Burra Charter process, or sequence of investigations, decisions and actions, is illustrated in the flowchart (below).

6.2 The policy for managing a *place* must be based on an understanding of its *cultural significance*.

6.3 Policy development should also include consideration of other factors affecting the future of a *place* such as the owner's needs, resources, external constraints and its physical condition.

Article 7. Use

7.1   Where the *use* of a place is of *cultural significance* it should be retained.

7.2   A *place* should have a *compatible use*.

The policy should identify a use or combination of uses or constraints on uses that retain the cultural significance of the place. New use of a place should involve minimal change, to significant fabric and use; should respect associations and meanings; and where appropriate should provide for continuation of practices which contribute to the cultural significance of the place.

Article 8. Setting

Conservation requires the retention of an appropriate visual *setting* and other relationships that contribute to the *cultural significance* of the *place*.

New construction, demolition, intrusions or other changes which would adversely affect the setting or relationships are not appropriate.

Aspects of the visual setting may include use, siting, bulk, form, scale, character, colour, texture and materials.

Other relationships, such as historical connections, may contribute to interpretation, appreciation, enjoyment or experience of the place.

Article 9. Location

9.1   The physical location of a *place* is part of its *cultural significance*. A building, work or other component of a place should remain in its historical location. Relocation is generally unacceptable unless this is the sole practical means of ensuring its survival.

9.2   Some buildings, works or other components of *places* were designed to be readily removable or already have a history of relocation. Provided such buildings, works or other components do not have significant links with their present location, removal may be appropriate.

9.3   If any building, work or other component is moved, it should be moved to an appropriate location and given an appropriate *use*. Such action should not be to the detriment of any *place* of *cultural significance*.

Article 10. Contents

Contents, fixtures and objects which contribute to the *cultural significance* of a *place* should be retained at that place. Their removal is unacceptable unless it is: the sole means of ensuring their security and *preservation*; on a temporary basis for treatment or exhibition; for cultural reasons; for health and safety; or to protect the place. Such contents, fixtures and objects should be returned where circumstances permit and it is culturally appropriate.

Article 11. Related places and objects

The contribution which *related places* and *related objects* make to the *cultural significance* of the *place* should be retained.

Article 12. Participation

Conservation, *interpretation* and management of a *place* should provide for the participation of people for whom the place has special *associations* and *meanings*, or who have social, spiritual or other cultural responsibilities for the place.

Article 13. Co-existence of cultural values

Co-existence of cultural values should be recognised, respected and encouraged, especially in cases where they conflict.

For some places, conflicting cultural values may affect policy development and management decisions. In this article, the term cultural values refers to those beliefs which are important to a cultural group, including but not limited to political, religious, spiritual and moral beliefs. This is broader than values associated with cultural significance.

Conservation Processes

Article 14. Conservation processes

Conservation may, according to circumstance, include the processes of: retention or reintroduction of a *use*; retention of *associations* and *meanings*; *maintenance, preservation, restoration, reconstruction, adaptation* and *interpretation*; and will commonly include a combination of more than one of these.

There may be circumstances where no action is required to achieve conservation.

Article 15. Change

15.1 Change may be necessary to retain *cultural significance*, but is undesirable where it reduces cultural significance. The amount of change to a *place* should be guided by the *cultural significance* of the place and its appropriate *interpretation*.

When change is being considered, a range of options should be explored to seek the option which minimises the reduction of cultural significance.

15.2 Changes which reduce *cultural significance* should be reversible, and be reversed when circumstances permit.

Reversible changes should be considered temporary. Non-reversible change should only be used as a last resort and should not prevent future conservation action.

15.3 Demolition of significant *fabric* of a *place* is generally not acceptable. However, in some cases minor demolition may be appropriate as part of *conservation*. Removed significant fabric should be reinstated when circumstances permit.

15.4 The contributions of all aspects of *cultural significance* of a *place* should be respected. If a place includes *fabric, uses, associations* or *meanings* of different periods, or different aspects of cultural significance, emphasising or interpreting one period or aspect at the expense of another can only be justified when what is left out, removed or diminished is of slight cultural significance and that which is emphasised or interpreted is of much greater cultural significance.

Article 16. Maintenance

Maintenance is fundamental to *conservation* and should be undertaken where *fabric* is of *cultural significance* and its *maintenance* is necessary to retain that *cultural significance*.

Article 17. Preservation

Preservation is appropriate where the existing *fabric* or its condition constitutes evidence of *cultural significance*, or where insufficient evidence is available to allow other *conservation* processes to be carried out.

Preservation protects fabric without obscuring the evidence of its construction and use. The process should always be applied:

● where the evidence of the fabric is of such significance that it should not be altered;

● where insufficient investigation has been carried out to permit policy decisions to be taken in accord with Articles 26 to 28.

New work (e.g. stabilisation) may be carried out in association with preservation when its purpose is the physical protection of the fabric and when it is consistent with Article 22.

Article 18. Restoration and reconstruction

Restoration and *reconstruction* should reveal culturally significant aspects of the *place*.

Article 19. Restoration

Restoration is appropriate only if there is sufficient evidence of an earlier state of the *fabric*.

Article 20. Reconstruction

20.1 *Reconstruction* is appropriate only where a *place* is incomplete through damage or alteration, and only where there is sufficient evidence to reproduce an earlier state of the *fabric*. In rare cases, reconstruction may also be appropriate as part of a *use* or practice that retains the *cultural significance* of the place.

20.2 *Reconstruction* should be identifiable on close inspection or through additional *interpretation*.

Article 21. Adaptation

21.1 *Adaptation* is acceptable only where the adaptation has minimal impact on the *cultural significance* of the *place*.

21.2 *Adaptation* should involve minimal change to significant fabric, achieved only after considering alternatives.

Adaptation may involve the introduction of new services, or a new use, or changes to safeguard the place.

Article 22. New work

22.1 New work such as additions to the *place* may be acceptable where it does not distort or obscure the *cultural significance* of the place, or detract from its *interpretation* and appreciation.

22.2 New work should be readily identifiable as such.

New work may be sympathetic if its siting, bulk, form, scale, character, colour, texture and material are similar to the existing fabric, but imitation should be avoided.

Article 23. Conserving use

Continuing, modifying or reinstating a significant *use* may be appropriate and preferred forms of *conservation*.

These may require changes to significant *fabric* but they should be minimised. In some cases, continuing a significant use or practice may involve substantial new work.

Article 24. Retaining associations and meanings

24.1 Significant *associations* between people and a *place* should be respected, retained and not obscured. Opportunities for the *interpretation*, commemoration and celebration of these associations should be investigated and implemented.

24.2 Significant *meanings*, including spiritual values, of a *place* should be respected. Opportunities for the continuation or revival of these meanings should be investigated and implemented.

For many places associations will be linked to use.

The results of studies should be up to date, regularly reviewed and revised as necessary.

Article 25. Interpretation

The *cultural significance* of many *places* is not readily apparent, and should be explained by *interpretation*. Interpretation should enhance understanding and enjoyment, and be culturally appropriate.

Statements of significance and policy should be kept up to date by regular review and revision as necessary. The management plan may deal with other matters related to the management of the place.

Conservation Practice

Article 26. Applying the Burra Charter process

26.1   Work on a *place* should be preceded by studies to understand the place which should include analysis of physical, documentary, oral and other evidence, drawing on appropriate knowledge, skills and disciplines.

The results of studies should be up to date, regularly reviewed and revised as necessary.

26.2   Written statements of *cultural significance* and policy for the *place* should be prepared, justified and accompanied by supporting evidence. The statements of significance and policy should be incorporated into a management plan for the place.

Statements of significance and policy should be kept up to date by regular review and revision as necessary. The management plan may deal with other matters related to the management of the place.

26.3   Groups and individuals with *associations* with a *place* as well as those involved in its management should be provided with opportunities to contribute to and participate in understanding the *cultural significance* of the place. Where appropriate they should also have opportunities to participate in its *conservation* and management.

Article 27. Managing change

27.1   The impact of proposed changes on the *cultural significance* of a *place* should be analysed with reference to the statement of significance and the policy for managing the place. It may be necessary to modify proposed changes following analysis to better retain cultural significance.

27.2   Existing *fabric, use, associations* and *meanings* should be adequately recorded before any changes are made to the *place*.

Article 28. Disturbance of fabric

28.1   Disturbance of significant *fabric* for study, or to obtain evidence, should be minimised. Study of a *place* by any

disturbance of the fabric, including archaeological excavation, should only be
undertaken to provide data essential for
decisions on the *conservation* of the place, or
to obtain important evidence about to be
lost or made inaccessible.

28.2   Investigation of a *place* which
requires disturbance of the *fabric*, apart
from that necessary to make decisions, may
be appropriate provided that it is consistent
with the policy for the place. Such investigation should be based on important
research questions which have potential to
substantially add to knowledge, which
cannot be answered in other ways and
which minimises disturbance of significant
fabric.

Article 29. Responsibility for decisions

The organisations and individuals responsible for management decisions should be
named and specific responsibility taken for
each such decision.

Article 30. Direction, supervision and implementation

Competent direction and supervision
should be maintained at all stages, and any
changes should be implemented by people
with appropriate knowledge and skills.

Article 31. Documenting evidence and decisions

A log of new evidence and additional decisions should be kept.

Article 32. Records

32.1   The records associated with the
conservation of a *place* should be placed in a
permanent archive and made publicly available, subject to requirements of security and

privacy, and where this is culturally appropriate.

32.2   Records about the history of a *place* should be protected and made publicly available, subject to requirements of security and privacy, and where this is culturally appropriate.

Article 33. Removed fabric

Significant *fabric* which has been removed from a *place* including contents, fixtures and objects, should be catalogued, and protected in accordance with its *cultural significance*.

Where possible and culturally appropriate, removed significant fabric including contents, fixtures and objects, should be kept at the place.

Article 34. Resources

Adequate resources should be provided for *conservation*.

The best conservation often involves the least work and can be inexpensive.

The Burra Charter Process

Sequence of investigations, decisions and actions

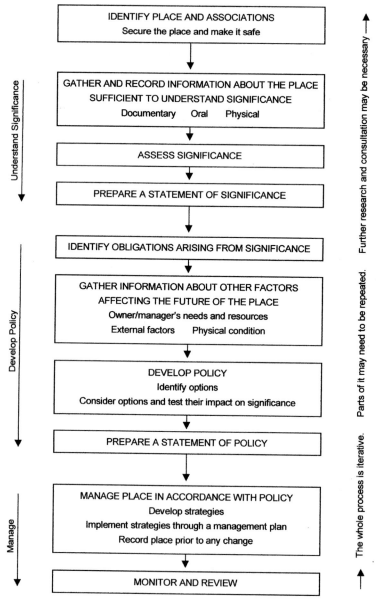

Editor's note:

An illustrated paperback book, giving a comprehensive explanation of the charter and its implications, is available and thoroughly recommended:

Peter Marquis-Kyle and Meredith Walker, *The Illustrated Burra Charter: Making Good Decisions About the Care of Important Places*, Australia ICOMOS, 1992, revised 1994 (ISBN 0 646 12403).

It is available through the ICOMOS London office (see Appendix 1)

142

Appendix 3

The Australian Pipe Organ Preservation Standards of the Organ Historical Trust of Australia (OHTA), revised 1998

Introduction

Pipe organs are a unique and very significant part of the heritage of Australia and the country is well known internationally for its extensive collection of these instruments. The *Pipe Organ Conservation and Maintenance Guide* is designed for owners, users and conservators of pipe organs.

The organ is a very specialised heritage item – primarily a musical instrument but also part-machine, part-decorative furniture and part of the form of a building. The detailed conservation of organs cannot be guided exclusively by the general conservation charter for heritage items in Australia, the ICOMOS *Burra Charter*, which addresses places (see Further Reading). The present guide is linked to the fundamental principles of the general heritage guidelines but adapts these principles to the unique circumstances of the organ. Unlike the earlier version, however, it seeks to achieve greater conformity with universal heritage principles by linking more closely the general heritage guidelines with the specific and long-practised principles of organ conservation.

These pipe organ guidelines address **conservation and maintenance** only. **Assessment of significance** is the first step in the process of managing an organ and must be undertaken in order to guide subsequent conservation and maintenance work. *The Burra Charter*, supported in NSW by *the NSW Heritage Manual* and *Caring for Heritage Objects* (see Further Reading), should be used to help assess significance and a conservation management plan should be produced to guide conservation. (Bear in mind that this assessment should address all aspects of an organ, from its musical quality to its historical, social and aesthetic contexts in the building and community in which it resides.) This process has barely commenced with pipe organs in Australia and much existing assessment is too narrow in scope. However, there is a good body of information in earlier technical documentation undertaken by the Organ Historical Trust of Australia (OHTA) and other published historical studies (see Further Reading).

This guide has been prepared by the NSW Heritage Office to update and supersede both OHTA's *Australian Pipe Organ Preservation Standards* and the New South Wales Heritage Council's *A Guide to the Conservation and Maintenance of Pipe Organs*, both originally published more than a decade ago. *The Australian Pipe Organ Preservation Standards*, from which this guide is directly adapted, were originally drafted by John Stiller in 1978 and were based on the German organ conservation document *Weilheimer Orgelregulativ* (1970). Some amendments have been made to the text of the OHTA document to maintain conformity with the language and principles of the general heritage guidelines.

Individual state requirements

NEW SOUTH WALES

These guidelines should be consulted prior to commencing work on a significant organ or prior to applying for funding under the NSW Heritage Assistance and Heritage 2001 grants programs. Note that some organs in NSW may be protected by conservation orders under the *NSW Heritage Act*, 1977. Contact the NSW Heritage Office for advice. The guidelines refer in a number of places to the need for specialist advice. Lists of pipe organ consultants and builders/conservators can be obtained from the NSW Heritage Office.

OTHER STATES

Heritage Victoria lists significant instruments and can provide conservation funding. The ACT also has controls under its heritage legislation which can be used to protect pipe organs. Contact the relevant state or territory government heritage agency for further information. The relevant state National Trusts can also be approached for assistance if there is concern about an organ.

Pipe organ conservation standards

1. CONSERVATION

Conservation is the process of looking after an organ so as to maintain its heritage significance. In principle, *conservation* embodies all processes directed to this end (that is, including those listed below such as *maintenance* and *restoration*). In a specific sense, it also means preservation or preventative conservation: the steps taken to maintain an organ in its existing state and to prevent its deterioration.

In practical terms, the *conservation* of an organ can be ensured through the maintenance of favourable climatic and room conditions. If the room is heated, attention must be given to room temperature; regular control of the relative air humidity is also recommended, to prevent the wooden parts from drying out. Quick heating, stirring up of dust, and large temperature fluctuations are to be avoided. Wood-damaging insects must be combated by insecticides. In short, the best conservation often means leaving the organ itself alone but ensuring that it has a favourable environment and is maintained so that the need for restoration work does not arise.

2. MAINTENANCE

Maintenance is the continuous protective care of an organ. This signifies the regulation, tuning and *repair* (see below) of **minor** defects in an organ.

2.1 Significant organs require especially careful maintenance.

2.1.1 Instruments which are significant because of their tonal qualities may be tuned twice per year, at the end of each of the cold and warm seasons. When this is done, the original pitch, temperament and voicing (if still in original form) should not be altered. Maintenance also includes playing through every note on every register (i.e. a stop or rank of pipes) at frequent time intervals for organs that are seldom used, in order to prevent the settling of dust and dirt in pipes and other parts vital to wind conduction. Maintenance of old organs also includes ensuring that the necessary degree of air humidity exists.

2.1.2 The organ is a working heritage item and components will thus wear out through use. It is permissible to renew such perishable materials such as leather, felt and key coverings. (See also 3.4 below.)

2.2 All work connected with the maintenance of an organ should be carried out by professionals. This work should remain in the hands of one person or firm and it should be governed by contract.

2.2.1 Only an organbuilder who can be trusted with, and has a demonstrated appreciation of historic values, should be commissioned with the maintenance of such instruments.

2.2.2 The repair of minor faults and defects discovered during tuning should be included in the tuning and maintenance contract.

2.2.3 Also to be included in the tuning and maintenance of an organ is the observation and reporting of the instrument's current condition, especially in regard to the appearance of wind leaks, cracks/splits, oxidation of metal components, wood-damaging insects, decay, water penetration, deterioration or wear.

2.3 The organist should be a person who can be trusted with the organ.

2.3.1 It is recommended that appointed organists should be persons who:

- have understanding and appreciation of the instrument entrusted to them;
- are capable of observing, assessing and reporting the current condition of the instrument.

2.3.2 Only in extraordinary circumstances should the resident organist be allowed to tune, and then only the reeds, after appropriate instruction from the usual tuner, and if they are accessible without disturbance to other pipes.

Admission to the inside of the organ should be restricted only to organ specialists, or to persons under their supervision.

The interior of an organ should never be used for storage of furniture, flower vases and other church materials.

If major damage is discovered, the owners of the organ, the maintenance contractor, and either the Organ Historical Trust of Australia or the National Trust in each state should be advised. In NSW, the NSW

Heritage Office should also be consulted, so that the required repairs can be initiated.

3. REPAIR

This term refers to the *repair* of damage which influences the appearance or function of the instrument and is **undertaken in the course of maintenance**. As defined here, this terminology is only valid if the old parts of the organ are not changed and should not involve *restoration* or *reconstruction* (see below).

Repair aims to preserve an endangered or deteriorated instrument in its present form.

3.1 As a rule, repairs are undertaken on instruments which have remained unaltered, but which nevertheless are damaged or worn. The term *repair* is also used when an instrument is not in completely original condition, and a return to the original condition, due to particular circumstances, cannot be considered, so that only a repair of what exists can be undertaken.

3.2 Thorough cleaning and dust removal throughout the whole organ, rounding-out crushed or dented pipes, regulation and re-bushing of the action, measures taken against wood-damaging insects, oxidation and deterioration are all included in the term *repair*. In combating insects, oxidation and deterioration, only preservatives which have proved themselves practically and have no residue should be used, and it is most important that an expert should be consulted.

3.3 No alterations should be made during the process of repairing. The original voicing must be carefully preserved.

3.4 For the treatment of parts affected by damage or wear, the following measures must be taken into consideration, according to the degree of damage:

    3.4.1 Treatment with proven impregnation preparatives, whereby the instrument must be dismantled. (This may also include the dismantling of the soundboard or wind chest with the opening of the note channels.)

    3.4.2 If the damage is so far advanced that the treatment with preservative preparations cannot guarantee the instrument's further preservation or playability, the affected parts must be exchanged for new parts. Any such parts which affect the sound of the instrument must be remade as exact (but distinguishable) copies of the original parts. This is *reconstruction* (see below for further advice).

    3.4.3 The addition of an electric blower should not occur when the instrument is a special furniture or museum piece (e.g. organs of D. H. Lemke). With such instruments all technical details concerned with wind supply must be remade (if this is necessary) as exact copies of the original. (See under *Restoration and Reconstruction*.)

3.5 For any repair work, section 2.2 above is to be strictly adhered to. Therefore, only an organbuilder who possesses a personal and professional guarantee that the work will be carried out faultlessly in accordance with the assessment of significance may be entrusted with repair work on historic organs. Above all, the organbuilder must have experience in the type of work to be undertaken.

3.6   If not already done, a detailed documentation should be undertaken prior to major repair work, and a work program prepared from this documentation.

4. RESTORATION AND RECONSTRUCTION

Together with preservation (see *Conservation*), these are the main processes associated with work which is needed to return an organ to a former higher standard.

Restoration is the returning of an altered instrument to an earlier documented condition by removing additions or by reassembling existing components without the introduction of new material (excepting, in the case of an organ, the components which perish with the working of the instrument such as felt, leather, wire and ivory or their acceptable substitutes).

Reconstruction is the returning of an altered instrument to as near as possible to an earlier documented condition and is distinguished from *restoration* by the introduction of lost or missing materials (new or old) into the organ. New material should be clearly distinguishable from the original, by labeling or documentation if necessary. [See also 5.1 *Conjectural construction*.]

4.1   In contrast to preventative conservation or preservation, *restoration* and *reconstruction* strive not only to preserve the existing historic parts of the organ, but at the same time, to undo alterations which the instruments may have previously undergone. Note, however, that it is not necessary that a *restoration* or *reconstruction* must return an organ to its original form. That is, not all alterations need to be undone, but more importantly, it is preferable to return the organ to an artistically-worthy form and condition that is advantageous to the organ. It is usually inadvisable to take the organ back in time past a condition or form which itself has historic value. (For example, an organ built in the 1860s which was enlarged in the 1880s and was further altered, rebuilt or electrified in the 1950s might be restored only to its 1880s rather than 1860s form – the prior assessment of significance will guide the decisions on this.)

4.2   Occasionally, an historic organ only altered in the twentieth century need not be restored, but only *maintained* (with minor *repairs*), especially when the instrument sounds satisfactory, and if unfavourable conditions exist for a good *restoration* or *reconstruction* to take place (e.g. when the original specification is unknown).

4.3   Before *restoration* or *reconstruction*, a thorough detailed documentation of the organ should be undertaken before the instrument is dismantled. On the basis of this documentation, a work program will be scheduled, which can be adapted to any new factors which may become apparent when the organ is dismantled. The course of the work must be thoroughly recorded in a written report. There may be a need for review of the conservation management plan if significant new information is revealed during dismantling.

4.4 During *restoration* or *reconstruction*, influences and elements foreign to the style of the organ are to be removed.

    4.4.1 When considering in the conservation management plan which alterations are to be removed, the following points should be taken into consideration:

Alterations which change the tonal structure of the organ:

I.   Alterations to the specification, especially of a significant reduction of the principal chorus, or the replacement of mutations or reeds by 8-foot stops (e.g. removal or alteration of upperwork and mixtures, or the replacement of a Twelfth $2^2/_3$ by a Dulciana 8, or vice versa).

II.   Alterations to the soundboards or wind chests. Due to the significant influence of the type of soundboard or wind chest on the tonal qualities of the organ, old organs must always have sliderchests or their original form of chest.

III.   Alterations to the action. Old organs should have (or have restored to them) their original type of action – usually mechanical or pneumatic. The existence of several different types of actions within a single organ is to be especially avoided unless originally present.

IV.   Alterations to the voicing and intonation:

- Wherever possible, with the flue pipes, non-original foot restrictions are to be removed. The same applies to non-original nicking and tuning and voicing aids. Flue and lip positions must be returned to their original settings, and the height of cut-up must be restored to the original.

- With reeds, non-original leathering and voicing aids are to be removed.

- Completely ruined pipes are to be replaced by new pipes having the same measurements and forms in all parts (including ornamentation, diapering etc., if present) and of identical metal composition or wood. The original pipes should be retained and stored.

V.   Alterations to the wind pressure. Wind pressures must be returned to the original values. Any alterations to the voicing which may have occurred when wind pressure was raised must be restored to the original. [See (IV) above.] The same applies to wind pressures which may have been reduced.

VI.   Alterations to the pitch. Pitch alterations also cause tonal alterations, and the temptation to retune an old organ to present-day standard or a non-original pitch is not acceptable. If the original pitch has been altered over the years, it should be restored to its original, if at all possible, and non-original tuning aids removed. If an old organ is not ideal for accompaniment purposes on account of its unusual pitch, the purchase of an additional accompanying organ, quite independent from the old organ, is recommended.

VII. Alterations due to the addition of another manual which is not suited tonally or structurally to the original concept of the particular organ.

Alterations which interfere with the original style of the case are to be removed. Such alterations include:

- Painting-over of decorated display pipes – the original decoration should be restored, if possible.
- Disfiguring enlargements and additions such as light fittings, heaters, switches, electrical conduits, etc.

Stylistic alterations which fit in tonally and architecturally with the original may remain.

4.5 In a restoration of museum quality, repairs that remove patina, and other evidence of aging, should be avoided. In organs that remain in constant use it may, for example, be desirable to protect timber surfaces by repolishing, where the original polish has disintegrated. Great care must be taken to avoid finishes not envisaged by the original builder.

5. Conjectural construction, enlargement and rebuilding

5.1 *Conjectural construction* is outside the scope of usual heritage practice, but may be necessary to bring an organ to complete working condition. It involves the new manufacture of lost or missing parts whose original condition is wholly or partly unknown. That is, no documented construction methods are available. Conjectural construction work on a significant organ should be fully documented and identified and be suited in quality and function to existing work.

5.2 A significant organ should not be altered through *enlargement* or *rebuilding* as its significance may be compromised. *Enlargement* means the fitting or addition of parts which were not present in the original, but without any changes to existing parts. *Rebuilding* means the free alteration of the existing form of the organ with no intention of serving any of the purposes of conservation. (Note that the removal of a non-original register and its replacement by another register which was present in the original is not part of a rebuild but is *reconstruction*. The replacement of single pipes which have become unusable is *repair*.)

6. Additional points

6.1 In respect of all types of conservation work (including repair, restoration and reconstruction) correct procedure must be observed by both organ adviser (consultant) and organbuilder. It is especially important to indicate which parts of the organ are to be renewed. Also during this work, all the required measurements and documentation can be undertaken and completed.

6.2 The following should **not** occur:

- Replacing old stop labels with new ones which have a different style of lettering. Old stop labels which have lettering which has become illegible should be restored to their original appearance or replaced by new ones which are in the same style as the originals.

- Replacing old stop knobs with new ones of a different style. It is possible to make exact copies of old stop knobs which may have become unusable due to wear and deterioration, and this is the course which should be followed.

- The replacement of original single, double or triple-rise bellows with an electric fan supplying a constant pressure or with spring regulators. Bellows (and other components such as wind trunks) which affect the wind characteristics of a particular organ should be restored rather than replaced. Pre-electric blowing apparatus should also be retained, together with other associated objects such as telltales, etc. Even if it is not possible to restore or repair these objects, they should still be retained as part of the historic interest of the organ.

- Replacing mechanical key and stop action. Even the use of modern mechanical action (using modern materials) is questionable when applied to instruments of historic value.

- The installation of slider seals, telescopic joints, etc. in soundboards or wind chests. It has been found that these alterations affect the tone of the instrument. Also the introduction of such devices is out of character with the style and practice of the original builder, and in some instances they have been shown to have had a short life.

- The replacement of a hitch down or lever swell shutter control with a balanced swell pedal, and the replacement of an old pedal board with one conforming to modern standards should not occur. While these adaptations may make the instrument easier to play for some present day performers, they constitute a departure from the original instrument and the style in which that instrument was played.

6.3 Other principles should be noted, as follows:

- The treatment of pipework needs very special attention in the context of preservation. Alteration of those parts of a pipe that affect speech should be avoided, except where damage has occurred. Regulation should be minimised.

- Original cone tuning should be preserved or *restored* wherever possible. The fitting of tuning slides to metal pipes should only take place, if at all, where the smallest pipes of a rank have been extremely badly damaged by cone tuning and pipes should not be trimmed down. Even then, tuning slides should only be added to these smallest pipes and their addition should be most carefully considered since this method of tuning is not in keeping with the organbuilding practices of the original builder. In cases where an accredited conservator considers metal pipework to be of such delicate or inferior construction that damage is likely to result from ongoing cone tuning, consideration may be given to the fitting of tuning slides on small pipes. The cutting of slots in any pipes should not be necessary. Naturally, all of these practices lead to tuning instability. The practice of cone tuning must be undertaken with the utmost care.

- The practice of newly varnishing or painting pipes during the course of any preservation work is open to question. Many vital inscriptions have been removed in the past by these practices; all inscriptions on wood and metal pipes should be preserved.

- The revoicing of undamaged pipework has no place whatever in any organ conservation work unless the existing voicing is non-original. [Refer to 4.4.1 IV.]

- Pipework must be handled with the utmost care during dust removal and cleaning and when it is transferred from one place to another. The delicate and sensitive mouth parts of metal pipes are easily damaged and the regulation of a particular rank of pipes can be easily upset by any but the most careful handling.

- Organ pipes should not be cleaned by washing, except in unusual circumstances, and the use of extremely hot water, with or without detergent or cleaning solutions, should be avoided.

6.4   In the conservation of significant organs the use of traditional materials is preferred. However, organs are working heritage items and in some instances the introduction of modern materials may be unavoidable and may be done under professional guidance. For example, various synthetic resins may be substituted for ivory and selected grades of alternative timber can be used where the original type of timber in a suitable size is unavailable.

7. Expert advice

7.1   An *organ consultant* should be engaged in any conservation project (other than *maintenance*) for any organ of heritage significance. The consultant can also investigate the significance of the organ beforehand, if necessary, and prepare a conservation management plan and can, of course, advise on a maintenance program. The NSW Heritage Office can provide a list of consultants in that state. The Organ Historical Trust of Australia can also be contacted for advice regarding consultants.

7.2   Many organbuilders are also conservators. The Australian Guild of Master Organbuilders (and, in New South Wales, the NSW Heritage Office) can provide the names of builders who are familiar with implementation of these standards.

Further reading

Australia ICOMOS, *The Illustrated Burra Charter*, Australia ICOMOS, Sydney, 1992. [See Appendix 2]

NSW Heritage Office, *NSW Heritage Manual*, NSW Heritage Office, Sydney, 1996.

[The *Heritage Manual* is the official NSW procedural guidelines for heritage and includes general guidelines for assessment and management of all types of heritage items.]

Organ Historical Trust of Australia, *Australian Pipe Organ Preservation Standards*, OHTA, Camberwell, 1992.

[See notes in Introduction above.]

Rushworth, G., *Historic Organs of New South Wales*, Hale and Iremonger, Sydney, 1988.

[Commissioned by the Heritage Council, this is the major reference on organ history in NSW.]

Townley, P. and Parris, R., *Caring for Heritage Objects*, Powerhouse Museum, Sydney, 1994.

[Commissioned jointly by the Heritage Council and the Powerhouse Museum, this is a first attempt at a universal heritage standard for movable heritage and includes a movable heritage charter and general management guidelines.]

There are some overseas guides to organ conservation which may be useful for comparative purposes. Apart from the German *Weilheimer Orgelregulativ* (1970) mentioned in the Introduction, there is an Italian guide by Oscar Mischiati and Luigi Ferdinando Tagliavini: *Estratto da: L'organo Rivista di Cultura organaria e organistica direzione e redazione* (Bologna, 1996).

Disclaimer

Any representation, statement, opinion or advice expressed or implied in this publication is made in good faith but on the basis that the State of New South Wales, its agents and employees are not liable (whether by reason of negligence, lack of care or otherwise) to any person for any damage or loss whatsoever which has occurred or may occur in relation to that person taking or not taking (as the case may be) action in respect of any representation, statement or advice referred to above.

Appendix 4

The Organ Historical Society: *Guidelines for Conservation and Restoration* (1986)

1. To Be Regarded as Historic:

    A. Any organ or organ case in the United States which was built prior to 1850 may be said to be of major historic importance. Its significance increases with its age, its rarity, and the extent to which its components remain in unaltered condition.

    B. Any substantially unaltered organ built prior to 1900 which is an outstanding example of a particular style or of a particular builder's work, or is unique in some other way (e.g., the only remaining example of a particular builder's work).

    C. The above criteria may also be applied to certain 20th-century organs, especially if they represent important periods in a given builder's work, or milestones in the development of a particular style.

    D. Instruments which have been so radically altered tonally and/or mechanically that they no longer represent the style of a period or the original builder may be regarded as having minimal historic importance, even though such instruments may still contain older material.

2. Historic organs in the United States should be considered the equal of those in Europe, and as worthy of preservation and restoration.

3. Restoration may be defined as the process of returning an organ to its original state, provided always that sufficient original material remains to make this feasible. In some cases a totally unaltered organ may be in such basically good condition that simple repair and cleaning will accomplish this. If a substantial number of original components are missing and must be made anew the process is more properly termed reconstruction. Some guidelines for restoration include the following:

    A. In general, all extant original components should be preserved and properly repaired. Severely damaged components may be replaced by new if incapable of being put into reliable working order and missing parts replaced by reproductions. All replacement parts should conform as closely as possible to the originals with regard to materials and method of construction.

    B. Pipework should be carefully repaired by a professional pipemaker, replacements for missing pipes being made of the same material and construction details as the originals. The original means of tuning should be preserved wherever possible. An effort should be made to ascertain the original temperament and restore it. Voicing should be limited to the re-regulation of repaired pipes and the voicing of any replacement pipes in the style of the remaining originals.

C.   Keyboards, stop controls, and other console components should be kept in, or restored to, their original condition. A possible exception may occur in cases where the extension of a short pedal-board compass is necessary to the continued acceptance and use of an organ. Key and stop action should always be restored in such a way that any new materials conform to the original materials.

D.   Slider and pallet windchests should be very carefully restored and checked for soundness. When replacement of pallet covering is necessary, it should be with material corresponding to the original.

E.   Pitman, ventil, and other forms of tubular-pneumatic or electro-pneumatic windchests should be restored using original techniques of design and construction and compatible materials and replacement parts. Replacement of such actions with all-electric units, even though the chest structure is retained, must be regarded as a major alteration. Similarly, replacement of original stop, combination, or player actions with ones of a different type constitutes an alteration, even though this may in some instances be necessary for financial reasons.

F.   Original bellows, reservoirs, wind trunks, concussion bellows, and other components which determine the wind characteristics of an organ should always be retained and releathered; if missing they should be replaced by new components conforming to the originals. Chest-mounted 'schwimmers' should not be added to organs not originally having them, nor springs added to a bellows which was originally weighted. Tremulants should be restored and adjusted; if replacement is necessary, it should conform to the style of the original. Feeder mechanisms, where extant, should be restored and made operable when feasible. The retention or addition of a modern electric blower does not detract from the historical value of an organ if installed with as little alteration to the original winding components as possible, but it is recognized that there is a discernible difference between fan-blown and hand-raised winding systems in organs which have both.

G.   If the original finish of an organ case has been altered, an effort should be made to determine the nature of the original finish and to restore it whenever feasible. The same is true of front pipes, particularly those which were originally decorated in polychromed designs but have since been painted over. In repairing damage to case woodwork, particularly in unpainted cases, care should be taken to match new wood to old.

H. In instances where financial or other considerations dictate that some original part of the organs be removed or left unrestored (e.g., a badly damaged set of pipes, or feeders and blowing handle) these should be packed up and stored in a safe part of the building, properly labelled as to their significance. The same applies when on the insistence of the owner some original part (such as a short pedalboard) is replaced.

I. It is highly desirable that a restorer keep detailed records, measurements, photographs, etc. during the course of the restoration work. Copies of such records sent to the Archives of the OHS are always greatly appreciated and may provide valuable information to future researchers and restorers.

J. Restoration of historic organs should always be done by an experienced professional restorer specializing in work on the particular type of organ involved and never entrusted to unsupervised amateurs. For the sake of the owner's own financial investment as well as the preservation of the organ, it is incumbent upon the owners of historic instruments to thoroughly investigate the reputation, previous work, and references of any prospective restorer. Quality of work, rather than price, should be the criterion in the choice of a restorer. A fine and historic organ may be irreparably altered or damaged by incompetent or unqualified workers but a well-restored historic organ can be a musical treasure and a legacy to future generations.

For further reference

A. Berner, J. H. van der Meer, & G. Thibault, *Preservation and Restoration of Musical Instruments*, International Council of Museums, 1967.

Mary Karp, 'Restoration, Conservation, Repair, and Maintenance: Some Consideration on the Care of Musical Instruments', *Early Music*, **7** (1979); 'Richtlinien zum Schutz Denkmalwertiger Orgeln: Neufassung des Weilheimer Regulativs', *Ars Organi*, Heft 36, July 1970.

OHS editor's note:

The Society's *Guidelines for Conservation and Restoration* were compiled in 1973 by the Historic Organs Committee and have been refined and published several times. This version was completed in 1986 after much study and appeared in *The Tracker*, **30** 2, following their adoption by the National Council. These guidelines may be reprinted and distributed without further permission from the Organ Historical Society or Church House Publishing.

Appendix 5

The British Institute of Organ Studies:
Guidelines for Conservation and Restoration
(January 1991)

1. Introduction

BIOS includes amongst its activities efforts to preserve important or interesting organs in Great Britain. This document suggests which instruments may be worthy of such attention, and indicates ways in which their qualities may be preserved for the enjoyment of generations to come.

Sadly, the number of surviving unaltered historic organs in Britain has been greatly diminished in recent years by neglect, by the closure of many little-used churches, and by ill-advised rebuilding or other changes. BIOS stresses that any such instruments remaining are of incalculable significance to our national heritage, and that in most other western countries they would be protected by law.

BIOS believes that the musical success of a good organ is due to a happy combination of the builder's skill and a particular date of construction. Subsequent alterations to keep pace with changes in fashion, whether to pipes or mechanism, will weaken the builder's original artistic concept and make the organ a less good musical instrument than before. Where no alterations have been made, they should be avoided; where alterations have been made, they should be reversed if this is reasonable.

This document reflects generally accepted views on musical instrument restoration at the time of writing (1991). It does not attempt to deal with all the questions that may arise, nor can it be used as a set of hard and fast rules for all circumstances. However, it reflects the kind of attitudes that will help anyone contemplating the maintenance or repair of an historic instrument. Standards are continually improving, and expert and impartial advice should be sought if necessary.

BIOS is happy to offer advice if asked. BIOS cannot normally help with fund-raising.

2. Organs to be regarded as worthy of conservation or restoration

The significance of an old organ increases with its age, rarity, and the extent to which it remains in its original state. Broadly speaking, any unaltered organ by a well respected builder should be maintained in or restored to its original state, or a state as near the original as possible, without any concession to modern taste being felt necessary. If restoration to the original state is impossible, the instrument may be restored to a chosen former state, usually decided as being that state when the organ last represented, in a coherent and recognisable way, the work of one builder or school of builders.

Organs of any size from the seventeenth, eighteenth or first half of the nineteenth centuries in any state of preservation are now so rare and of such historic importance that their preservation, and, if necessary, faithful restoration, should be assumed as a matter of course. Organs of the period 1850–1920 survive in somewhat greater numbers, but again their preservation and restoration should normally be the rule. Organs from 1920 onwards may not be historic as such, but nevertheless major unaltered examples of the work of good builders should be preserved in their original state.

Organs that have been so radically altered tonally and/or musically that they no longer represent the style of the original builder may be of lesser interest, though some such instruments may still contain important historical material worthy of preservation. Any pipework or mechanism more than a hundred years old should be considered for preservation according to its merits.

Organs, like other musical instruments, are works of art. The most significant examples rank alongside famous violins and paintings by great masters, though as they are fixtures and not often marketable, their monetary value may not reflect this. Even the most humble examples represent great care and skill on the part of their makers, and the temptation to alter them to conform to tastes in playing that the maker did not envisage should be avoided. Nor should it be imagined that the non-sounding parts of the organ are just mechanism, and can be changed at will; each part has a vital role in affecting the way the instrument can be played, and therefore the way it will sound.

3. Conservation

Conservation may be defined as work carried out to prevent decay. Even if an organ does not require restoration it may require careful attention to keep it in good order.

An historic instrument should be maintained by a skilled professional. When choosing an organ builder to tune and maintain the instrument, it is advisable that the choice should be made bearing in mind his experience and reputation in work with historic organs. The recommendations of an organ builder should be taken seriously. However, there is the possibility that they may be motivated by the prospect of financial reward, and impartial expert advice should be sought where necessary.

Responsibility for maintenance does not lie only with the organ tuner. Like furniture and other musical instruments, organs suffer badly from extremes of temperature and humidity. Sudden changes of climate, whether extreme heat, extreme dryness or extreme damp, can all cause serious damage to an organ. New heating systems are often to blame: most historic organs were built at a time when heating was inefficient or non-existent and are not made with such systems in mind. A temperature of 10°C–16°C and a relative humidity of 55% are ideal. The organ and its surroundings should be kept free of dirt and rubbish and should be guarded against interference or vandalism. Moderate use of an organ will not usually do any damage and is better than complete disuse.

4. Restoration

Restoration may be defined as the process of returning an organ to its original state, or to as near its original state as is possible, or to some other chosen earlier state. The word is often mis-used to cover various forms of rebuilding or alteration. In some cases a little-altered instrument may be restored to its original state by a simple programme of cleaning, repair and adjustment. Other instances may require the reproduction of missing or damaged parts. In severe cases the whole organ may be rebuilt in the style of the original builder round some surviving material, in which case the work is likely to be of a more speculative nature, and should perhaps be termed reconstruction.

All original components should be preserved and properly repaired. Components that have been severely damaged or altered beyond repair, and are incapable of being put into reliable working order, may be replaced by reproductions. All repairs and replacement parts should be made in a manner consistent with the original work, both in materials used and method of construction. Any repairs or changes necessary during the course of restoration should be reversible, in case it be found at a later date that the work needs to be done again, either through further wear or deterioration, or because the original restoration was defective or that techniques have advanced since restoration took place.

Certain organs that have been greatly altered may be incapable of restoration. If returning the instrument to a former state would involve considerable speculative reconstruction and/or considerable further alteration to original material, then restoration should not be carried out. In the case of derelict organs, this may mean that they remain silent.

5. Appropriate technical procedures in restoration

The following paragraphs deal specifically with some of the technical problems to be found in restoration. While no document of this kind can hope to provide the right solutions to every problem, the examples given generally illustrate the kinds of methods that will lead to a successful restoration.

5.1   Pipework

Pipework should be carefully repaired, always by an expert pipemaker. Replacements for missing pipes should be made of similar materials and to similar details of construction as the original. The original means of tuning should be preserved where this survives. If it does not survive, it may be restored provided that this requires no further alteration to the pipes. Tuning slides should not be fitted if this involves the cutting of any pipe, nor, if they are fitted, should they be removed when this would require the lengthening of many pipes. Efforts should be made to discover the original pitch and temperament of the organ and to restore this when possible. Voicing should be limited to the re-regulation of repaired pipes and the voicing of any replacement pipes in the style of the originals.

5.2 Console and fittings

Keyboards, pedalboards, stop knobs and other controls and accessories should be maintained in, or restored to, their original state. Original key coverings, felts and bushings should be retained wherever possible and if they must be replaced, every effort should be made to use similar materials and techniques of construction.

5.3 Mechanical key action

Mechanical key action should be retained when it is present; its simplicity and reliability is often a factor in the survival of an historic organ, and the sensitivity of a good mechanical key action cannot be equalled. Some may seem heavy to those used to organs with other mechanisms. A good player will quickly become used to the touch of an organ, and careful maintenance or restoration may make the touch lighter. The heaviness of the action of a Victorian organ when the manuals are coupled is a good indication that the couplers are designed for occasional use only. During the course of restoration, no efforts need be made to change the design of the action or its components in order to change the quality of touch, though the key action and couplers should be repaired and adjusted to give the best operation possible consistent with the design. Where an organ originally had mechanical action and it has since been removed, the original action should ideally be restored, in the style of the original maker.

5.4 Pneumatic key action (including pneumatic lever actions)

Pneumatic key actions are variable in quality, but almost all examples made by reputable builders are capable of good response and, if they are well maintained and operate in good atmospheric conditions, should be reliable; however, it should be noted that some variation in response and reliability may be apparent at different seasons of the year. (Tubular pneumatic actions are particularly susceptible to unreliability caused by heating in the building.) An existing pneumatic action should be retained and restored if necessary. The skills and materials for such restoration are available; though they may sometimes be expensive, restoration will usually be cheaper than a new action of similar quality.

5.5 Electro-pneumatic and electric-actions

At the time of writing, relatively few organs with electro-pneumatic or electric-action are regarded as historic. However, some examples from before about 1940 may be of considerable interest as examples of early electrical engineering, and specialist advice should be sought before discarding switchgear etc. from this period.

5.06   Stop and combination action

Stop and combination action should be maintained in or restored to its original condition. The type of stop and combination action has a profound effect on the way an organ sounds. A simple stop action, or the absence of any combination action, will prevent anachronistic quick changes from one registration to another, and the retention or restoration of an original stop action will help ensure that the instrument sounds as the maker envisaged. Thus neither mechanical nor pneumatic stop actions should be electrified, though where this has already taken place the process may be reversed.

5.07   Slider soundboards

Slider soundboards should be restored and checked for soundness. Appropriate materials should be used in their repair, especially as concerns pallet coverings and springs, pull-downs, pull-down seals, slide lubrication and so on. Where upperboards are held down with old or unusual screws or even nails, these should be kept and matched to their holes. Where flooding is needed, the glue should be carefully matched to the original material; synthetic glue should not be used where natural glue was used originally. Slides running in leather should be restored. The repair of split or lifted tables and warped slides and upperboards should be carried out with care, using the minimum of additional material or screws, and the minimum of planing or grooving away of timber. A certain amount of minor running may be allowed where the alternative would involve the loss of considerable thickness in tables, slides or upperboards. Slide seals should not be fitted where they are not already present.

5.08   Sliderless chests

Sliderless chests, where they survive as part of an organ being restored, should be restored to their original state using the same care over materials and techniques as would apply to a slider soundboard.

5.09   Winding systems

Original feeders, bellows, reservoirs, regulators, wind trunks, concussions and other components that determine the wind characteristics of the organ should be retained and restored where necessary. Bellows winding systems should not be replaced by other types of regulators. Double-rise reservoirs should not be releathered in single rise form. Hand-blowing mechanisms, where these survive, should not be removed, even if they are not restored to working order; however in normal circumstances their restoration should be considered as part of the whole project. The retention or addition of a rotary fan blower does not detract from the value of an historic organ if it causes no alteration to the winding system or to the case or structure of the organ, but it must be understood that there is a difference in sound between hand blowing and electric blowing in organs which have both.

5.10   Casework

If the original finish of an organ case has been altered, an effort should be made to discover the original finish and restore this where possible. This may involve the employment of now rare skills, such as french polishing, graining or gilding. However, in all cases the careful application of an original finish is always preferable to the modern alternatives – cheap varnish, gold paint etc. – and if the proper finish is too expensive, then no restoration is preferable to a cheap face-lift.

5.11   Storage of unwanted parts

All original parts not used in the restoration should be carefully labelled, packed, and stored in safety in the organ or as near to it as possible.

5.12   Financial restrictions, partial restoration

When financial limitations prevent all of a restoration project being carried out immediately, it is almost always advisable to wait until sufficient funds have accumulated to carry out the work in one go. If an organ is restored in stages, it will decay in stages, and work will be necessary indefinitely. An unrestored organ, though disappointing will usually be preferable to a half finished restoration. The absence of any restoration may not be a bad thing: many historic instruments have been preserved through disuse, though this should not be confused with decay.

5.13   Records

When work is carried out on a historic organ, the restorer should make a report before he starts, covering the history of the organ and its present condition, as well as detailing the work proposed. He should also keep a record of the work as it is carried out, as well as taking photographs before and after, and taking measurements of those parts of the organ not normally accessible for inspection. A copy of this record should be given to the church or customer. The restorer should allow for the cost of this work in his estimate. Copies of such records sent to BIOS's British Organ Archive are always appreciated, and may provide valuable information for future restorers and researchers.

5.14   Restorers

The restoration of historic organs should always be carried out by a professional specialising in work on the type of organ involved, and should never be entrusted to amateurs. For the sake of the owner's own investment as well as the preservation of the organ, it is incumbent on the owners of organs and their advisers to investigate the reputation, previous work and references of any prospective restorer. A fine or historic organ may be irreparably damaged by incompetent or unqualified workers, but a well-restored historic organ can be a musical treasure and a legacy to future generations.

Appendix 6

The British Institute of Organ Studies:
Sound Advice: The Care of Your Pipe Organ

A pipe organ is a valuable resource . . .

Pipe organs have been used in Christian worship for more than a thousand years. The pipe organ is still unsurpassed as an instrument for leading congregational singing and accompanying church choirs.

A pipe organ is both a musical instrument and a refined piece of machinery. Often it will have an architectural case which may be an integral part of the church's furnishings.

Well-made pipe organs will give excellent service for many years provided they are properly cared for. It is not uncommon to find pipe organs functioning efficiently after a century or more, with only occasional cleaning and minor repairs.

Consequently many churches now contain organs which have already given years of reliable service. Many of these (and some more recent instruments, too) should be carefully preserved, both for their own sake as part of our heritage, and also because they have many more decades of useful service ahead of them.

What is an historic organ?

This is a difficult question to answer concisely but an arbitrary answer might be that an historic organ is one that:

> is a good and intact example of its style or period;

> incorporates material (e.g. pipework) from an earlier instrument of good quality; or,

> retains an interesting or architecturally distinguished case.

What to do?

Like any other piece of machinery a pipe organ requires maintenance from time to time. With a simple mechanical action organ this should involve no more than cleaning, regulation and small repairs. Less frequently (every seventy or eighty years) a more thorough overhaul is needed, when parts may have to be taken back to the organ-builder's workshop for renovation.

It is tempting to use these occasions as opportunities to make alterations to the organ. The temptation should be resisted. Like a piece of antique furniture, a pipe organ is easily spoiled by needless changes. Once its integrity is lost it can never be regained.

Restoration, not alteration, is nearly always the right policy when dealing with a pipe organ which survives intact and is well made. In order to achieve this, BIOS offers the following general guidelines.

Do

- Seek independent advice; e.g. from your Church's advisory body, the Council for the Care of Churches or BIOS.
- Make sure you employ an organbuilder with the necessary skills. There are good firms, both national and local, but (inevitably) there are also some unreliable ones. Seek more than one estimate, and make informal enquiries of others for whom your preferred builder has done similar work recently.
- See what you can find out about the history of your organ. Parish archives and the local history library may be able to help; also the British Organ Archive and the National Pipe Organ Register (see Appendix 1).
- Consider applying for a grant. Although the sums of money are seldom large, a number of bodies will consider making grants for restoration of historic organs (again BIOS can advise on this, though the society does not make grants itself).

Don't

- Make tonal alterations (except to restore original features), transpose pipework or alter mixture compositions.
- Replace non-standard pedalboards.
- Replace lever-type swell pedals with balanced swells.
- Introduce tuning slides, unless your organbuilder and adviser agree that this is the only way to preserve the pipes.
- Paint interior wood surfaces, making it impossible to distinguish old materials from new.
- Try to introduce extra console accessories (e.g. thumb pistons); this usually involves costly alterations to the organ's internal mechanism, and compromises its integrity.
- Fix unsightly switches, light fittings, clips or mirrors to the console woodwork.
- Replace ivory key coverings or stop faces unnecessarily; always reproduce original features, e.g. style and colouring of lettering.
- Paint over original decoration on front pipes (e.g. Victorian stencilling); if it is getting shabby, explore the possibility of having it conserved professionally.
- Use an unqualified organbuilder.

Appendix 7

Council for the Care of Churches: General conditions of grants awarded by the Conservation Committee

The Conservation Committee is a sub-committee of the Council for the Care of Churches with special responsibility for conservation advice and the administration of grant-giving. The Conservation Committee in turn is advised by a number of specialist committees on particular areas of expertise, for example organs, stained glass, sculpture and furnishings, etc. However, the final responsibility for all matters regarding conservation and conservation grants remains with the Council.

1. The parish shall send a letter to the committee accepting the grant on the terms and conditions stated below, to arrive within two months of the date of the offer letter.

2. A Faculty must be obtained before work begins.

3. The parish shall commission the conservator, in writing, to carry out the work for which grant aid is offered.

4. The work shall be carried out by the conservator who prepared the specification and estimate, submitted in support of the application, and in accordance with that specification and estimate, but taking account of alterations or additions required by the committee. If, after an offer of grant has been made, the parish wishes to change either the conservator or the specification, the agreement of the committee shall be sought before any work begins.

5. The request for payment of the grant shall be made by the *parish*, accompanied by a copy of the relevant invoice or invoices. Conservators should not send invoices directly to the Council. Payment can only be made by cheque, made payable to the PCC or to an appropriate appeal fund if requested. Cheques cannot be made payable to conservators.

   For smaller grants, please claim one payment at the completion of the project. For larger grants, interim payments can occasionally be made, providing requests for payment are accompanied by copies of invoices for at least the amount of grant requested. The grant, or final instalment of the grant, will only be paid on receipt of a complete written and photographic record of the conservation work (see condition 7), as well as a copy of the final invoice.

6.   The grant is made on condition that the project for which it is offered is completed within two years of the date of the offer letter. If payment has not been requested at the expiry of the two years, the grant will be automatically revoked. If work cannot reasonably be completed within the two-year period, it is the responsibility of the parish to seek such extensions as may be reasonable, explaining in writing to the committee the cause of delay.

7.   Record of Conservation: the Conservation Committee insists on full recording of all work it assists financially. The submission of a record of the completed conservation is a condition of the payment of grant.

The record consists of:

i)   *Three* copies of a detailed written record of work carried out. Copies of the appropriate forms will be enclosed with the Grant Offer Letter. These should be passed on to the conservator with whom responsibility for providing photographs (see below) should be agreed. Some conservators have their own format of conservation record but it is the parish's responsibility to ensure that *all* the information required is included in any record provided, including details of photographs. The form must also be completed by the inspecting architect who, if not actually supervising the work, must be kept informed of progress.

ii)   A photographic record (with three copies of each photograph), which must include colour pictures of the object before and after treatment, and during treatment if relevant.

All photographs should be clearly labelled on the reverse with the name of the parish, the subject of the photograph and the date it was taken.

All three copies of the written record and the three sets of photographs should be returned by the parish. On receipt, one copy is filed in the Library of the Council, one deposited in the National Monuments Record, and one is returned to the parish for insertion in the Church Log Book.

N.B. **The importance of the record cannot be stressed enough. It will form the only evidence available to future generations.** A proportion of the grant will be withheld until the completed record is received.

8.   The parish shall ensure that the object is generally accessible to visitors as well as to worshippers. The degree of public access which is reasonable depends on the nature and location of the object.

9.   The parish shall take all reasonable steps to ensure the future safety and security of the object concerned.

10.   Any works proposed in the future, which materially affect an object in respect of which a grant has been made, shall be submitted to the Conservation Committee before any work begins. If this condition is not complied with the committee reserves the right to require repayment of the grant.

11. If the parish should consider disposing of the object for which grant aid has been obtained, they shall give the committee an opportunity to comment before disposal. The committee may require repayment of the grant if disposal of the object takes place.

12. If any of the above conditions are not complied with the committee reserves the right to cancel all or part of the offer of grant aid and to require repayment of all or part of the grant already paid.

Appendix 8

Council for the Care of Churches: Guidelines for minimum information required in conservators' reports accompanying faculty and grant applications

Church furnishings

1. DESCRIPTION

(Good quality clear labelled colour photographs must illustrate this section.)

1.1 Name of parish, dedication of church, diocese and county.

1.2 Name and dates of artist. If monument, whom commemorating, and date.

1.3 Location within church.

1.4 Materials and overall dimensions. Whether attached to the structure of the building.

1.5 General description of furnishing to include special surface treatments, inscriptions, signatures, etc.

2. ENVIRONMENT

2.1 Overall perceived condition of the fabric of the building with particular reference to the area in the immediate vicinity of the subject of the report.

2.2 Relationship of object to outside ground levels, windows, rainwater goods and heating appliances.

2.3 Indicate any characteristic of the building environment that may have a detrimental effect on the wellbeing of the object.

3. CONDITION

(Labelled colour photographs must illustrate this section. Photographs should be referred to in the text. Diagrams or translucent overlays may be used for illustration of detail given below.)

3.1 State whether the object has been inspected from a scaffold, ladder or ground, and if a further inspection would be advisable.

3.2 State whether you have carried out any tests on cleaning or consolidation giving details and results. State whether samples of pigment, salts, mortar etc. have been taken. State whether readings have been taken for levels of dampness in walls/floors, RH of surrounding environment and detector readings.

3.3 Describe general condition of the object concentrating on main manifestation of deterioration.

3.4 Give full description of structural condition and of surface deterioration. Support your assessment with scientific analysis reports and other supporting evidence, such as measurement of movement, X-rays, etc.

3.5 Condition of pigmented areas. Indicate integrity of pigment/ground.

4. ANALYSIS OF CAUSES OF DETERIORATION

4.1 Evaluate the seriousness of the deterioration and whether further monitoring/testing is required to discern the causes/rate of decay/disruption.

4.2 Assess the causes of deterioration affecting the object.

4.3 If it appears to you that the causes of deterioration are inherent in the fabric of the building (e.g. defects in the external wall facings/pointing, in the rainwater goods, in the ground level/draining, in the roofing, in the heating or in the ventilation), have you discussed this with the parish architect? If so, with what result? If not, do you recommend that a meeting with the architect is necessary?

5. GENERAL OUTLINE OF CONSERVATION PROGRAMME

5.1 Evaluate possible alternatives (e.g. *in situ* conservation, removal to studio, etc.). Indicate any important practical or ethical issues particular to this case.

5.2 Indicate whether there is a choice between different materials or material-based approaches to the conservation.

6. RECOMMENDATIONS FOR CONSERVATION

6.1 If any remedial work to the fabric of the building needs to take place before conservation begins:

(a) indicate whether you have reached agreement with the parish architect as to what remedial work is required;

(b) assess what interval (if any) should elapse between the completion of this work and the start of the conservation.

6.2 Indicate if any emergency work on the object is necessary pending the full conservation. Give details.

6.3 Describe, step-by-step, the conservation work you recommend, giving details of both methods and materials you may use. Indicate in sequence any works to be carried out by architect/builders, etc. during the programme.

6.4 Indicate why, if there were alternatives possible, you have preferred these particular measures.

6.5 Indicate why methods/materials normally employed in similar situations would not be suitable here.

6.6 Assess the urgency of the programme/elements of the programme.

6.7 Discuss any problems in the integration and preservation of the conserved object.

6.8 Give details of proposed photographic record.

7. FUTURE RECOMMENDED CONSERVATION REQUIREMENTS

7.1 Describe what, if any, additional steps you would recommend should be taken following completion of conservation to ensure the continuing well-being of the object. Indicate frequency of post-conservation visual monitoring required. Indicate frequency of maintenance required.

7.2 Describe what preliminaries and attendance you would require the parish to provide for your work, e.g. scaffolding, electricity, the architect, a builder, etc.

8. ESTIMATE

8.1 State accurately the time and cost for carrying out the above work. If a phased programme is envisaged show estimates for phases separately. All on-costs such as materials, accommodation, and travel should be included (unless accommodation is the subject of a specific agreement with the parish).

8.2 Ensure the estimated cost includes the time to produce the record of conservation work.

8.3 Indicate VAT as a separate item.

8.4 State terms of payment and duration of validity of the estimate.

8.5 Indicate any other terms of contract e.g. insurance liability.

Appendix 9

Delegate list

Jonathan Ambrosino	USA
Michael Anderson	Worcester DOA
Andrew Argyrakis	Conservation Officer, CCC
David Atkinson	BIOS, NPOR
Ian Bell	IBO; CCC Organs Committee
Michael Bell	Rochester DOA
Jim Berrow	BIOS Secretary; CCC Organs Committee
Ian Black	Carlisle DOA
Jonathan Boston	Norwich DOA
John Bradley	Bristol DOA
David Brindle	
Douglas Carrington	
Linda Carrington	
John Clare	Historic Buildings Adviser
Barrie Clark	CCC Organs Committee; Southwark DOA
Rolf Claus	
Peter Collins	Peter Collins Ltd, organ builders; CCC Organs Committee
Anthony Cooke	Ripon DOA
Mervyn Cousins	Liverpool Metropolitan Cathedral
C. Hilary Davidson	Peterborough DOA
Etienne De Munck	
Geoffrey Donald	
William Drake	Organ builder
Bruce Draycott	Cambridge Reed Organs
Michael Gillingham	Royal College of Organists, London DAC
Sebastian Gluck	Gluck Orgelbau, Inc., USA, organ builders
Richard Godfrey	Salisbury DOA
Martin Goetze	Goetze & Gwynn, organ builders
Göran Grahn	Stiftelsen Musikkulturens Främjande, Sweden
Christopher Gray	BIOS Case Officer
Dominic Gwynn	Goetze & Gwynn, organ builders; CCC Organs Committee
John Harper	Director General, Royal School of Church Music
Richard Hird	BIOS Treasurer; CCC Organs Committee; Durham DOA
José Hopkins	AIOA Administrator
Peter Hopps	Harrison & Harrison, organ builders
Peter Horton	Royal College of Music
Paul Houghton	BIOS, NPOR
Richard Howell	BIOS

Bryan Hughes	BIOS
Kerr Jamieson	BIOS Membership Secretary
Christopher Kent	University of Reading; Salisbury DOA
Peter King	Bath & Wells DAC
John Kitchen	University of Edinburgh
David Knight	Conservation Adviser, CCC
Marcus Knight	*Organists' Review*
William Lapina	New York Law School, USA
John Mander	N.P. Mander Ltd, organ builders
Duncan Matthews	Harrison & Harrison, organ builders
Tim McEwen	Goetze & Gwynn, organ builders
William McVicker	Southwark DOA
Colin Menzies	Archbishops' Council
Geoffrey Morgan	Guildford DOA
Adrian Mumford	Europe DOA
John Norman	AIOA; CCC Organs Committee; London DOA
Eric Pask	St Albans DOA
John Pemberton	Lincoln DOA
James Pinder	
Nicholas Plumley	Chichester DOA
Sarah Plumley	
Paul Ritchie	Newcastle DOA
John Rowntree	Roman Catholic Organ Advisory Group
John Sayer	
Robert Shaftoe	Organ builder
Nigel Stark	
Gordon Stewart	IAO Education Officer
Gerry Sumner	Blackburn DOA
Norman Taylor	United Reformed Church Musicians' Guild
Nicholas Thistlethwaite	Guildford Cathedral; CCC Organs Committee
Alan Thurlow	Chichester DOA; Chairman, CCC Organs Committee
Axel Unnerbäck	GOArt, Riksantikvarieämbetet, Sweden
Philip Walden	
David Walters	Coventry DOA
John Watson	Colonial Williamsburg Foundation, USA
David Wells	David Wells Organ Builders
Ian Wells	Liverpool Cathedral
Michael Whitehall	
David Wickens	BIOS, British Organ Archive
John Witham	BIOS
Alan Woolley	
David Wyld	Willis & Son, organ builders
Michael Young	Peter Wood, organ builders

Notes and references

Dedication

1 John Betjeman, 'Hymn' (1932) in *John Betjeman's Collected Poems*, 2nd edn, London, John Murray, 1962, pp. 3–4.

Introduction

1.   There was an added, unforeseen bonus that during the month of August, presumably because of the absence of student trade, properly made beer was available at the adjacent pub at half-price!

2.   Access to the Rushworth Collection was anticipated, but was not possible due to work in one of the Liverpool galleries and the consequent use of the space which would have provided a temporary viewing area.

3.   An accurate replica of a *Vickers Vimy* twin-engined bomber, of First World War design, recently flew to Australia. However, the modern Pontiac engines failed and it had to make an emergency landing on a deserted Pacific island.

4.   *Standards in the Museum Care of Musical Instruments*, London, Museum and Galleries Commision, 1995.

5.   Drafted by John Stiller in 1978, first published in 1979, with the 1998 edition available on the OHT web site.

6.   Drafted by Dr Nicholas Thistlethwaite.

7.   Grant O'Brien, 'Attitudes to musical instrument conservation and restoration', *JBIOS*, **6**, 1982, p. 78. The absence of Dr O'Brien was keenly felt, for he has done much to focus attention on these matters.

8.   Ibid., p. 80.

10. *Musical World*, **2**, 1836–7, p.174.

11. Information from Kate Clark, English Heritage.

12. Alfred Reichling (quoting Egon Frilled), 'Problems in the preservation and restoration of organs', *JBIOS*, **12**, 1988, p. 4.

Chapter 1

1.   Edward Rimbault, *Early English Organ Builders and Their Works*, 1865, facsimile edition, Oxford, Positif Press, 1996, p. 2.

2.   Peter Holman, editorial in *Early Music*, **27**, no. 2, 1999, pp. 180–81.

3.   William McVicker, *IBO Newsletter*, **14**, June 1999, pp. 6–9.

4.   'A list of historically important organs', MS in the Library of the CCC, 1956.

5.   Cecil Clutton and Austin Niland, *The British Organ*, 2nd edn, London, Eyre Metheun, 1982, p. 265.

6. *Sound Advice*, Reading, BIOS, 1994.

7. Stephen Bicknell, *History of the English Organ*, Cambridge, Cambridge University Press, 1996, p. 370.

8. Nicholas Thistlethwaite, 'Hill, Norman & Beard: the heyday of the Hills', *Organists' Review*, **2**, 1999, p. 117.

9. Nicholas Thistlethwaite, preface to Rodney Tomkins, *Historic Organs in Derbyshire: A Survey of the Millennium*, Cromford, Scarthin Books, 1998, p. 6.

10. *Ibid.*, p. 6.

11. Stephen Bicknell, 'Village organs, a neglected heritage', *Conservation and Repair of Ecclesiastical Buildings*, July 1998, p. 40.

12. Simon Webb, programme note, BBC Promenade concert, 27 July 1999, p. 15.

Chapter 2

1. English Heritage, *Joint Grant Scheme for Churches and Other Places of Worship*, Heritage Lottery Fund and English Heritage, London, 1999.

2. John Norbury, *The Box of Whistles, an Illustrated Book on Organ Cases; with Notes on Organs at Home and Abroad*, London, 1877.

3. *La loi du 31 décembre 1913. Décret du application du 18 mars 1924. La loi No. 66-1042 du 30 décembre 1966. Circulaire du 12 juillet 1968. Décret du 10 septembre 1970. Décret du 15 novembre 1984.*

4. *Bundesgesetz vom 25 September 1923, BGBl 1923/533, betreffend Beschränkungen in der Verfügung über Gegenstände von geschichtlicher, künstlerischer oder kultureller Bedeutung (Denkmalschutzgesetz) idF BGBl 1959/92 und BGBl 1978/167.*

5. *La Ley 16/85, de 25 de junio, del Patrimonio Histórico Español. Decreto Foral 4 diciembre 1985, núm 233/1985 [Gobierno de Navarra] PATRIMONIO HISTORICO DE NAVARRA. Regula ayudas a la conservación y restauración de bienes meubles.*

6. Jerzy Golos, *The Polish Organ*, Vol. 1, Warsaw, Sutkowski Edition, 1993, quoted in *Organists' Review*, **79**, May 1993, p. 164.

7. 'A guide to the conservation and maintenance of pipe organs', *Heritage Bulletin*, no. 1, Heritage Council of New South Wales, Australia, 1983.

8. John Newman, *A Review of the Ecclesiastical Exemption from Listed Building Controls*, Department for Culture, Media and Sport and the Welsh Office, 1997, p. 120.

9. Ibid., p. 28, para. 5.3.

10. *House of Commons Official Reports, Parliamentary Debates* (Hansard), 6th series, **163**, London, 1989, column 658, 11 December.

Chapter 3

1.   Jonathan Ambrosino, 'Over there . . .', *IBO Newsletter*, June 1996, p. 3.

Chapter 4

1.   Bertil Wester, *Gotisk resning i svenska orglar*, dissertation, Stockholm, Sweden, 1936.

2.   Some leading organists gave recitals on these old organs and such music was broadcast every Saturday (an initiative of Dr Erici), which did a great deal to make them known and appreciated by a wider public.

Chapter 5

1.   Einar Erici and R. Axel Unnerbäck, *Orgelinventarium, Bevarade Klassiska Kyrkorglar i Sverige*, Stockholm, Proprius, 1988, p. 13.

Chapter 7

1.   Edward Hopkins and Edward Rimbault, *The Organ, its History and Construction*, London, 1855, p. 75.

2.   Dominic Gwynn, 'Voicing developments in the eighteenth-century English organ', *The Organbuilder*, **4**, 1986, p. 26.

Chapter 8

1.   Ewa Smulikowska, *Organ Cases in Poland*, Warsaw, Poland, 1993.

2.   The *Harley Monographs*: a list is available from Goetze & Gwynn, 5 Tan Gallop, Welbeck, Worksop, Notts S80 3LW; web site: www.creswell.co.uk/goetzegwynn.

3.   Analytical Services (Sheffield Assay Office), PO Box 187, 137 Portobello Street, Sheffield S1 1AY.

4.   *Paraloid* B72 is a long-lasting and non-yellowing acrylic polymer widely used in conservation in a range of concentrations as a fixative, consolidant and adhesive. It is soluble in acetone, toluene and isopropanol.

5.   John Bolton, *The Vicar's Gift: The Organ attributed to Christiopher Shrider in the Parish Church of St Mary the Virgin, Finedon, Northamptonshire*, Kettering, Organotes, 1996.

Chapter 9

1.   A partial account of the author's reconstruction of Kirkman's methods of work is the subject of the article, 'An eighteenth-century harpsichord workshop contributes two new technologies', in James M. Gaynor (ed.), *Eighteenth-century Woodworking Tools*, Colonial Williamsburg Foundation, USA, 1997.

2.   For a compelling description of the meaning of microstructures in historic objects, see Cyril S. Smith, *A Search for Structure*, Cambridge, Mass., MIT Press, quoted in W. David Kingery (ed.), *Learning from Things*, Washington DC, Smithsonian Institution Press, 1996, p. 189.

3.   John Barnes dramatically illustrated this in 'Does restoration destroy evidence?', *Early Music*, **8**, no. 2, April 1980, p. 213. Barnes cited an early (1970) initiative by Edwin M. Ripin to argue against the destructive restoration of musical instruments. 'Ripin saw that museums were destroying the information he wished to collect and that the destruction was largely caused by restoration. He felt like a collector of folksongs whose singers were dying before he had time to write down their songs.' Organologist Grant O'Brien has also demonstrated the wealth of historical information revealed by historic instruments, pointing out the implications for their conservation and restoration. See his, *Ruckers: A Harpsichord and Virginal Building Tradition*, Cambridge, Cambridge University Press, 1990, pp. 233–5.

4.   Quoted from provision II and guideline 21, *Code of Ethics and Guidelines for Practice*, American Institute for Conservation, 1994.

5.   Aspects of this metaphor may be implied in the common phrase 'point of view', or in calling a book or object 'a window on . . .'. However, the author knows of no previous description of the window metaphor with its many implications, except in his own usage.

6.   J. J. Rousseau, 1783, quoted in I. M. Lewis, *Social Anthropology in Perspective*, Cambridge; Cambridge University Press, 1976, p. 16.

7.   Also assisting in the examination were organ builders George Taylor and James Collier, and conservator David Blanchfield.

8.   For background on the Hunstanton Hall organ, see Barbara Owen, 'A "Payer of Organs" and a "Voyall"', *The Tracker*, Richmond, VA, USA, 41, no. 2, 1997, pp. 4–11.

9.   The only way documentary condition can improve is if the instrument gains sufficiently important additional historical associations. This might be true of a cathedral organ with a succession of historically important composer/organists or an instrument that received a celebrated remodelling by a historically important organ builder.

Chapter 11

1.   *Editor's note*: See also *Training in Musical Instrument Conservation*, CIMCIM *Publications* (International Committee of Musical Instrument Museums and Collections), no. 2, 1994. Part 1 is a 'Survey on training for musical instrument conservators'; Part 2, 'The conservator of musical instruments: a critical analysis of the position and tasks in the museum'; and Part 3, 'The role of the musical instrument conservator'. It is aimed at museum conservators and offers only a limited picture, with very little more than enthusiasm to show in the UK.

Chapter 15

1.   Roger Tebbet, 'The legacy of W. T. Best', *Organists' Review*, November 1997 and February 1998.

2.   Relf Clark, 'Transcriptions', *JBIOS*, **18**, 1994, pp. 126–36.

Chapter 17

1.   The London diocesan organ database lists the names and addresses of any organ builder recorded as working on an organ. The database includes the noted eighteenth-century builder Abraham Jordan but, strangely, leaves blank his current business address!

Chapter 18

1.   In the preparation of this article John Clare acknowledges the inspiration of English Heritage (and Historic Scotland) in general, and Kate Clark in particular. See *Conservation Plans in Action*, English Heritage, 1999.

Index

Note: Places (towns etc.) are indexed, but not individual churches or halls. The abbreviation 'o.b.' after an entry indicates an organ builder or builders.